The Handbook of
Conflict Resolution
Education

RICHARD J. BODINE
DONNA K. CRAWFORD
FOREWORD BY JUDITH M. FILNER

The Handbook of Conflict Resolution Education

A Guide to Building Quality Programs in Schools

NID*R NATIONAL INSTITUTE FOR DISPUTE RESOLUTION

JOSSEY-BASS PUBLISHERS ▪ San Francisco

Chapter Four excerpts and adaptation from GETTING TO YES 2/e by Roger Fisher, William Ury, and Bruce Patton. Copyright © 1981, 1991 by Roger Fisher and William Ury. Reprinted by permission of Houghton Mifflin Company. All rights reserved.

Chapter Five material from *Making Choices About Conflict, Security, and Peacemaking Part I: Personal Perspectives* by Carol Miller Lieber © 1995 Educators for Social Responsibility, Cambridge, MA, adapted with permission.

Substantial discounts on bulk quantities of Jossey-Bass books are available to corporations, professional associations, and other organizations. For details and discount information, contact the special sales department at Jossey-Bass Inc., Publishers (415) 433–1740; Fax (800) 605–2665.

Jossey-Bass Web address: http://www.josseybass.com

Manufactured in the United States of America.

Library of Congress Cataloging-in-Publication Data
Bodine, Richard J.
      The handbook of conflict resolution education : a guide to
   building quality programs in schools / Richard J. Bodine, Donna K.
   Crawford ; foreword by Judith M. Filner. — 1st ed.
          p.   cm. — (The Jossey-Bass education series)
      Includes bibliographical references and index.
      ISBN 0–7879–1096–1 (alk. paper)
      1. School violence—United States—Prevention—Handbooks, manuals,
   etc. 2. Conflict management—Study and teaching—United States—
   Handbooks, manuals, etc. 3. Schools—United States—Safety
   measures—Handbooks, manuals, etc. I. Crawford, Donna K.
   II. Title. III. Series.
   LB3013.3.B63 1998
   371.7'8—dc21   97–33873

FIRST EDITION
PB Printing   10 9 8 7 6 5 4 3 2

The Jossey-Bass Education Series

CONTENTS

FIGURES, TABLES, AND EXHIBITS   xi

FOREWORD   xiii
     Judith M. Filner

RED RIDING HOOD REVISITED   xvii

PREFACE   xxiii

ACKNOWLEDGMENTS   xxix

THE AUTHORS   xxxi

PART ONE

The Case for Conflict Resolution Education

CHAPTER 1
Conflict Resolution and the Mission of Education   3

CHAPTER 2
The Capacity of Schools to Develop
Responsible Citizens   17

CHAPTER 3
Understanding Conflict as a Learning Opportunity   35

PART TWO

Approaches to Conflict Resolution Education

CHAPTER 4
Essential Goals and Principles   47

CHAPTER 5
An Overview of Exemplary Programs   61

CHAPTER 6
Research Findings on What Works   103

PART THREE _____

Establishing Programs in Schools

CHAPTER 7
Ensuring Developmentally Appropriate Practices   117

CHAPTER 8
Developing and Implementing Programs   129

CHAPTER 9
Conducting a Strategic Plan   159

APPENDIX A
Consultation and Training Organizations   171

APPENDIX B
Curriculum Resources   175

APPENDIX C
Selecting Curriculum and Staff Development
Providers   191

APPENDIX D
Recommended Reading   203

NOTES   207

INDEX   213

FIGURES, TABLES, AND EXHIBITS

CHAPTER 7

Figure 7.1   Circle of Learning   119

Table 7.1   Conflict Resolution Developmental
Sequence   122

CHAPTER 8

Exhibit 8.1   Five Phases of a Comprehensive Conflict
Resolution Education Program   132

Exhibit 8.2   Conflict Resolution in Schools:
Needs Assessment Form   138

Exhibit 8.3   Implementation Time Line   141

Exhibit 8.4   Sample Peer Mediation Budget,
Under $5,000   145

Exhibit 8.5   Sample Peer Mediation Budget,
Over $50,000   145

Exhibit 8.6   Peer Mediator Application Form   147

Exhibit 8.7   Peer Mediator Student Nomination
Form   147

Exhibit 8.8   Peer Mediator Faculty Nomination
Form   148

CHAPTER 9

Exhibit 9.1   Sample Staff Development Action Plan   166

Exhibit 9.2   Sample Discipline Policy Action Plan   167

Exhibit 9.3   Sample Development of a Cooperative
Context Action Plan   169

APPENDIX C

Exhibit C.1   Conflict Resolution Program and
Curriculum Assessment Form   193

Exhibit C.2   Foundation Abilities of Conflict
Resolution   194

Exhibit C.3   Fundamental Principles of Conflict
Resolution   194

Exhibit C.4   Problem-Solving Methods of Conflict
Resolution   195

Exhibit C.5   Learning Opportunities and Styles   195

Exhibit C.6   Implementation   196

Exhibit C.7   Conflict Resolution Staff Development
Provider Assessment Form   198

Exhibit C.8   Conflict Resolution Staff Development
Provider Assessment Criteria   200

FOREWORD

Thousands of America's schools are incorporating conflict resolution skill development into their basic educational strategies. The Conflict Resolution Education Network of the National Institute for Dispute Resolution (NIDR) estimates that there are at least eighty-five hundred conflict resolution programs in schools today. This means that at least 10 percent of public schools have a program.

Most of these are peer mediation programs, but many take a much more comprehensive approach to making the skills of problem solving part of the formal or informal curriculum of the school. These programs are in place to achieve a variety of purposes: developing responsible citizens, creating nonviolent and safe schools, enhancing the social and emotional growth of young people, expanding law-related education, supporting bias awareness or multicultural education, providing a component of cooperative education, and improving the learning environment through better classroom management and more student-centered discipline.

Since 1983, NIDR has promoted the development of fair, effective, and efficient conflict resolution processes and programs in all of our nation's institutions. Its work in schools and universities has focused on serving as a national resource to educators and educators-in-training who are striving to bring conflict resolution expertise to young people. Its goals have included increasing the number and improving the quality of conflict resolution programs.

Parents, teachers, and school administrators are confronted daily by statistics and reports that tell them youth violence is increasing. Deborah Prothrow-Stith's 1991 book, *Deadly Consequences*,[1] identified youth violence as a public health problem, and one of major proportions. The current data on youth violence give us some insight into using conflict resolution as a prevention strategy:

- Sixty-six percent of U.S. high school students who fought reported that their most recent physical fight had been with an acquaintance or family member.[2]
- A large proportion of violent acts "occur in the context of personal relationships."[3]
- Among children and youth, most violence occurs between people who know each other, usually of similar age and of the same race.

Violence prevention research gives us additional insight. There are measurable characteristics of students who are at risk for violence. And there are measurable characteristics of students who are at risk for violence but who manage to choose more socially productive means of achieving their needs or solving differences. Having identified youth violence as a public health issue, researchers are now finding causes and prevention strategies for addressing it. One of these strategies, conflict resolution life skills for young people, is showing promising results.

Students in conflict resolution programs learn and ultimately master a set of core abilities essential to positive interpersonal and intergroup relationships. The programs achieve improved student attitudes toward conflict, increased understanding of nonviolent problem solving, and enhanced communication skills. They also yield positive changes in classroom climate, moderate or significant decreases in physical violence in the classroom, less name calling and fewer verbal insults, improved self-esteem among children receiving training, and greater acceptance of differences. Many programs report fewer incidents of trips to the principal, suspensions, and expulsions after conflict resolution training or peer mediation programs are in place in schools.

The teachers, counselors, and school administrators who have pioneered bringing these programs to their schools knew that there was something very powerful about the programs well before research began to substantiate the belief. They knew that if we can teach our children how to ride a bike or perform any of the numerous skills that are part of everyday life, we can also teach children skills that improve their competency in interpersonal and intergroup problem solving.

In *Emotional Intelligence,* Daniel Goleman identified the role of emotional success in life success. He reports that there are ways of developing the social and emotional intelligence of young people for success in personal relationships, at school, and on the job. He concludes the overview of his book with these words: "I can foresee a day when education will routinely include inculcating essential human competencies such as self-awareness, self-control, and empathy, and the arts of listening, resolving conflicts, and cooperation."[4]

Conflict resolution education has proven to be one of the key components of school strategies that not only assist young people in finding alternatives to violence but also support them in developing the social competencies of cooperation, empathy, creative problem solving, social cognitive skills, and relationship skills.

Conflict resolution education is based on underlying principles of cooperative problem solving. Fundamental to conflict resolution is the notion that conflict is normal and natural; individuals can learn constructive problem-solving skills and processes to resolve interpersonal and intergroup conflict. The skills and processes are founded on principles of cooperation rather than competition. Conflict resolution is not solely about compromise. It is about identifying underlying needs or interests and finding solutions that meet everyone's needs or interests to the fullest extent possible. The challenge is to focus on everyone's needs and find a resolution that is lasting and meaningful. The process provides the building blocks for problem solving; these process building blocks are critical to resolving a conflict.

Conflict resolution is a generic term that covers negotiation, mediation, peer mediation, and collaborative problem solving. A school conflict resolution curriculum or program includes (1) an understanding of conflict, (2) principles of conflict resolution (win-win interest-based problem solving), (3) process steps in problem solving (for example, agreeing to negotiate and establishing ground rules for the negotiation, gathering information about the conflict, exploring possible solution options, selecting solution options, and reaching agreement), and (4) skills required to use each of the steps effectively (for example, active listening, reframing, understanding, and factoring into the process the impact that cultural differences have on the dispute).

In my capacity as the director of conflict resolution education programs at NIDR, I found that schools—perhaps in their haste to institute a program that seeks to reduce violence—did not fully understand how to establish a conflict resolution program in their school system. People intuitively understood the importance of conflict resolution skills, but they were not fully knowledgeable about the underlying principles, philosophy, and processes of conflict resolution. I found the same to be true in schools of education, where tomorrow's teachers and administrators learn about teaching. My colleagues, conflict resolution education consultants and experts such as Donna Crawford and Dick Bodine, confirmed that this was their experience as well. We began a lengthy dialogue to explore how we might assist schools—teachers, counselors, administrators, and parents—in developing and implementing effective conflict resolution programs for young people. We knew that these individual schools were not aware of the fundamentals of conflict resolution education, that they did not have a way of identifying best practices, and that they did not have easy access to state-of-the-art conflict resolution strategies. *The Handbook of Conflict Resolution Education: A Guide to Building Quality Programs in Schools* offers a fundamental, comprehensive resource to every school or school district that wants to incorporate conflict resolution principles, skills, and philosophy into the way it educates our children. It is the resource that schools and schools of education have been asking for.

Donna Crawford and Dick Bodine are dedicated educators, each with an extensive history as a public school teacher and administrator. They know firsthand the burdens on schools to meet modern standards of student success, provide the best of modern information and technology, incorporate parent participation in a child's education, find ways to unite school and community goals, and find and hire talented and competent staff. They also have a vision that each and every school will provide a safe and welcoming environment for children. It is in this context that children learn best, and it is to achieve this vision that Donna Crawford and Dick Bodine have written this book. I am extremely gratified that this practical and comprehensive resource is now available to educators.

Judith M. Filner
Former director, Conflict Resolution Education Network
National Institute for Dispute Resolution

RED RIDING HOOD REVISITED

Step 1: Agree to Negotiate

Red: I'm Red Riding Hood. I agree to take turns talking and listening and to cooperate to solve the problem.

Wolf: I'm the Wolf. I also agree to take turns talking and listening, and I agree to cooperate with you, Red Riding Hood, to solve the problem.

Step 2: Gather Points of View

Red: I was taking a loaf of fresh bread and some cakes to my granny's cottage on the other side of the woods. Granny wasn't well, so I thought I would pick some flowers for her along the way.

I was picking the flowers when you, Wolf, jumped out from behind a tree and started asking me a bunch of questions. You wanted to know what I was doing and where I was going, and you kept grinning that wicked grin and smacking your lips together. You were being so gross and rude. Then you ran away. I was frightened.

Wolf: You were taking some food to your grandmother on the other side of the woods, and I appeared from behind the tree and frightened you.

Red: Yes, that's what happened.

Wolf: Well look, Red, the forest is my home. I care about it and try to keep it clean. That day, I was cleaning up some garbage people had left behind, when I heard footsteps. I leaped behind a tree and saw you coming down the trail carrying a basket of goodies.

I was suspicious because you were dressed in that strange red cape with your head covered up as if you didn't want anyone to know who you were. You started picking my flowers and stepping on my new little pine trees.

Naturally, I stopped to ask you what you were doing. You gave me this song and dance about going to your granny's house with a basket of goodies.

I wasn't very happy about the way you treated my home or me.

Red: You were concerned when you saw me in a red cape picking your flowers. You stopped me and asked me what I was doing.

Wolf: That's right.

Red: Well, the problem didn't stop there. When I got to my granny's house, you were disguised in my granny's nightgown. You tried to eat me with those big ugly teeth. I'd be dead today if it hadn't been for the woodsman who came in and saved me. You scared my granny. I found her hiding under the bed.

Wolf: You say I put on your granny's nightgown so you would think I was your granny, and that I tried to hurt you?

Red: I said you tried to eat me. I really thought you were going to eat me up. I was hysterical.

Wolf: Now wait a minute, Red. I know your granny. I thought we should teach you a lesson for prancing on my pine trees in that get-up and for picking my flowers. I let you go on your way in the woods, but I ran ahead to your granny's cottage.

When I saw Granny, I explained what happened, and she agreed that you needed to learn a lesson. Granny hid under the bed, and I dressed up in her nightgown.

When you came into the bedroom you saw me in the bed and said something nasty about my big ears. I've been told my ears are big before, so I tried to make the best of it by saying big ears help me hear you better.

Then you made an insulting crack about my bulging eyes. This one was really hard to blow off, because you sounded so nasty. Still, I make it a policy to turn the other cheek, so I told you my big eyes help me see you better.

Your next insult about my big teeth really got to me. You

see, I'm quite sensitive about my teeth. I know that when you made fun of my teeth I should have had better control, but I leaped from the bed and growled that my teeth would help me to eat you.

But, come on, Red! Let's face it. Everyone knows no wolf could ever eat a girl, but you started screaming and running around the house. I tried to catch you to calm you down.

All of a sudden the door came crashing open, and a big woodsman stood there with his ax. I knew I was in trouble. . . . There was an open window behind me, so out I went.

I've been hiding ever since. There are terrible rumors going around the forest about me. Red, you called me the Big Bad Wolf. I'd like to say I've gotten over feeling bad, but the truth is I haven't lived happily ever after.

I don't understand why Granny never told you and the others my side of the story. I'm upset about the rumors and have been afraid to show my face in the forest. Why have you and Granny let the situation go on for this long? It just isn't fair. I'm miserable and lonely.

Red: You think that I have started unfair rumors about you, and you are miserable and lonely and don't understand why Granny didn't tell your side of the story.

Well, Granny has been sick—and she's been very tired lately. When I asked her how she came to be under the bed, she said she couldn't remember a thing that had happened. Come to think of it, she didn't seem too upset . . . just confused.

Wolf: So you think it is possible that Granny just doesn't remember because she is sick.

Step 3: Focus on Interests

Red: I want to be able to take flowers to Granny when I visit her because she is lonely and flowers help cheer her up.

I want to be able to go through the forest to Granny's house because it is too far to take the road around the forest.

I want you to stop trying to scare me or threaten me in the forest because I want to feel safe. Besides, I think the forest is a fun place.

Wolf: You want to go through the forest to visit Granny, who is lonely, and you want to feel safe because you think the forest is a neat place.

Red: Yes, and I want to take flowers to Granny.

Wolf: I want you to watch where you are walking and to stop picking my flowers because I want to keep my forest home looking nice.

I want the rumors to stop because I want people to like me, and I want to be able to enjoy the forest without being afraid that someone is hunting for me.

Red: You want the forest to be pretty, you want people who visit the forest to like you and not be afraid of you, and you want to be safe in the forest.

Wolf: Right, the forest is my home. I should be free to enjoy my own home.

Step 4: Create Win-Win Options

Red: In order to solve this problem, I could try to stay on the path when I walk through the forest.

Wolf: I could try to remember to call out when I hear you coming instead of quietly stepping out from behind a tree. I could plant some flowers over by Granny's house for you to pick.

Red: I could pick up trash I see in the forest and take it to Granny's trash can.

Wolf: I could check up on Granny to make sure she is OK on those days when you can't make it. She is my friend, you see.

Red: Granny and I can talk to the woodsman and tell him we made a mistake about you. I could tell my friends that I'm not afraid of you anymore—that you can be nice.

Wolf: I could meet your friends on the edge of the forest and show them through it.

Step 5: Evaluate Options

Wolf: Do you think if you tell the woodsman and your friends that you made a mistake about me and that I'm really nice, then I won't have to worry about the woodsman and his hunters catching me?

Red: I think that will work.

Wolf: Maybe I could go with you to talk to the woodsman.

Red: Yes, that would help. You could also go with me when I tell my friends I'm not afraid of you anymore. . . . I'd like to help you plant some flowers at Granny's, and I could also help you plant some in the forest. It would be nice to visit Granny together. She's pretty lonely.

Wolf: That sounds good.

Red: I agree.

Wolf: I don't think it will work for you to stay on the path all the time. I can show you where to walk so you don't harm anything.

Red: I think that's fair.

Wolf: I agree.

Red: Will it work for you to check on Granny when I can't visit her?

Wolf: Yes, if you call me early in the morning.

Red: I think it would be a good idea if I ask my friends for a donation when you give them a tour of the forest, and we could use the money to buy more trees to plant and start a recycling program for the trash we pick up.

Wolf: I think we've taken care of both of our interests.

Red: This solution will help both of us.

Step 6: Create an Agreement

Red: I'll arrange for Granny and myself to talk to the woodsman. I'll try to get an appointment for this afternoon, and I'll let you know when.

Wolf: I'll get some flowers to plant at Granny's. I'll have them ready to plant Saturday. I'll draw up a possible forest tour map and give it to you.

Red: As soon as I get your tour map, I'll bring some friends over to try it out. That's when I'll introduce you and tell them you're nice.

Wolf: I'll put a donation box at the edge of the forest for our tree-planting and recycling program.

Red: And I'll call you by seven o'clock if I can't go visit Granny.

Wolf: OK. I've agreed to get flowers to plant by Saturday, to draw a tour map of the forest, to go along with you to talk with the woodsman, to meet your friends and lead a tour through the forest, to take care of the donation box, and to visit Granny when you can't do it.

Red: I've agreed to arrange for an appointment with Granny and the woodsman, to plant flowers with you, to bring my friends to tour the forest and introduce you as a nice wolf, and to call you by seven o'clock if I can't visit Granny.

(The two shake hands.)[1]

PREFACE

Conflict is a natural, vital part of life. When conflict is understood, it can become an opportunity to learn and create. The challenge for people in conflict is to apply the principles of creative cooperation in their human relationships.

Richard Bodine, Donna Crawford, and Fred Schrumpf
Creating the Peaceable School[1]

Fairy tales and folktales are entertaining to children, but they also communicate common ideas and modes of thinking about relationships, morals, values, and how to get along in the world. Fairy tales present children with a model of how to think and act. In the familiar story of Little Red Riding Hood, one of the morals is to beware of strangers. The two sides in the fairy tale are sharply drawn: one good, one bad; one innocent, one cunning; one right, one wrong. If our retelling of the tale seems odd, it is because it challenges the stereotype of the "big bad wolf" and asks us to consider the wolf's side of the story.

The tenets of conflict resolution present a new model of interacting with and thinking about other people—one that challenges us to go beyond stereotypes, to consider the other's point of view, and to reach mutually satisfactory agreements in which all parties win. "The Story of Little Red Riding Hood and the Wolf, Retold Through Negotiation" is an illustration of one of the problem-solving processes of conflict resolution. If, in our schools and our communities, we can succeed in teaching youth this framework for resolving their disputes, the results for them and for our society could be profound. The world could be a different place within twenty years. If we can create in our youth a generation of peacemakers, that future will be welcomed.

U.S. Attorney General Janet Reno and Secretary of Education Richard W. Riley, in their joint foreword to *Conflict Resolution Edu-*

cation: A Guide to Implementing Programs in Schools, Youth-Serving Organizations, and Community and Juvenile Justice Settings (1996), stated that

> safe and orderly environments in our nation's schools are essential to promoting high standards for learning and ensuring that all children have the opportunity to develop to their fullest potential. No teacher should ever fear to walk into a classroom, and no child should ever stay home from school because he or she is afraid. Too often, however, young people face conflicts before, during, and after school. They are subjected to bullying, teasing, and senseless, sometimes fatal, disputes over clothing and other possessions. Many of these conflicts either begin at school, or they are brought into school from the home or the community.
>
> A growing body of evidence suggests that we are not powerless to prevent these destructive behaviors. We can intervene successfully to prevent conflicts from escalating into violent acts by providing young people with the knowledge and skills needed to settle disputes peacefully. Conflict resolution education can help bring about significant reductions in suspensions, disciplinary referrals, academic disruptions, playground fights, and family and sibling disputes. It is important to understand that conflict resolution education is a critical component of comprehensive, community based efforts to prevent violence and reduce crime. . . .
>
> As adults, we cannot solve young people's problems for them. We can, however, provide them with the knowledge, skills, and encouragement to resolve conflict in a nonviolent manner, using words instead of fists or weapons. Conflict resolution education includes negotiation, mediation, and consensus decisionmaking, which allow all parties involved to explore peaceful solutions to a conflict. When these problem solving processes to conflict and strife become a way of life, young people begin to value getting along instead of getting even or getting their way.
>
> We urge you to help make our schools and communities safer places. . . . Give our youth the skills, techniques, and tools they need to learn and to resolve disputes in a safe and nonviolent environment.[2]

To fulfill the mission of educating youth and preparing them to function effectively in adult society, schools must first be safe places. Schools are challenged to provide an environment in which (1) each learner can feel physically and psychologically free from threats and danger and can find opportunities to work and learn with others for the mutual achievement of all and (2) the diversity of the school's population, in all its multiple dimensions, is respected and celebrated.

Conflict resolution education programs can help schools promote the individual behavioral change necessary for responsible citizenship, and the systemic change necessary for a safe learning environment.

As a reference tool that offers both basic information and the experience of experts in the field of conflict resolution education, this book is designed to assist educators in building quality conflict resolution education programs in schools and school systems. Based on a shared vision that youth of all ages can learn to deal constructively with conflict and live in civil association with one another, *The Handbook of Conflict Resolution Education* challenges educators to act on the premise that conflict resolution skills are essential for having successful relationships and lives in homes, schools, workplaces, and communities. The goal is to build the capacity of educators to successfully meet that challenge.

Presented here is a comprehensive digest of the state of the art of conflict resolution in schools. The program examples presented in Chapter Five represent the best practices of organizations that have been key players in the history and development of the field. Programs for conflict resolution in schools began to emerge in the early 1970s. One of the pioneers in the field was Children's Creative Response to Conflict (CCRC). Their work grew from the nonviolence training programs of their parent organization, the New York Quaker Project on Community Conflict, in response to the query, "Why not apply the theory and practice of nonviolence to children?" The thinking prompted by this question suggested that if children were taught the skills of nonviolence and nonviolent conflict resolution at an early age, they would be less likely to use violence later.

Another pioneer organization, Educators for Social Responsibility (ESR), which also began working with schools in the early 1980s, drew from their work in equitable, nonviolent resolution of community social issues. In the mid-1980s, the New York chapter of ESR and the New York City Board of Education began collaborating to develop the Resolving Conflict Creatively Program, a comprehensive conflict resolution education program now disseminated by the national ESR office.

The Teaching Students to Be Peacemakers program emerged in 1972 as a logical extension of the work of the Cooperative Learning Center at the University of Minnesota. The Peace Education Foundation (PEF), which began developing materials and training programs for schools in 1980, came from a parent organization with a long history of work on peace education and global issues.

The Community Board Program (CBP) began working to develop programs in schools in 1982, applying what had been learned in its community mediation programs and trainings since 1976. Also in 1982, another program with a community mediation focus, the New Mexico Center for Dispute Resolution (NMCDR), began to work in schools in that state. These two groups did much to advance peer mediation programs in schools throughout the country and have recently pioneered efforts to use the strategy in youth detention facilities and to resolve gang related disputes.

In the mid–1980s, the National Association of Mediation in Education (NAME) formed as a networking and resource organization for conflict resolution in schools. The National Institute for Citizen Education and the Law (now known as Street Law, Inc.) began developing school-based programs and classroom curriculum materials.

Although many of the conflict resolution organizations, especially in urban areas, had been dealing for years with issues of racism, sexism, anti-Semitism, and homophobia, a diversity-education element was incorporated into the work of nearly all training providers by the late 1980s. NAME and the Society of Professionals in Dispute Resolution (SPIDR) made diversity and bias awareness a major program goal.

With the advent of the nineties, the field of violence prevention developed rapidly. Conflict resolution was embraced by many of the spokespersons in this field as a major prevention strategy. The Centers for Disease Control presented violence as a public health issue, and the U.S. Department of Justice began to promote conflict resolution and violence prevention as part of their role. "Safe Schools" government funding resulted in more long-range planning toward program efforts in violence prevention, thus spurring implementation of youth-centered conflict resolution programs in schools.

In 1992, the Illinois Institute for Dispute Resolution (IIDR), a partnership between the Illinois Bar Association and the Illinois State Board of Education, received federal law-related education funding to provide training and technical assistance to educators, with the purpose of developing conflict resolution education programs in schools throughout the state of Illinois. The Program for Young Negotiators (PYN) began applying the work of the Harvard Negotiation Program (often credited with initiating principled negotiation theory) with school-age youth in school settings in 1993. In 1996, IIDR was awarded a grant by the Office of Juvenile Justice and Delinquency Prevention of the Justice Department. As a national center for conflict resolution education and in partnership with the organizations whose programs are highlighted in this book along with other conflict resolution educators, IIDR is pursuing a mission of developing conflict resolution education programs in all schools of our nation.

What has been learned about conflict and conflict resolution during the recent decades provides the foundation for this book:

- Conflict exists.
- It is not going away.
- Conflict can be a welcome opportunity for growth.
- Learning the foundation abilities and the processes of conflict resolution enable us to deal with those inevitable conflicts creatively and constructively.
- Everyone can learn these alternative skills.
- There may be many definitions of a problem—and many ways of responding.
- As we learn to express feelings and points of view, we can all become better at creatively resolving our conflicts and finding win/win solutions.

We are no longer in a time where the primary goal of the conflict resolution education field is to convince people of its importance. Our current task is to create an approach to conflict resolution education that sets new standards for excellence. The goal is movement toward changing the school or community culture by establishing a critical mass of teachers, community members, and youth who practice conflict resolution and peacemaking to live day-to-day in civil association with all others. The twenty-first century will present a unique combination of necessity and interest for (1) creating new models for resolving conflict in our increasingly diverse population and (2) coordinating our efforts toward building a friendly community on our small planet.

How the Book Is Organized

The Handbook of Conflict Resolution Education is designed to provide teachers, administrators, school board members, school site-based management teams, and others involved in the work of schools with sufficient information and the tools to initiate and sustain development of comprehensive youth-centered conflict resolution education programs. It provides a framework for making informed decisions about implementing conflict resolution education programs in schools and about selecting resources to support program development.

Chapter One, "Conflict Resolution and the Mission of Education," presents conflict resolution as being integral to the educational mission rather than as yet another add-on program. The rationale for conflict resolution education is its efficacy as a medium that enables schools to address their mission of safe schools and development of responsible, effective citizens.

Chapter Two, "The Capacity of Schools to Develop Responsible Citizens," outlines the potential of conflict resolution education for promoting both the individual behavioral change that is necessary for responsible citizenship and the systemic change necessary for creating effective learning environments.

Chapter Three, "Understanding Conflict as a Learning Opportunity," defines conflict as a natural condition and examines origins, responses, and the outcomes of the responses.

Chapter Four, "Essential Goals and Principles," details the essential elements of a quality program and presents the foundation abilities and the problem-solving processes of conflict resolution.

Chapter Five, "An Overview of Exemplary Programs," defines the four basic approaches of conflict resolution education: *process curriculum, mediation program, peaceable classroom,* and *peaceable school;* the chapter then provides exemplary descriptions of each approach.

Chapter Six, "Research Findings on What Works," reviews the findings from research and assessment of conflict and conflict resolution education efforts in schools; it also relates risk-and-resiliency research on individuals to conflict resolution.

Chapter Seven, "Ensuring Developmentally Appropriate Practices," provides a developmental view of how the foundation abilities and the problem-solving processes might fit into a preschool through high school scope and sequence.

Chapter Eight, "Developing and Implementing Programs," presents a continuum for program development and details the program implementation phases for the various approaches.

Chapter Nine, "Conducting a Strategic Plan," offers a conflict resolution needs assessments and a strategic planning process for designing a program to address identified needs of a school or community.

Appendices A through D include comprehensive listings of organizations that provide national leadership in the field of conflict resolution in education and of conflict resolution curriculum resources, and a conflict resolution reading list. Also provided are tools for assessing conflict resolution curricula and staff development providers.

ACKNOWLEDGMENTS

This book grew from a publication, *Conflict Resolution Education: A Guide to Implementing Programs in Schools, Youth Serving Organizations and Juvenile Justice Settings,* that we developed for the U.S. Department of Justice and the U.S. Department of Education. We feel considerable gratitude to Donni LeBoeuf, Senior Program Manager at the Office of Juvenile Justice and Delinquency Prevention, Office of Justice Programs, for her diligence, clarity and enthusiasm for the initial conflict resolution education publication that ultimately enhanced our ability to contribute this *Handbook* to the field of education.

We are indebted to Cheryl Niro of the Illinois State Bar Association and to Judith Filner of the National Institute for Dispute Resolution for recognizing the need for and the potential of this publication, for contributing time and expertise in brainstorming sessions to develop the initial outline, and for their endless support and dedication to our work.

We are grateful to the following individuals for their counsel, guidance, and written contributions throughout the development of this book: Terry Amsler and Irene Cooper-Basch of the Community Board Program, Jared Curhan and Bruce Richman of the Program for Young Negotiators, Larry Dieringer and Laura Parker Roerden of Educators for Social Responsibility, Linda Lantieri of Resolving Conflict Creatively Program, David Johnson and Laurie Stevahn of the Cooperative Learning Center at the University of Minnesota, Priscilla Prutzman and Judith Johnson of Children's Creative Response to Conflict, and Judith Zimmer of Street Law, Inc. This handbook would have been incomplete without their efforts, expertise, and contributions to the field of conflict resolution.

Finally we wish to express our appreciation to the staff and consultants of the Illinois Institute for Dispute Resolution, Topper Steinman, Vernessa Gipson, Fred Schrumpf, and Ethel Enoex-Godonoo, for being catalysts, for translating our visions into reality, for their inspiration and challenges, and for their devotion and harmony.

R. J. B.
D. K. C.

THE AUTHORS

Richard J. Bodine is education program director of the Illinois Institute of Dispute Resolution. He holds an undergraduate degree in teaching mathematics and chemistry and has taught in elementary, middle, and high schools and junior college. He has a master's degree in special education, specializing in gifted children, and an advanced certificate of education in administration from the University of Illinois. He has been a secondary school administrator and director of special regional education programs. Bodine has consulted with numerous schools on gifted education, individualized learning programs, and administrative issues and has directed teacher training institutes on innovative practice. He has taught graduate-level courses in administration at the University of Illinois, including a course on the principalship. For twenty years, he served as principal of Leal Elementary School in Urbana, Illinois. In 1992 he was the recipient of the Illinois State Board of Education "Those Who Excel" award as an outstanding administrator. He holds training certificates from CDR Associates of Boulder, Colorado, for mediation, for dispute management systems design, and for conflict resolution in organizations. He is the coauthor (with Crawford and others) of several books on conflict resolution education regularly cited in this work.

Donna K. Crawford is the executive director of the Illinois Institute for Dispute Resolution. She has been a public school teacher and administrator, teaching in and serving as principal of an early childhood center and as a district special education administrator with supervisory responsibility for a regional program for students having emotional and behavioral disorders. She is an experienced mediator, reality therapist, and dispute resolution trainer. She holds a master's degree in special education and an advanced certificate of education in administration from the University of Illinois. Her training in alternative dispute resolution methods was at the Justice Center of Atlanta, the Illinois State Board of Education Department of Specialized Services, and the Harvard University Law School. She serves as a practicum supervisor for the Institute for Reality Therapy in Los Angeles and is reality therapy certified. She has served on the joint committee of the National Association for Mediation in Education and the National Institute for Dispute Resolution to bring conflict resolution programs to colleges of education. Presently, she serves as project director for the U.S. Department of Justice Office of Juvenile Justice and Delinquency Prevention's National Youth Centered Conflict Resolution Education Program. She coauthored several books in the field of conflict resolution education that are cited in this work.

The Handbook of
Conflict Resolution
Education

PART ONE

The Case for Conflict Resolution Education

CHAPTER 1

Conflict Resolution and the Mission of Education

In a recent interview, U.S. Attorney General Janet Reno declared that "importantly, we have a juvenile justice system that in many states is bankrupt and is starting too late. You cannot start with a 16- or-17-year-old who has dropped out of school and who was the drug dealer's gofer when he was 13. You've got to start earlier. . . . We can do tremendous amounts of good through conflict resolution [education] programs in our public schools."[1]

There are valid, even compelling, reasons why every school should teach conflict resolution problem-solving techniques to students.[2] Three elements of the educational mission shared by all schools in America are safe schools, social justice, and cooperative learning environments. More often than should be acceptable, the challenges schools face are difficult to meet. Consider, for example, what is needed to achieve these mission elements and create an ideal setting for learning:

- An environment in which each learner feels physically and psychologically free from threats and danger

- An arena in which all present can find opportunities to work and learn together to the mutual enhancement of all

- An environment for respecting, cherishing, enhancing, and celebrating the diversity of its population

- An arena that provides equal access and opportunity to each learner, free from consideration of diversity issues based on race, ethnicity, culture, gender, sexual orientation, physical and mental abilities, or social class

Safe Schools, Social Justice, and Cooperative Learning Environments

Charged by the constitutional mandate to prepare youth to live productively in a democratic society, safe schools, social justice, and cooperative learning environments are essential features of the American educational system. The field of conflict resolution education responds directly to the educational challenges inherent in executing this mandate. Conflict resolution education embraces the mission of providing these three essential features. The potential of conflict resolution education, both for individual behavioral change and—through individuals collectively—for systemic change, offers significant promise that schools can build the capacity to achieve their mission. Conflict resolution education addresses both the individual behavioral issue of violence prevention and the exercise of responsible citizenship, and the systemic issues of promoting safe schools, social justice, and cooperative learning environments. The knowledge of the means for constructively dealing with conflicts, both for individuals and for the collective, that is provided through conflict resolution education is a crucial component in building the capacity of schools to achieve their societal mandate.

Behavior Change and System Change

The relationship between conflict resolution education and the issues of violence prevention, social justice, and responsible citizenship is somewhat easy to conceptualize. What may not be so obvious is the necessity for *systemic* change: the collateral requirement that institutional philosophies and practices must be adaptable to new patterns of thought. Nonetheless, for individual behavioral change to occur beyond isolated individual cases, the school system must be reconceptualized. The necessary institutional changes are those that support the individual changes and allow youth to practice and live the behaviors of peaceful conflict resolution in a significant context of their lives: school, a place where they spend a considerable amount of their time. When behaviors are consistently used in one context, they can become internalized; this results in more prevalent use in other life contexts, present and future. For the behaviors to be employed consistently in the original context, however, the organizational precepts and practices of that context must support and encourage the behaviors.

The specific system reconceptualizations to support individual behavioral change that is promoted through conflict resolution education are addressed in more detail in the next chapter of this book. Briefly, this paradigm shift calls at the very least for system changes to operationalize cooperation as the normative expectation, both behaviorally and academically, and to allow adults to interact noncoercively with youth. Most professionals in the field of conflict resolution education argue that for conflict resolution education programs in schools to realize maximum results, these system changes are needed to provide a context that facilitates the development and sustenance of the program.

Conflict resolution programs can provide effective alternatives to traditional discipline programs. Such alternatives provide for long-term changes in attitudes and in behavior, the desired outcome of any effective discipline program. Conflict resolution programs constitute an important part of those alternatives primarily because they invite participation and expect that those who choose to participate will plan more effective behaviors and then employ those behaviors.[3]

As the elements of the educational mission are addressed, it should be obvious that realizing safe schools demands that actual or implied violence be extinguished—psychological trespasses, as well as physical ones. Processes that empower students to deal constructively with interpersonal conflicts, cultural differences, and the violence embedded in American culture need to be grounded in the day-to-day school experience. Conflict resolution education provides youth with the understandings, skills, and strategies needed to choose alternatives to self-destructive, violent behavior when confronting interpersonal and intergroup conflict. The fundamental challenge is for schools to engage students in learning skills and processes that allow them to constructively manage and resolve the conflicts significant to them.

The Pervasive Problem of Violence

There is a disturbing scenario playing itself out in households across the land:

> "Mom, can I tell you something? I'm worried. All of the boys I grew up with are dead. I lie awake at night and think about it. What am I supposed to do?" The question was from a thirteen-year-old boy in New Orleans and caused his mother to realize that, of a group of

six-year-olds who started school together seven years earlier, only her son was still living. All the others had met violent deaths.[4]

Violence among the nation's youth occupies a prominent place on the national agenda. Attention to the issue of youth violence has increased in recent years because it is perceived to be accelerating and because of the use of weapons by youths committing violent acts. We have been bombarded in recent years with staggering facts and statistics testifying to this trend:

- Adolescence is a period of heightened risk among all youth. More than one-fourth of male adolescents commit at least one violent offense before reaching adulthood. The median age of first gun ownership is twelve-and-a-half. The peak age of arrests for serious violent crimes in America is eighteen.[5]

- The Centers for Disease Control and Prevention found that one in twenty-five high school students carry a gun.[6] Suicide, murder, and gunfire are wiping out American children at higher rates than their counterparts in the rest of the industrialized world. The CDC reports that 2.57 out of every 100,000 Americans under age fifteen are killed, compared with an overall rate of 0.51 in twenty-five other industrialized countries included in their survey. Deaths caused by firearms amount to 1.66 out of every 100,000 children the United States, compared with 0.14 in other nations. The child suicide rate here is twice as high: 0.55 out of every 100,000 compared with 0.27.

- About 40 percent of arrests for all serious crime are accounted for by youths between ten and twenty years of age. Yet despite the prevalence of delinquent behavior, a small proportion of adolescents—about 6 percent—are responsible for two-thirds of all violent crimes committed by juveniles.[7]

Youth involvement in and with violence is a pervasive problem that touches every school and neighborhood, cutting across lines of race, religion, and gender. Feelings of frustration and hopelessness have become deeply ingrained among educators and other adults directly involved with youth. These individuals increasingly find themselves overwhelmed by students who are hostile, aggressive, violent, and disconnected. One of every five teachers can cite incidents of verbal or physical threats from students during the past twelve months.[8] Physical aggression and intimidation are often young people's first response to problems and disagreements.

Psychological Violence

Violence is behavior by persons against persons that threatens, attempts, or inflicts physical or emotional harm. Although acts of physical violence capture our attention and mobilize our concern and outrage, more subtle psychological violence may well be the predominantly devastating factor in efforts to combat violence. Verbal abuse and other nonphysical acts of violence are more pervasive; often the victims are not recognized as victims. If violence begets violence, as many contend, these victims of psychological violence present a significant threat. Exemplifying this is a nine-year-old girl with mild cerebral palsy who wrote to a radio station in a small Midwestern city, saying that all she wished to have for Christmas was one day free from teasing. In her public school, both the teasers and those who do not intervene to stop such behavior are practicing violence that perhaps causes more far-reaching destruction than the violence of those comparatively few who wreak havoc with guns and other weapons of physical violence.[9]

Some schools think they have far more than their fair representation of violent youth, while others think that violence by youth has no impact on them. But the issue for schools is not only serious and violent crime. Unkindness and transgressions toward and among youth have a long history. Such interchanges are universally observable, appearing wherever youths interact. Every child, and thus every school, feels the impact of violence whether physical harm is evident or not.[10]

Conflict Resolution and Violence Prevention

Kids everywhere, like the teenage boy in New Orleans, are crying out to us to do something. When their anguish was quiet or self-directed, we did not respond with sustained vigor and concern. But now their feelings are turning outward. They are enraged and disenfranchised; they feel they have little to lose, no future to compromise. The problem is there for us to see: school must be a place where all children feel valued, useful, and needed.[11] School may well be the last remaining collective experience of our society. If youth do not otherwise find themselves in a supportive environment—and many do not—then schools must develop effective ways to compensate, even as other systems are working to change the problematic conditions. What we cannot do is throw away any more generations of children as we wait and hope for things to get better. Schools must stop acting as though parents are sending them the wrong kids; they must stop wishing that if "better" kids would just start showing up in our schools everything would be OK. *We have the kids we have; there are no others to replace them.* So, what proactive measures can be chosen to try to improve the current state of affairs in our schools? To continue focusing concern and action on the occurrence of violence—the modus operandi of many schools and other youth-serving agencies—is to treat a symptom; it offers little for the future. Focusing concern and action on educating students in alternatives to violence (in all its various forms) offers hope that those alternatives will more and more frequently become the behaviors of choice.[12]

The goal of making the school a safe haven in which youths can gain respite from violence in order to think and learn is a good one, but it cannot be created apart from improving what and how teachers teach, how principals administer school rules, and how an antiviolent vision is created and shared by everyone in the building.[13] The best school-based violence prevention programs seek to do more than reach the individual child. Instead, they try to change the total school environment, to create a safe community that lives by a credo of nonviolence and multicultural appreciation.[14]

Schools alone cannot change a violent society. Schools can, however:

- Stop making the problems worse
- Teach alternatives to violence
- Teach students to act responsibly in social settings
- Teach students to understand and accept the consequences of their behavior
- Improve the quality of learning[15]

Making schools safe havens is not likely to stamp out all of the violence embedded in our society. But that constraint should not deter us from the effort.[16]

Youth Empowerment

Education is living, not the preparation for living. Students must be involved in dealing with real problems in order to learn what they need to know now and later. The fact is, students are involved with real problems constantly. When the school does not accept this fact and commit to teaching students the tools to deal with those problems, students and the school disjoin. Conflict resolution education prevents this disassociation: students can learn to constructively resolve problems in need-fulfilling ways. If students are empowered—and encouraged—to solve their own real problems in the school environment, they will likely become more accepting of the school's effort to expand their repertoire of information and skills in other areas of learning.[17]

Three principles are paramount in any program to counteract school violence:

1. *Whatever is illegal outside of school cannot be treated as if it were not a crime inside of school.* Making schools a safe haven for youngsters does not mean creating a medieval sanctuary where civil authorities may not enter. Crimes are not transformed into something else because they are perpetrated in schools.

2. *The process of school management and discipline are more important than the outcomes.* [Adults in schools must repeatedly demonstrate] that thinking, reasoning, and working through problems are respectable alternatives to violence [and] are the behaviors to be reinforced and learned. If school officials begin by assuming they do not have enough time or person power to administer individualized, careful processes, they are, in effect, conceding that they cannot decrease the violence. Indeed, we can be certain that a system of only enforcement and control, impersonally administered with an emphasis on punishments, will make matters worse. It will play into the limited view of the world held by most youth . . . that power is everything and it is the school's responsibility to make them behave in much the same way as it is the school's responsibility to make them learn.

3. *Problems of school violence are not intrusions on the school program; they are an integral part of the school program.* Making the building safe is a necessary but incomplete condition; teaching students to care about and predict the consequences of their behavior is the goal. Options to violence . . . must be actively modeled every day in every classroom and school.[18]

Conflict resolution education programs do provide a proactive means of addressing these principles for counteracting school violence. Conflict resolution especially offers a means for individuals to address the far more pervasive, but frequently institutionally ignored (and often institutionally perpetrated), issues of psychological violence. The problem-solving processes of conflict resolution are better suited to allowing individuals to confront issues of psychological trespass than issues of physical trespass.

How Youth Learn About Conflict, Violence, and Peace

Educational opportunities that equip students to deal constructively with interpersonal conflicts, cultural differences, and the violence embedded in our social fabric are often absent from the day-to-day school experience. While youths are particularly vulnerable to the effects of violence, they are also resilient and reachable. School counselors, social workers, deans, psychologists, teachers, principals, administrators, and superintendents are in important positions to create primary prevention programs. Educators are often discouraged by the notion that prevention is not possible without total social reforms to end problems such as poverty, racism, and drug abuse. What is wrong with this view is that it can justify inaction, even as there are "doable" interventions that can make a significant difference in breaking the cycle of violence.[19]

The American Psychological Association's Commission on Violence and Youth (1993) reports, "We overwhelmingly conclude, on the basis of the body of psychological research on violence, that violence is not a random, uncontrollable, or inevitable occurrence . . . Although we acknowledge that the problem of violence involving youth is staggering . . . there is overwhelming evidence that we can intervene effectively in the lives of young people to reduce and prevent their involvement in violence."[20] The report recommends that schools play a critical part in any comprehensive plan for preventive intervention to reduce youth violence. It calls for inclusion of school-based curricula and teaching strategies to build young people's resistance to violence. Educators can play an important role in reversing patterns of conflict and aggression by implementing comprehensive conflict resolution programs in schools, programs that are characterized by students resolving their conflicts both with and without adult involvement. Against the backdrop of escalating violence that involves our nation's youth—both as perpetrators and as victims—adults (especially those involved in youth services, which includes educators) must be fully cognizant of their role in initiating and nurturing peacemakers.

A Proactive Tool

Just as it is important that all schools attend seriously to violence prevention, it is also important that conflict resolution education be included as an integral component in that prevention framework. Although conflict resolution in and of itself is not a solution to preventing violence, it does have a significant place in any violence-prevention strategy. When considering the role of conflict resolution education in this framework, school decision makers should understand that conflict resolution as detailed in this book is not a reactive tool, but a proactive one. Conflict resolution is not a program for reacting to a violent incident in a school; it is a tool to further the educational mission of the school to develop and promote a safe environment and an effective citizenry.[21] The relationship to violence prevention is that a conflict resolution education program affords youth the understandings, skills, and strategies needed to choose alternatives to self-destructive and violent behaviors when confronting intrapersonal, interpersonal, or intergroup conflicts.

Because the problem-solving processes of conflict resolution are better suited for allowing individuals to confront issues of psychological trespass than issues of physical trespass, the vision is that prevention-oriented, proactive uses of these processes will diminish psychological violence as well as physical incidents. The expectation is that by constructively addressing issues of conflict that often precede physical engagement, the incidence and intensity of physical engagement will diminish.[22]

Conflict Resolution and Social Justice

It is a major challenge to any school to realize the mission of social justice for all. Few if any institutional models of effective practice exist—in or outside of education. Many conflicts in schools are about diversity issues: cultural conflicts often based on differences in national origin or ethnicity, but also based on social differences such as gender, sexual orientation, social class, or physical or mental abilities. Personal and institutional reactions to diversity often take the form of prejudice, discrimination, harassment, and hate crimes. Diversity conflicts are complex because they are rooted not only in prejudice and discrimination related to these cultural and social differences but also in the resulting structures and relationships of inequality and power. Conflict resolution education programs are arenas in schools where prejudice can be challenged; they promote tolerance, respect, and acceptance through new ways of communicating and understanding.

It is equally important for schools to foster a learning climate that is committed to equity and social justice. Providing conflict resolution education is a way to act upon that commitment. Conflict resolution education offers schools strategies to begin to respond affirmatively to crucial questions:

- Does the school community possess the skills and knowledge to successfully nurture an environment in which diversity thrives?

- Is there a cultivated willingness to accept the inevitable conflict that arises from differing values and cultures?

- Is there an understanding that conflict is an opportunity for growth, self-awareness, and development of understanding and respect for others?
- Is there an articulated vision that this inevitable conflict can enrich and strengthen our school community?[23]

One short-term goal of educational institutions must be to move students from simply recognizing that they live in a multicultural and often violent society to feeling prepared to contribute and live peacefully in their diverse communities. Looking ahead, educators and the educational system must challenge young people to believe and act on the understanding that a nonviolent, pluralistic society is a realistic goal.[24]

Conflict Resolution and Cooperative Learning Environments _____

A cooperative learning environment is a requisite element to improving school climate and providing an enhanced learning environment. Necessary environmental conditions include increasing levels of respect, trust, cohesiveness, and morale, and providing opportunities for input, continuous academic and social growth, and school renewal and caring. Conflict resolution, when used not only as a curriculum to be taught but as a lifestyle to be lived, contributes to most if not all of these qualities. When conflict resolution practices are applied, then respect, caring, tolerance, and community building become "the way we do things around here."[25] Creating a cooperative learning environment where controversies enhance learning and where self-discipline and self-responsibility prevail is a primary objective of conflict resolution education.

Cooperative, collaborative problem solving is the essence of conflict resolution education. The processes of conflict resolution (negotiation, mediation, and consensus decision making) are workable dispute resolution models that provide potential nonviolent and nonadversarial alternatives to the jurisprudence process of our legal system, or to our schools' problem-solving and discipline processes.

Conflict Resolution and Responsible Citizenry _____

The mandate to prepare youth to live productively in our democratic society is clearly a charge to educate for responsible citizenship. The ability to express and resolve conflicts is central to peaceful expression of human rights. Skills and strategies of conflict resolution are also skills of peace. Conflict resolution and peacemaking can be viewed as a responsibility inherent in citizenship in a democratic society. When persons are able to peacefully express their concerns and seek resolutions to problems that take into account common interests, they promote the values of human dignity and self-esteem as well as advance democracy. A conflict resolution education program gives young people the theoretical understanding and practical experience necessary to become effective, balanced, flexible adults. The school whose structures and teaching enable the learner to behave peacefully truly serves the highest ideal of education: individual acceptance of responsibility to guarantee the universal human rights of all. In the absence of effective prevention, employment of tougher law enforcement and stricter sanctions is unlikely to reduce violence significantly, if at all. A democratic society relies on the acceptance of individual self-responsibility; it is incompatible with the philosophy of democracy to believe responsibility can be simply mandated and then enforced.[26]

Schools have to be places from which viable and positive future pathways for young people can be forged. Above all, they must be places where children can learn to live and get along with one another and prepare to assume their future roles as responsible citizens of a democracy, as parents, as community members and leaders, and as productive members of the workforce. Many children have no other place from which to gain these experiences. Only schools can extend these possibilities equally to all children—and that is the constitutional mandate to the schools.[27]

Civil Association

How we "get along" seems important. The debates of our time that relate to the very essence of our social fabric, especially the issues of racial and cultural division, community and communitarianism, volunteerism and philanthropy, the common good, public virtues and values, and even collaborative conflict resolution suggest that we are defined by the very questions we are trying to answer:

> One of these questions relates to citizenship and how we live in civil association with one another. . . . We may understand citizenship not simply as membership in a state, but the condition of people participating in the exercise of governing themselves, and with the capacity to effectively carry on the public's business. We act more as citizens not in private, but together, in relationship to each other, to our community and to our country. Our relationships with each other are impacted by how we live our lives in the modern world,

and there are many forces at work which make these relationships problematic. Conflict resolution skills are increasingly needed to let us lead successful public lives in our schools, communities, and workplaces. This does not simply refer to the need for complex problem-solving processes, but suggests that our ability to solve larger issues depends, at least to some extent, on how we regularly deal with each other. Building effective relationships among citizens is important not just for 'reaching agreements,' but for how people may choose to disagree.[28]

Rationale for Conflict Resolution Education

In summary, a rationale for establishing conflict resolution education programs presents powerful reasons for every school to teach conflict resolution to youth:

- Using the conflict resolution processes of group problem solving, negotiation, and mediation to resolve school-based disputes can improve the school climate.

- Conflict resolution strategies can result in reduced violence, vandalism, chronic school absence, and suspension.

- Conflict resolution training helps students and teachers deepen their understanding of themselves and others.

- Conflict resolution training provides the recipient of the training with important life skills.

- Training in group problem solving, negotiation, and mediation encourages high-level citizenship activity.

- Shifting the responsibility for solving some school conflicts to students frees the adults to concentrate more on teaching and less on discipline.

- Behavior management systems that are more effective than detention, suspension, or expulsion are needed to deal with conflict in the school setting.

- Conflict resolution training increases skills in listening, critical thinking, and problem solving—skills basic to all learning.

- Conflict resolution education emphasizes seeing other points of view and the peaceful resolution of differences, skills that assist one to live in a multicultural world.

- Negotiation and mediation are problem-solving tools that are well suited to the problems that young people face, and those trained in these approaches often use them to solve problems for which they would not seek adult help.[29]

Education can be and should be turned into a force for reducing intergroup conflict. It can serve to enlarge our social identifications in light of common characteristics and communal goals. It can establish a basis for fundamental human identification across diverse cultures in the face of manifest conflict. The question is whether human beings can learn more constructive orientations toward those outside their group while maintaining the values of group allegiance and identity. It seems reasonable to believe that, in spite of very bad habits from the past and very bad models in the present, we can indeed learn new habits of mind: "It is not too late for a paradigm shift in our outlook toward human conflict. Perhaps it is something like learning that the earth is not flat. Such a shift in child development and education . . . might at long last make it possible for human groups to learn to live together in peace and mutual benefit."[30] Since we are, in fact, a single, interdependent, meaningfully attached, worldwide species, effective citizenry is an issue for our country and a global one as well. Where will effective citizenry emerge if not in our schools?

We, the educational community collective, have the power to decide what vision we wish for the future. Our world will be a different place in twenty years. Reconstituting our schools to realize the elements of mission addressed by conflict resolution education offers hope that the future will be characterized by an improved human experience for all. Conflict resolution education supports equipping individuals to be peacemakers. Peace is made moment by moment, day by day, by each of us. Peace will be realized only when a critical mass practices peacemaking: honoring self, honoring others, and honoring the environment.[31] These are the behaviors that allow individuals to live in civil association—that is to say, in responsible global citizenship. Where will youth learn these behaviors if not in our schools?

CHAPTER 2

The Capacity of Schools to Develop Responsible Citizens

Through implementing comprehensive conflict resolution education programs, school communities can improve the school learning climate and have an impact on the future. The skills of conflict resolution and the behaviors of peacemaking are life skills that apply not just in the school community but in every context of life and that release the potential within each for a life of quality. Creating a generation of individuals who possess the skills of constructive, creative conflict resolution and peacemaking offers hope for a less violent culture. It cannot be assumed that students have the ability to behave as peacemakers unless they have been taught the skills of peacemaking and allowed to experience the joy and power of peace. Schools alone may not be able to accomplish a peaceable society, but society cannot succeed in creating peace without educating our country's youth in peacemaking behaviors.[1]

A Comprehensive Approach

To reduce violence among youth in the community and lead young people to be responsible citizens, we must build the capacity of school-communities to establish quality comprehensive conflict resolution programs. Communities must challenge youths to believe and act on the understanding that a nonviolent, pluralistic society is a realistic goal. This societal goal comes alive for students only when they can live it in one context significant to their life.

School can be that context. When the adults in that context visualize the goal and commit themselves to action to achieve it in the total school environment, students can embrace the vision and contribute to the goal of a nonviolent, pluralistic society.[2] The fundamental challenge is for schools to provide community leadership toward realizing this vision by engaging students in learning skills and processes that allow them to constructively problem solve. When students experience success with these processes in the context of school, they are more likely to choose the processes in their other life contexts. By demonstrating that the processes work for youth in the school environment, the school challenges the community to provide youths with the opportunities to use the processes outside the school.[3]

Learning and Transfer

Humans beings learn, remember, and think. We also plan, solve problems, and use language. We can, and usually do, learn to modify our behavior when confronted with new situations. We are capable of using prior learning to generalize to differing circumstances. We pursue acquisition of concepts and strategies to cope with both current and anticipated events. This flexible, adaptive character of human behavior illustrates the significance of learning and provides the basic rationale for learning about conflict and conflict resolution. Through learning, human beings acquire the capacity to behave in a variety of circumstances, always driven by the goal of attempting to attain satisfaction of basic needs from the experience: to belong, to achieve or gain recognition, to exercise choice or control, to enjoy. Since conflict is perpetually present, nearly every circumstance affords the opportunity to manage conflict, and each individual is constantly required to do so. Everyone learns to do something with and about conflict. Unfortunately, many have no personal experiences from which to draw and no significantly involved models from which to learn other than the mostly dysfunctional approaches to conflict of "fight" or "flight." For these individuals, the only alternative in order to try to gain satisfaction of needs from an experience involving conflict is to try harder at what they do know: flee faster or farther, or fight longer and harder.

Teaching individuals the foundation abilities and the problem-solving processes of conflict resolution provides behavioral alternatives to flight-or-fight that may be chosen to effectively manage conflicts. At first glance, attaining this purpose appears to be a simple matter of providing sufficient skills training to use a specific step-by-step problem-solving process. However, to realize the goal for an individual to actually choose a different behavior in conflict situations entails much more than training in a specific process. Each new situation the individual confronts contains elements of uniqueness and requires him or her to use previous learning in a new way. The individual must not only remember but also select from his or her experiences those responses that are appropriate. When what has been learned is creatively employed in new situations, transfer of learning has been achieved. Transfer is highly unlikely unless the individual has a profound understanding of why the problem-solving process is constructed the way it is. Following a procedure simply as a ritual established through repeated practice, one is unlikely to transfer the use of the procedure to circumstances that are perceived as different. Whereas it is possible through repeated practice to train an individual to follow a specific problem-solving technique, it requires education for the individual to know when to apply the technique and how to modify it to fit varying circumstances. Conflict resolution education, as the name suggests, provides the necessary education in understanding conflict, peacemaking, and the principles of conflict resolution.

There is little reason to teach conflict resolution if the learning does not transfer. It is impossible to predict for a person exactly in what situations he or she will use the problem-solving processes of conflict resolution. Nevertheless, it is clear that these processes are life skills, and transfer of learning is stipulated in the view that conflict resolution education provides skills for living. The foundational understanding of conflict and peacemaking allows one to assimilate the perceptions of an unknown circumstance into the framework of known responses and to integrate the two to generate unique but socially acceptable behavior. On the one hand, technique alone may not find sincerity. On the other hand, an individual whose sincere intent to resolve issues peaceably is underpinned with understanding of the intentions behind the foundational principles of conflict resolution finds a personally workable technique for peacemaking.

Violence prevention efforts in schools have concentrated mostly on actual infliction, or attempts to inflict, physical harm and have dealt little with intimidation and harassment or other issues of emotional harm. Programs that do focus more on these issues of psychological violence are directed toward helping youths learn peaceful, effective ways of resolving conflicts. Despite what appears to be broad-based concern regarding youth involvement in violence and, as advanced in Chapter One, the viability of conflict resolution education to address that concern, even a cursory examination of current school programs indicates that there has not existed a widely recognized need to integrate conflict resolution principles and skills development into all levels of educational curricula. Notwithstanding the heroic efforts of many teachers, organizations, and schools today, the number of schools in the nation with comprehensive conflict resolution education programs falls far short of what is desperately needed. Even though the field of conflict resolution in education has grown dramatically over the past few years, the number of schools without conflict resolution education programs far exceeds the number of schools with such programs. Further, existing programs all too often do not provide conflict resolution education to all students, choosing instead to provide intensive education to a few peer mediators who then make their services available to other students. Most children in our schools get no sustained exposure at any grade level to such basic skills as active listening, empathy, appreciation of diversity, brainstorming, and joint problem solving. Few schools offer an integrated curricular approach in which basic conflict resolution skills are developed, practiced, and applied again and again in simulated and real situations until they become fully internalized.

Even when there exists a recognized need for educating students in nonviolent problem solving, educators often lack knowledge about conflict resolution and effective implementation of conflict resolution education programs. For example, students have conflicts with each other, but they also have conflicts with parents, teachers, school administrators, employers, neighbors, and others. Educators who implement conflict resolution education programs addressing only conflict among students limit the impact of these programs and deprive school faculty, students, families, and the larger community of opportunities to develop and practice conflict resolution skills in all areas where they are desperately needed.

Prevention and Intervention

Conflict resolution education programs exemplify the capability to make operational for youth the value that intervening without violence is an act of courage, not weakness, and the capability to nurture prosocial behavior in youth. Programs that are successful in intervening with youth involved in violent or self-destructive behavior have abandoned the failed policies of striking back at them. No amount of righteous anger can teach delinquents self-worth or cause them to empathize with their victims. Instead, the goal of such programs is to open lines of communication with troubled youths in order to effectively confront and overcome the destructive thoughts, feelings, and values that perpetrate antisocial behavior. Such programs resist the call for harsher, swifter punishments and instead pursue more pragmatic courses to not only avert further or future damage but also to provide to these perpetrators education in behavioral alternatives.

Clearly, there are issues affecting youths, and affected by them, that go beyond the purview of conflict resolution education programs in schools. For a multiplicity of causes, only some of which are self-inflicted, many young people are in need of therapy. Programs of conflict resolution education are not therapy programs. This is not to say that youths with therapy issues cannot participate in and profit from conflict resolution education programs. Also, not all young people are inclined toward violent behavior or otherwise in need of therapy, but all will encounter conflict. Conflict resolution education programs, however, are not designed to deal, or are not capable of dealing, with many of the underlying causes of deviant behavior; nor should such programs be designed to deal directly with the occurrence of violent antisocial behavior.

Full Range of Services

It is not a matter of choosing between providing conflict resolution education or offering therapy to youth. These two paths of intervention address different concerns, and youth deserves the opportunity to reap benefits from both. Brendtro and Long assert that breaking the cycle of violence requires a full range of services, therapy, and education, including but not limited to school-based programs. If we are going to really "get smart" and reverse patterns of conflict and aggression, we must prepare to fight a three-front war of primary prevention, early intervention, and restoration of social bonds.

Primary Prevention. Research shows that once launched, troubled behavior is often self-perpetuating across the life span. Therefore, the highest priority should be interventions that affect the lives of young children in families and schools:

- *Preventing broken belongings.* We developmentally immunize children against violence as we meet their most basic needs to be reared in consistent, safe, loving environments. Therefore, any meaningful violence prevention begins with comprehensive early childhood and family support services. We must move beyond the rhetoric of family values and start nurturing our embryonic child-citizens in order to plant solid family values in future generations.

- *Teaching children self-discipline.* We can either turn our schools into police states or teach our students responsibility. Teachers can be trained to use naturally occurring discipline problems as a curriculum for "ethical literacy" and create school cultures of nonviolence.

- *Teaching conflict resolution.* Students need specific competencies to resolve conflicts with peers and authority problems with adults. Such programs are not affective frills but basic training in life survival skills.

Early Intervention.   We can now identify students at risk of violence in the first years of school and provide them with a variety of effective and comprehensive experiences in school, home, and the community. There are research-validated interventions that should be part of a logical system for reducing delinquent and self-defeating behavior:

- *Mentoring children at risk.* Every child needs at least one adult who is irrationally crazy about him or her. Millions of children suffer from attention starvation, and there are not enough professional caregivers to combat this famine. Mentoring programs offered by schools, social agencies, churches, and businesses can help fill that void and can have profound impact.

- *Mentoring and training parents.* Since much early antisocial behavior is caused by inconsistent and harsh discipline, parent training curricula are important tools for breaking coercive cycles and instilling positive parent-child interactions.

- *Targeting school bullying.* Peer harassment is an early indicator of lifelong antisocial problems. Without intervention, childhood bullies often develop into violent adults.

- *Disengaging from punitive cycles.* Counselors, social workers, psychologists, teachers, and administrators need nonpunitive skills for managing behavior and inevitable conflicts in schools.

Restoring Social Bonds.   With our most damaged youth, the real choice is between reclaiming options and nonreclaiming ones. Our culture is producing a growing population of hostile, unattached children with weak conscience development. We must have the guts to stand up to those who would discard an entire generation of children in conflict. We now have indisputable research evidence that punitive settings imposing external control can actually escalate a youth's aggression. Research also validates that alternative approaches are effective in creating positive treatment environments that empower these youths to change:

- *Fostering attachment.* The more troubled and "beset" youths are, the more they need close personal attachments in order to reconstruct their lives. These positive bonds should characterize both adult and peer relationships.

- *Fostering achievement.* Delinquent behavior is often provoked by school failure. Teachers in successful school programs give students "uncommonly warm emotional support" and prevent them from failing. Youth who become interested in school and make achievement gains have better subsequent community adjustment.

- *Fostering autonomy.* Adult domination and authoritarian control fuel negative peer subcultures. Involving youth in decision making fosters the turnaround to prosocial behavior.

Successful programs find ways to address the developmental needs of youth as well as societal needs to stop destructive behavior. This requires adults who are authoritative, but not authoritarian. Troubled youths need safe, positive environments in which they can create corrective social bonds with adults and peers.[4]

Prevention and intervention clearly demand more than conflict resolution programs in schools, but schools and conflict resolution programs have a role—a major one—in the total effort to provide quality-of-life skills to youth. Rational interventions demand a clear perception of the worldview of youths growing up in cultures of violence. Many youths are personally immersed in such a culture; however, through the omnipresent messages of the media, no youth today can escape exposure to such a culture. Empathy is not bleeding-heart emotionalism, but a higher-order thinking process that suspends blame and seeks to understand another person. It takes great courage to communicate with troubled youths in times of crisis. Schools can provide the structures and programs to allow those who work there real opportunity to be empathetic toward and courageous with youth.

Conflict resolution education as a prevention strategy, and certainly as an intervention strategy, is not a quick fix; it takes time. It takes time for adults in schools to integrate conflict resolution into their own lives and to use it consistently when under pressure, especially in the workplace. It takes time for adults to learn to translate the concepts of conflict resolution for their students. It takes time for students to integrate conflict resolution into their lives and to use it consistently when under pressure, especially from peers who are choosing other behaviors. It takes time for even the most effective school and classroom instruction to have a significant impact upon individual behavior and upon the collective climate of the school. Obviously time is an issue, but it is in actuality an issue of pay now or pay later. If time is not invested in developing programs to provide youth alternatives to self-destructive and violent behaviors, then time will be constantly invested in reacting to those behaviors. As with nearly every other example in life, if one chooses to pay later one must pay more. Interest accrues.[5]

Conflict resolution takes time because its problem-solving strategies are not employed in a vacuum. To be effective, conflict resolution must be viewed not as isolated interactions between individuals but as a pervasive, systemic culture change. Thus, whether a conflict resolution education program is planned for implementation in a single classroom or in an entire school, more is involved than just providing students with the foundation abilities and the problem-solving processes. Sustaining and expanding a program requires attention to systemic change issues. Policies and rules governing the school, and implementation of those policies and rules, often provide powerful contradictory messages to peaceful resolution of conflicts. Two areas of practice that require examination are the degree of competition promoted by or inherent within the system and the manner in which behavioral expectations are enforced.[6]

Cooperative Context

Conflict resolution is problem solving for mutual benefit; thus cooperation is an operational value of conflict resolution. Johnson and Johnson assert that "it makes little sense to teach students to manage conflicts constructively if the school is structured so that students have to compete for scarce rewards (like grades of 'A') and defeat each other to get what they want."[7] The nature of the reward system is an extremely important dimension of the classroom and school context. The primary reward system of nearly every classroom and school is grades, and grades exemplify a competitive context:[8]

> It makes no sense to talk of constructive conflict management in schools structured competitively. Even aside from the issue of competition for grades, most learning activities in schools are structured as an activity for an individual—even though all individuals in the classroom are usually involved simultaneously in the same activity. It is generally perceived by the learner that he or she is competing against all the other learners. Although competition may not be the intent in the learning activities, there is a virtual dearth of cooperative learning in our schools. The first step in teaching students the

procedures for managing conflicts, therefore, is creating a cooperative context in which conflicts are defined as mutual problems to be resolved in ways that benefit everyone involved.[9]

The more cooperation becomes an integral feature of the school culture, the more it seems logical to expect individuals involved in a conflict to cooperate in finding a resolution.

Managing Behavior Without Coercion

Another operative value of conflict resolution is to refrain from coercive behaviors toward others and to choose problem solving instead. In the next chapter, it is noted that when individuals' basic needs conflict, each has only two behavioral alternatives: to elect problem solving or to coerce, that is, either try to get the other person to do as he or she wants them to do or else to give in. It is noteworthy that most school discipline plans are in fact based not on *discipline* but on *punishment*. Such programs are really designed to gain student compliance to externally imposed behavior expectations rather than to teach responsible, need-fulfilling behaviors. These programs resemble obedience training more than they do education. They place the adult in the system in the role of enforcer, and the enforcement can only occur through coercion. Thus the most significant observable behavior—the behavior of the adult model—is contrary to the message of respect, tolerance, and appreciation for differences. The behavior modeled is coercion, not problem solving. The following chart contrasts punishment practices and discipline practices:

Punishment Versus Discipline

Punishment	Discipline
Expresses power of an authority; usually causes pain to the recipient; is based upon retribution or revenge; is concerned with what has happened (the past)	Is based on logical or natural consequences that embody the reality of a social order (rules that one must learn and accept to function adequately and productively in society); concerned with what is happening now (the present)
Is arbitrary—probably applied inconsistently and unconditionally; does not accept or acknowledge exceptions or mitigating	Is consistent—accepts that the behaving individual is doing the best he or she can do for now

circumstances

Is imposed by an authority (done to someone), with responsibility assumed by the one administering the punishment and the behaving individual avoiding responsibility	Comes from within, with responsibility assumed by the behaving individual and the behaving individual desiring responsibility; presumes that conscience is internal
Closes options for the individual who must pay for a behavior that has already occurred	Opens options for the individual, who can choose a new behavior
As a teaching process, usually reinforces a failure identity; essentially negative and short-term, without sustained personal involvement of either teacher or learner	As a teaching process, is active and involves close, sustained, personal involvement of both teacher and learner; emphasizes developing ways to act that will result in more successful behavior
Is characterized by open or concealed anger; is a poor model of the expectations of quality	Is friendly and supportive; provides a model of quality behavior
Is easy and expedient	Is difficult and time-consuming
Focuses on strategies intended to control behavior of the learner	Focuses on the learner's behavior and the consequences of that behavior
Rarely results in positive changes in behavior; may increase subversiveness or result in temporary suppression of behavior; at best, produces compliance	Usually results in a change in behavior that is more successful, acceptable, and responsible; develops the capacity for self-evaluation of behavior[10]

If educators desire students to choose not to coerce others, they must consistently model an orderly, productive system accomplished through cooperation and persistent pursuit of quality behavior, rather than through actual or implied force to maintain a semblance of order. Further, students must be provided with alternative ways to behave—not just told to not behave in a particular manner. Rethinking the behavior management plan and processes is a paramount systemic change requirement in building a peaceable climate.

Making this notion operational requires as a prerequisite making clear the behavioral expectations for the system. Often conflicts occur because the individuals involved interpreted differently what is expected, or one or both believed that pursuing their behavior choice was worth the risk because the behavior had gone undeterred in the past. A successful conflict resolution education program is dependent upon adroit student self-evaluation of behavior and the self-generation of system-accepted alternative behavioral choices. Each student must fully understand the behavioral expectations of the school and be fully cognizant of the consequences of choosing to behave otherwise. Such understanding is simplified when expectations make sense to the student. Expectations make sense when there is a logical, age-appropriate explanation for their existence; when rules are few and simple; when expectations are predictable and can be applied in new situations; and when consequences for inappropriate behavior are known, nonpunitive, and consistently applied.

In brief, a sense-based system for determining acceptable and unacceptable behavior reduces confusion about rules, concerns regarding the uniform enforcement of rules, and the willingness to risk "not getting caught" behaving inappropriately. Most schools, however, are *rule-abundant systems* characterized by rules that are many and complex and that appear to be unconnected and unrelated, expectations that are not easily applied to new situations, and consequences for inappropriate behavior—usually punitive—that are often neither understandable nor consistently applied. A chart contrasts the two systems:

Sense-Based System	Rule-Abundant System
Has a logical organization.	Lacks organization.
Rules are few and simple, predictable, and generalizable.	Rules are many and complex, lack predictability, and cannot be generalized (situation-specific).
Consequences for inappropriate behavior are known and consistently applied.	Consequences for inappropriate behavior are unknown and/or inconsistently applied.
Authority derives from the system.	Authority derives from those in charge.
Reduces rule confusion.	Is characterized by rule confusion.[11]

To build the foundation for peace in the school where human dignity and self-esteem are valued, individuals must understand their human rights, respect those rights for self and others, and learn how to exercise their rights without infringing upon the rights of others. Rights and responsibilities provide a teachable, understandable system for framing behavioral expectations. Rights and responsibilities are the constitution under which the rules and conventions of behavior management and interactions are generated. The following is an example of how one school framed its expectations as rights and responsibilities:

My Rights

I have the right to be happy and to be treated with compassion in this school: This means that no one will laugh at me or hurt my feelings.

I have the right to be myself in this school: This means that no one will treat me unfairly because I am . . .
    black or white
    fat or thin
    tall or short
    boy or girl
    adult or child.

I have the right to be safe in this school: This means that no one will . . .
    hit me
    kick me
    push me
    pinch me
    threaten me
    hurt me.

I have the right to expect my property to be safe in this school.

I have the right to hear and be heard in this school: This means that no one will . . .

    yell
    scream
    shout
    make loud noises
    or otherwise disturb me.

My Responsibilities

I have the responsibility to treat others with compassion: This means that I will not laugh at others, tease others, or try to hurt the feelings of others.

I have the responsibility to respect others as individuals and not to treat others unfairly because they are . . .
    black or white
    fat or thin
    tall or short
    boy or girl
    adult or child.

I have the responsibility to make the school safe by not . . .
    hitting anyone
    kicking anyone
    pushing anyone
    pinching anyone
    threatening anyone
    hurting anyone.

I have the responsibility not to take or destroy the property of others.

I have the responsibility to help maintain a calm and quiet school: This means that I will not . . .
    yell
    scream
    shout
    make loud noises
    or otherwise disturb

I have the right to learn about myself and others in this school: This means that I will be free to express my feelings and opinions without being interrupted or punished.

others.

I have the responsibility to learn about myself and others in this school: This means that I will be free to express my feelings and opinions without being interrupted or punished, and I will not interrupt or punish others who express their feelings and opinions.

I have the right to be helped to learn self-control in this school: This means that no one will silently stand by while I abuse my rights.

I have the responsibility to learn self-control in this school: This means that I will strive to exercise my rights without denying the same rights to others, and I will expect to be corrected when I do abuse the rights of others as they shall be corrected if my rights are abused.

I have the right to expect that all these rights will be mine in all circumstances so long as I am exercising my full responsibilities.

I have the responsibility to protect my rights and the rights of others by exercising my full responsibilities in all circumstances.[12]

The concept of organizing expectations as rights and responsibilities is teachable and is understandable to students because it is based on a logical system of thought—a system fundamental to our democratic traditions. Rules allow everyone to know his or her responsibilities and safeguard the rights of all by making explicit the relationship between rights and responsibilities. Such a logical and fundamentally simple notion provides students with a framework they can use to determine what is and what is not acceptable behavior—a critical requirement in evaluating behavioral options in any conflict resolution process. In the context of our democratic culture, the notion of rights and responsibilities makes sense. Such expectations apply to all members of the school environment—adults or students.

Students cannot resolve behavioral conflicts within a system absent of behavioral norms. Nor is the absence of norms alleviated by the presence of confusing and ambiguous norms. If the authority and justification for rules are the sole domain of the adults in the system, students will be severely hampered in any efforts to engage successfully in conflict resolution unassisted by those adults. Conflict resolution is facilitated by clarifying behavioral expectations and the consequences of not meeting those expectations. This information becomes a major criterion for selecting options upon which to build an agreement.

Still another strong argument for developing a sense-based system is the understanding that conflict resolution is about designing future acceptable behaviors and does not involve fault finding and punishment for past behavior. When consequences for unacceptable behavior are clear, it is easier to determine which conflicts are appropriate for student-assisted resolution. The application of the consequence is not an issue for mediation or negotiation. Conflict resolution may be very appropriate to help those who engaged in a behavior that resulted in a consequence to plan for a future behavior that is acceptable, thus avoiding similar future consequences. Requiring participation in a conflict resolution process, however, should not be a consequence. Conflict resolution is a choice. For example, if the consequence for fighting is suspension, one should not be allowed to escape or reduce the suspension by choosing to mediate. Mediation is appropriate in this scenario if offered as an opportunity for the individuals involved to plan a way to behave toward each other that avoids future fighting, is acceptable to each of them, and is viewed as acceptable behavior by the school.

Alternative to Traditional Forms of Discipline

Most school reform initiatives espouse that alternatives to traditional forms of discipline are required to change student behaviors. If suspensions and expulsions worked, we would witness a decrease in the need for such measures; instead we see their increasing use. Punitive school measures succeed only in gaining student compliance to adult-imposed standards; they work initially only when the student believes the standards are reasonable or when the student fears the punishment. It is nearly impossible to "frighten" many of today's students into "behaving properly." Youngsters who grow up where they are socialized to violence, physical abuse, or even death are not brought readily into submission by such punishments as lowered grades, time-out, detention, suspension, or even expulsion. The harshest punishments available to schools can be ignored or even laughed at by students. The reward and punishment system no longer works—if in fact such a system ever worked.[13]

An attractive alternative to violence and coercion and a basic life skill is being assertive. Assertiveness is knowing how to take advantage of opportunities without victimizing another, knowing how to resist pressure or intimidation from others and how to do this without destroying relationships or isolating oneself, and knowing how to resolve conflicts in ways that make use of the full range of nonviolent opportunities that exist in a conflict situation. These skills do not just combat violence; they are necessary for a quality life. They are fostered by conflict resolution programs and can be taught in schools.[14]

Rewards and Punishments

Alfie Kohn asserts that

many educators are acutely aware that punishment and threats are counterproductive. Making students suffer in order to alter their future behavior can often elicit temporary compliance, but this strategy is unlikely to help students become ethical, compassionate decision makers. Punishment, even if referred to euphemistically as "consequences," tends to generate anger, defiance, and a desire for revenge. Moreover, it models the use of coercive power rather than reason and ruptures the important relationship between adult and student. As with punishments, the offer of rewards can elicit temporary compliance in many cases. Unfortunately, carrots turn out to be no more effective than sticks at helping students become caring, responsible people or lifelong, self-directed learners. Research and logic suggest that punishment and rewards are not really opposites, but two sides of the same coin. Both strategies amount to ways of trying to manipulate someone's behavior—in one case prompting the self-evaluative question, "What do they want me to do, and what happens to me if I don't do it?" and in the other instance leading the student to ask, "What do they want me to do, and what do I get if I do it?" Neither strategy helps students to grapple with the question, "What kind of person do I want to be?"[15]

The mandate to prepare youth to be effective citizens in our world calls for a system to manage behavior that teaches alternatives characterized as long-term changes in attitudes and behavior. Conflict resolution education programs can be an important part of those alternatives primarily because they invite participation and expect those who choose to participate to plan more effective behavior and then to employ those behaviors.[16]

Professionals in the field of conflict resolution education recognize that for conflict resolution education programs in schools to realize maximum results, practices and policies of the school often need to be reformed. Crucial changes are usually required to provide a context facilitative of conflict resolution processes. This, at the very least, calls for system changes to operationalize cooperation as the normative expectation, both behaviorally and academically, and a system for managing behavior that allows adults to interact non-coercively with youth. These two reconfigurations, seen as necessary to convey operationally the valued behavior of collaborative problem solving, often provoke highly charged emotional exchanges within the school community: "Without competition for scarce resources such as praise and grades, how will students be motivated to learn?" "Without punishment, how will students' behavior be controlled to create an atmosphere conducive to learning?" These questions frame conflicts that the adults in the system are challenged to confront and resolve.[17] These two issues—creating a cooperative context and managing behavior noncercively—are core considerations in creating the desired paradigm shift, but these questions speak to the ingrained nature of competitive and punitive practices of the system. The magnitude of the task of reconfiguring the system demands quality, comprehensive staff development to facilitate the paradigm shift.

Staff Development for Systemic School Change

In calling for a change in the total school environment that creates a safe community living by a credo of nonviolence and multicultural appreciation, William DeJong, a lecturer at the Harvard School of Public Health, concludes that for this to happen educators themselves must change: "They must learn and apply a new set of skills for managing and resolving conflict. Even more difficult, they must adopt a new style of classroom management, one that fundamentally involves a sharing of power with students so that students can learn how to deal with their own disputes."[18]

Staff development is the initial thrust required toward realizing broad-based youth-centered conflict resolution education programs in our nation's schools. Historically, staff development programs have often fallen short in translating what appeared to be desired change into sustained practice. The challenge is to go beyond the traditional staff development program approach, which is designed to assist educators in improving their skills and becoming more knowledgeable. A staff development program with these goals is designed to help educators develop the skills and knowledge to do their work better. What is needed for conflict resolution education programs to become institutionalized is an enhanced collective capacity of those involved to create and pursue an overall vision—a vision of school as a collection of individuals behaving very differently from what is currently observed in most schools.

To ensure the highest probability of success, a staff development program must be organized around team learning, focused on building a shared vision, and directed toward systems thinking. Systems thinking is required because systemic change is necessary for a youth-centered conflict resolution education program to be integral to, not an adjunct to, a school. In operationalizing a shared vision for a school community, it is indispensable to provide implementation support that involves coaching, mentoring, and technical assistance available to the adult segment of the school population as well as to the youth segment. Since learning always occurs in a context where one is taking action, the challenge is to find ways for the adults (historically isolated from each other in our schools) to really work together. Creation of an environment where adults can continuously reflect on what they are doing, and learn more about what it takes to work as teams, is critical in developing and implementing an action plan to address the issues of the school community. This learning is imperative in order to have the visionary systems thinking and concomitant action needed to involve all youth in developing the skills of conflict resolution and peacemaking.

Any school system that implements the staff development program necessary to implement and sustain a quality conflict resolution education program benefits directly in obtaining staff skilled in consensus decision making. Broad-based collaboration is essential in the school's ability to adapt to the changing needs of its clientele in all dimensions of operation, not just in efforts to provide a quality conflict resolution education program.

CHAPTER 3

Understanding Conflict as a Learning Opportunity

Conflict is a discord of needs, drives, wishes, or demands. Intrapersonal conflict involves an internal discord, interpersonal conflict means discord between two parties, and intergroup conflict is discord within a group of people or between groups of people. Each of these types of conflict has an impact on schools.[1]

Conflict is a natural, vital part of life. When conflict is understood, it can become an opportunity to learn and create. The synergy of conflict can create new alternatives—something that was not possible before. The challenge for people in conflict is to apply the principles of creative cooperation in their human relationships. When differences are acknowledged and appreciated—and when the conflicting parties build on one another's strengths—a climate is created that nurtures the self-worth of each individual and provides each with an opportunity for fulfillment.[2]

Without conflict, there would likely be no personal growth or social change. Unfortunately, when it comes to conflict most people's perceptions are profoundly negative. Negative perceptions and the reactions they provoke are extremely detrimental to successful conflict resolution. In every conflict, the individual has a choice: to be driven by negative perceptions or to take control of the situation and act positively. However, in the absence of educational opportunities to learn positive ways of approaching conflict, many individuals are seriously hampered in taking effective control of a conflict situation. Thus without training, these individuals actually do not have the ability to make positive choices. With more personal awareness and better understanding of available choices, one becomes able to approach conflict knowing that it can have either destructive or constructive results. When conflict is perceived as a positive life force, individuals in conflict become responsible for producing a result in which relationships are enhanced and they are empowered to control their own lives in ways that respect the needs of others. In brief, the power to create resolution lies within each person. Even so, perhaps largely because of the absence of observable models, this power is not often used. The purpose of a school-based conflict resolution education program is to give students and adults the knowledge and behaviors to unleash this power.[3]

It is important to realize that students' success in developing awareness of the positive potential of conflict is an outgrowth of the endeavors and commitment exhibited by the adults in the school to approach conflict positively. Educators who integrate positive ways of resolving conflict into their classroom and school see a powerful effect on their own lives and work, as well as on the lives and work of their students.[4]

Origins of Conflict

In his exposition of control theory, Dr. William Glasser explains that conflict originates from within.[5] Control theory explains why (and to a great extent how) all living organisms behave. Under this theory, everything we do in life is behavior; all of our behavior is purposeful, and the purpose is always to attempt to satisfy basic needs that are built into our genetic structure. Control theory is based on the assumption that all behavior represents the individual's constant attempt to satisfy one or more of five basic inborn needs. In other words, no behavior is caused by any situation or person outside of the individual.

Accepting this idea requires a paradigm shift on the part of those—including most educators—whose prior training supports the view of life according to stimulus-response theory. According to the stimulus-response paradigm, behavior is caused by someone or something (the stimulus) outside the individual; the action following is the response to that stimulus.

According to the control theory paradigm, people or events outside us never stimulate us to do anything. Rather, our behavior always represents the choice to do what most satisfies our needs at the time. When we repeat a choice that is consistently satisfying, we exercise less and less deliberation in making that choice. Even a quick action, however, is chosen and not automatic.

Basic Psychological Needs

All individuals are driven by genetically transmitted needs that serve as instructions for attempting to live our lives. These are the physiological need to survive and four psychological needs:

1. The need for *belonging:* fulfilled by loving, sharing, and cooperating with others
2. The need for *power:* fulfilled by achieving, accomplishing, and being recognized and respected
3. The need for *freedom:* fulfilled by making choices in our lives
4. The need for *fun:* fulfilled by laughing and playing

The needs are equally important, and all must be reasonably satisfied if individuals are to fulfill their biological destiny. The individual has no choice but to feel pain when a need is frustrated, and pleasure when it is satisfied. When any need goes unsatisfied, there is a continuous urge to behave. This urge is as much a part of human genetic instructions as is eye color. Instructions related to the physiological need of survival—such as hunger, thirst, safety, and sexual desire—are relatively distinct. Individuals quickly learn that a particular discomfort is attached to this need, and it is plain what they must do to satisfy the survival instructions. The psychological needs are challenging because it is often less clear what an individual must do to satisfy them. Psychological needs, like biological needs, have their source in the genes, even though they are much less tangible and the behaviors that fulfill them are more complex than the physical behaviors used to fulfill the survival need. Glasser holds that we are essentially biological beings, and the fact that we follow some of our genetic instructions psychologically rather than physically makes neither the instructions less urgent nor the source less biological.

The needs seem regularly to conflict with one another, and the constant challenge to satisfy them requires constant renegotiation of balance. For example, when a person chooses to work long hours, his accomplishments may help to meet his power need but he may not be involved with his friends and family in a need-fulfilling way. Perhaps another individual derives a sense of freedom from living alone, but she loses a sense of belonging when exercising this choice.

Even though individuals may not be fully aware of their basic needs, they learn that there are some general circumstances that strongly relate to the way they feel. As examples, people behave lovingly with their parents because it feels good; they realize that when people pay attention to their words or actions they feel powerful; by making choices they feel the importance of freedom; and through laughter they learn about fun.[6]

Quality World: Choices and Conflict

Even though human needs are essentially the same for everyone, the behaviors through which individuals choose to satisfy those needs may be quite different. Beginning at birth, individuals have unique experiences that feel either pleasurable or painful. Through these experiences, individuals learn how to satisfy their needs. Because individuals have different experiences, the things they learn to do to satisfy their needs differ as well. Each individual has memories of need-fulfilling behaviors specific to his or her unique life experiences. These pleasurable memories constitute the individual's *quality world* and become the most important part of the person's life. This quality world is composed of pictures (or, more accurately, perceptions) representing what they have most enjoyed in life. These perceptions become the standard for choosing behaviors. Unlike the basic survival needs, which are the same for everyone, the perceptions in each person's quality world are very specific and completely individual. Individuals choose to behave in different ways to fulfill their needs because their quality worlds are different. It is important to realize that the choice the individual makes in each situation is the choice he or she believes offers the best potential to meet his or her needs. In short, each is doing the best they know how to do to satisfy their needs.

However, one individual's choice may limit or disrupt another's choice. This is one significant source of conflict between individuals, especially in social situations like school, where the choice to disassociate from one another is nearly nonexistent. To be in effective control of one's life means integrating this knowledge into how one deals with others. *Making responsible choices that protect one's own rights without infringing on the rights of another is a basic precept of conflict resolution and the essence of effective citizenry in a democratic society.*[7]

Thus, even though all people are driven by the same four psychological needs, each person's wants are unique. Wants are like pictures in an album: it is impossible for two people to have the same picture album because it is impossible for two people to live exactly the same life. To understand conflict and perceive it positively, the knowledge that no two people can have exactly the same wants is central. For example, if two individuals wish to satisfy their need to belong through a friendship, they must learn to share their commonalities and respect and value their differences. As long as people have conflicting wants and as long as an individual's needs can be satisfied in ways that may conflict, the need to renegotiate balance persists. Thus, driven by our genetic instructions, we inevitably experience conflict and therefore we must learn how to deal with it constructively.[8]

Diagnosing Origins of Conflict

Diagnosing the origin or source of a conflict can help define a problem, and a definition of the problem is the starting point in any attempt to find a solution. Almost every conflict involves an endeavor by the disputants to meet the basic psychological needs for belonging, power, freedom, and fun. Limited resources and different values may appear to be the cause of conflicts, but unmet needs are truly at their root. Conflict resolution is next to impossible so long as one side believes its psychological needs are being threatened by the other. Unless unmet needs are expressed, the conflict often reappears even when a solution is reached regarding the subject of the dispute.[9]

Limited Resources

Conflicts involving limited resources (time, space, money, equipment, property) are typically the easiest to resolve.[10] People quickly learn that cooperating instead of competing for scarce resources is in their best interests. In cooperation, disputants share in problem solving, recognize each other's interests, and create choices. This process usually provides satisfaction because the psychological needs of belonging and power, perhaps even of freedom and fun, are addressed in the equitable allocation of limited resources. For instance, the student who is upset over the fact that a friend has not repaid a loan may really want to know that his friend respects him (a power need). He may not easily accept a payment solution unless his need for recognition and respect is addressed in the process. Limited resource conflicts may not be resolved because the resource itself may not define the problem. When solutions are crafted that deal only with the limited resource that seems to be the source of the conflict, the real problem is not solved, and the conflict will return.

Different Values

Conflicts involving different values (beliefs, priorities, principles) tend to be the more difficult to resolve. When a person holds a value, he or she has an enduring belief that a specific action or quality is preferable to an opposite action or quality. This belief applies to attitudes toward objects, situations, or individuals. The belief becomes a standard that guides the person's actions.

When the terminology used to express a conflict includes words such as *honest, equal, right,* and *fair,* the conflict is typically one of values. Many times disputants think in terms of right or wrong, or good or bad, when values are in opposition. Even conflicts over differing goals can be viewed as value conflicts: the source of a goal conflict relates either to the goal's relative importance for each disputant or to the fact that the disputants highly value different goals.[11]

When values are in conflict, the disputants often perceive the dispute as a personal attack or as a serious conflict between a trusted family belief and an alternative way of viewing the issue. They tend to personalize the conflict because their whole sense of self feels threatened and under attack. Strong stances on principle are therefore characteristic of value conflicts. When people feel attacked, they typically become defensive and stubbornly cling to their own convictions. The conflict exists because the disputants are governed by different sets of rules. Because the disputants evaluate the problem and each other according to conflicting criteria, resolution can be especially difficult.

Values disputes may be rooted in issues of social diversity (differences in cultural, social, or physical or mental attributes), often expressed as different beliefs, convictions, and principles, but they often also involve prejudice. Although complex, these conflicts can be resolved by increased awareness, understanding, and tolerance. When a conflict is rooted in prejudice or bias against a fellow student—as a member of a group that is perceived as inferior, unfamiliar, strange, even dangerous—ignorance, fear, and misunderstanding often guide behavior toward that person. Also, an unexamined sense of status or privilege may inadvertently hurt someone else through lack of recognition, exclusion, isolation, and so forth. Verbal expressions of this sense of ascendancy or privilege may even constitute racial or sexual harassment.

Psychological needs are enmeshed in value conflicts. For example, a person may be in conflict when a friend does not keep a promise. The person's picture of a friend is that of someone who is reliable, and her sense of belonging is threatened because her value system includes the assumption that friends do not make promises they cannot keep.

Rigid value systems can severely restrict one from meeting the need for belonging. The more one adheres to any value, the more one's belonging is limited to others who hold the same beliefs and the less exposure one has to diversity. Inflexible values are also almost always destructive to our need to be free. We see others as wrong if they do not hold our beliefs, and we see situations as bad if they do not meet our standards. When this is the case, our options in life to satisfy our needs for freedom, fun, and power, as well as our choice of friends, become limited.

Resolving a values conflict does not mean the disputants must change or align their values. Often a mutual acknowledgment that each person views the situation differently is the first step toward resolution. If the disputants can learn not to reject each other because of differences in beliefs, they are better able to deal with the problem on its own merits. This is the essence of one of the fundamental principles of conflict resolution: seeking to deal separately with the relationship issues and the substantive issues of the conflict. *To resolve values conflicts, the disputants must look for interests that underlie the conflicting values.* Again, psychological needs are enmeshed in values conflicts, and those needs likely frame the interests of each disputant.[12]

Responses to Conflict

Schrumpf, Crawford, and Bodine advance that responses to conflict can be categorized into three basic groups: *soft responses, hard responses,* and *principled responses.* For both soft and hard responses, participants take positions or stands on the problem. They negotiate these positions by trying either to avoid or else to win a contest of will. Soft and hard negotiations either bring about one-sided losses to reach an agreement or they demand one-sided gains as the price of the agreement. In the case of principled responses, participants use conflict resolution strategies designed to produce "wise agreements." A wise agreement is one that addresses the legitimate interests of both parties, resolves conflicting interests fairly, is durable, and takes contextual interests into account (how will others besides the disputants be affected by the agreement?).

Soft Responses

Soft responses usually involve people who are friends or people who just want to be nice to each other, probably because it is likely the contact between the parties will continue into the future. In such cases, they want to agree, and they negotiate softly to do so. Avoiding conflict is often the first soft response. People attempt to avoid conflict altogether by withdrawing from the situation, ignoring it, and denying that the conflict even matters. When people choose to avoid conflict, it is usually because they are not interested in maintaining the relationship or they lack the skills to negotiate a resolution. Accommodation—when one party adjusts to the position of the other without seeking to serve his or her own interests in the relationship—is a common soft response. Soft responses, especially avoidance responses, may have some merit for the immediate situation; for example, they may help a person control anger or protect herself or himself from the immediate danger of someone who responds aggressively. However, the soft response typically results in feelings of disillusionment, self-doubt, fear, and anxiety about the future. Many compromises are, in reality, soft responses to the conflict. The parties agree to something that addresses only some of each of their needs in order not to have to continue the confrontation.

Hard Responses

Hard responses to conflict usually involve people who are adversaries. The goal is victory. Hard responses to a conflict are characterized by confrontations that involve threats, aggression, and anger. Hard negotiators demand concessions as a condition of the relationship and insist on their position. They often search for a single answer to the problem: the one the other side will give in to. Hard negotiators frequently apply pressure, trying to win a contest of will. They use bribery and punishment (for example, withholding money, favors, and affection). When these intimidating tactics cause the other side to yield, the hard negotiator feels successful. Hostility, physical damage, and violence often result from this type of response to conflict. Furthermore, this attitude is always detrimental to cooperation.

Principled Responses

Principled responses involve people who view themselves as problem solvers; their goal is a wise outcome reached efficiently and amicably. These problem solvers have well-developed communication and conflict resolution skills. Principled negotiators understand that communication is fundamental to cooperative interaction, and they understand what it means to participate in developing a common understanding. Principled responses to conflict are characterized by first seeking to understand the other side, and then seeking to be understood. Principled negotiators are skilled active, empathic listeners. Principled negotiators examine the other side's frame of reference to see the problem as that person does and to comprehend the person emotionally and intellectually.

Principled responses to conflict create the opportunity for each participant to get his or her needs met. Principled responses to conflict are proactive, not reactive. When people behave proactively, they do not feel victimized and out of control; they do not blame other people or circumstances when in conflict. Instead, they take charge of their actions and feelings and use their principled negotiation skills to make resolution a possibility.

Outcomes of Soft, Hard, and Principled Responses

The three types of response to conflict produce different outcomes. Soft positional bargaining may be considered a *lose-lose* approach to conflict. When both parties deny the existence of the conflict or when they deal only with the superficial issues and not the interests at the root of the problem, neither person gets what he or she needs; they both lose. In a situation in which the response is to accommodate the other, the responder experiences a *lose-win* outcome. A person who avoids a conflict by accommodating the other person loses in the sense that he is intimidated and has little courage to express his own feelings and convictions. When conflicts are avoided, basic psychological needs are either unacknowledged or unmet. Thus, people who avoid conflicts are not in effective control of their lives; they see themselves as victims, and their relations with others invariably suffer.

Choosing a hard response may be considered a *win-lose* approach to conflict, where the responder is the more aggressive person and the adversary loses. This interpretation of winning and losing is usually in relation to the limited resource involved in the conflict. Hard positional bargaining often becomes *lose-lose* when the desire to punish or get even provokes adversaries to take vindictive actions that harm themselves as well as their opponent. These confrontations often are characterized by each party viewing the other as the enemy and each being driven to vindictive actions to punish or get even with the other. Hard responses produce stressful situations whenever the negotiators are required to continue to interact in some manner, perhaps in having to continue to work together toward common goals.

Both soft and hard responses are characterized by reactive communication indicating the individual is attempting to transfer responsibility and is unable to choose a response: "There is nothing I can do; I am not responsible."

Win-win or *principled* responses to conflicts change the game and the outcome. Principled methods of conflict resolution produce wise outcomes efficiently and amicably. This response to conflict focuses on interests instead of positions, and it brings people who are in conflict to a gradual consensus on a joint resolution without the transactional costs of digging into positions and without the emotional costs of destroying relationships. Principled responses are characterized by proactive communication, meaning that the individual takes responsibility for his or her actions and has the ability to choose a response. Principled negotiation is considered a *win-win* response to conflict.

The actions that people choose when they are involved in a conflict either increase or decrease the problem. When conflict escalates, the problem remains unresolved, and the effect can be destructive. As a conflict escalates, threats usually increase and additional people become involved with, and take sides in, the conflict. Anger, fear, and frustration are expressed, sometimes violently. As a conflict escalates, people become more and more entrenched in their positions. Conflicts deescalate when differences and interests are understood. People remain calm and are willing to listen to opposing viewpoints. Those involved focus on the problem rather than on each other, thus creating opportunity for resolution.[13]

In summary, conflict in and of itself is not positive or negative. Rather, the actions chosen turn conflict into either a competitive, devastating battle or else a constructive challenge where there is opportunity for growth. One always has the choice, when in conflict, to work for resolution. It is not our choice to not have conflict—it is an inevitable part of life. Our choice is how to deal with those inevitable conflicts. The ultimate goal of conflict resolution education is to provide tools for individuals to move beyond mere conflict deescalation (a conflict management strategy) to actual conflict resolution, which is true action planning for improved relations.

PART TWO

Approaches to Conflict Resolution Education

CHAPTER 4

Essential Goals and Principles

An authentic conflict resolution program has three components: (1) a set of problem-solving principles, (2) a structured process, and (3) the skills for creative cooperation between individuals and among groups.[1] Underlying a conflict resolution education program are certain precepts:

- Conflict is natural and normal.

- Differences can be acknowledged and appreciated.

- Conflict, when viewed as a solution-building opportunity, can lead to positive change.

- When the conflicting parties build on one another's strengths to find solutions, a climate is created that nurtures individual self-worth and opportunities for fulfillment of each individual's needs.

Practices for Managing Conflict in Schools

Clearly, conflict resolution differs from common perceptions of how problems are solved—especially in schools. Teachers, administrators, and other staff in schools charged with managing student behavior are all too aware of interpersonal and intergroup conflict. A considerable component of these adults' responsibilities within the school community is managing conflict. To suggest that schools do not have in place methodologies to manage behavior arising from conflict would be unconscionable. There are many possibilities for problem solving between people or groups of people. The use of arbitration as a problem-solving strategy is widely employed. Arbitration is the process whereby a party not involved directly in the conflict determines a solution to the conflict; the arbitrator rules and the disputants are expected to comply with the ruling. This is the process that is characteristic of adult involvement in most conflicts between students in schools.[2]

Conflict resolution programs, as discussed in this book, differ from the prevalent practices for managing student conflict. Conflict resolution is cooperative, collaborative problem-solving methodologies in which those with ownership of the problem participate directly in crafting a solution to the problem, with or without involvement of others. The following chart illustrates the differences:

Prevalent Practice	**Conflict Resolution**
Relies on a third party to settle disputes	Directly involves the conflicting parties in both resolution process and outcome
Reactively offers services after the conflict occurs	Proactively offers skills and strategies to participants prior to their involvement in the conflict
Focuses on conflict after a school rule has been broken; often offers advice to ignore problem if it is thought not to be major or serious	Intervenes in conflicts and prevents their escalation into the broken-rule stage or into violence
Uses arbitration almost exclusively to settle disputes	Maximizes the use of negotiation and mediation processes to resolve disputes
Requires adults to spend a disproportionate amount of time dealing with minor student conflicts	Uses teacher and virtually unlimited student resources to handle such conflicts and learn essential decision-making skills in the process
Relies on disciplinary codes that are ineffective at helping students reconcile interpersonal and intergroup differences	Focuses attention not on disciplinary offense but on how to resolve interpersonal and intergroup dimensions of a conflict[3]

Whereas the prevalent practices for managing conflict in schools rely on arbitration (with the adult authority serving as arbitrator to settle the dispute for the parties), conflict resolution involves bringing the parties of the dispute together, providing them with the processes to resolve the dispute, and expecting them to do so. The problem-solving strategies of conflict resolution are future directed. *The disputants craft and commit to a plan of action to behave differently from this point forward.*[4]

It is important to note that implementation of a comprehensive conflict resolution education program in a school is not likely to eliminate the adult role of arbitrator. Not all disputes are suitable for the problem-solving strategies of conflict resolution employed by students. There are instances where it may be deemed appropriate that an adult be involved in the conflict resolution process. There are other instances where the adult authority may determine that the obvious issue of the dispute, say, a fight between two students, is not appropriate for mediation or negotiation even though the long-term relationship issues of the dispute might be suitable for cooperative, collaborative problem solving between the parties of the dispute. There also exist cases in which the disputants choose, for any number of reasons, not to participate in the problem-solving process. If any of these scenarios is present and the problem requires resolution, then arbitration in some form is likely to be the most practical alternative available.

Schrumpf, Crawford, and Bodine (1997) discern that the problem-solving strategies of conflict resolution are consensual. The disputants must agree to participate in the cooperative, collaborative process and to work toward resolution. The concept of BATNA, or the best alternative to a negotiated agreement (Fisher, Ury, and Patton, 1991), is a prime determinant in deciding whether to elect the problem-solving strategies of conflict resolution. The reason one negotiates is to produce something better than the results that could be obtained without negotiating. A person would likely choose not to participant in consensual problem solving if she believes doing so might be detrimental to satisfaction of her needs—in other words, if she believes that the BATNA would be superior to a negotiated outcome. She volunteers to participate with the belief that doing so enhances the opportunity to satisfy her needs—that is, if *any* of the conceived outcomes seems superior to her BATNA. The question "What might happen if you don't reach an agreement?" is useful in assessing the BATNA.

BATNA is in actuality the individual's perception of the possible outcomes from problem solving. An outcome for conflict resolution education is to help people assess their BATNAs creatively and accurately, to bring these perceptions closer to reality. An accurate

BATNA protects the individuals from accepting agreements that are unfavorable and from rejecting agreements that would be in their long-term best interests. Becoming proficient in the principles of conflict resolution enables people to base assessment of the BATNA on understanding rather than fear, and to approach situations with an "abundance mentality" rather than one of "scarcity." When this happens, people are more likely to choose to be directly involved in determining the resolution of problems that affect them. They understand that their interests are more likely to be addressed when they inform others of those interests and advocate for them.

The following situation illustrates how the BATNA is involved in the choice of whether or not to use problem solving.

Sam and Terry have been friends for several years. In the hallway just before school started today, Terry accused Sam of spreading rumors about Terry and another student. A loud argument ensued, and Sam shoved Terry into the lockers. At that very moment, a hall supervisor came around the corner and witnessed the shove. The supervisor sent Sam to the dean's office.

The dean assigned Sam to in-school suspension and also suggested that Sam and Terry request a mediation to try to work out their problem.

Sam has no choice but to serve the suspension. The decision whether to mediate (negotiate an agreement) is a shared choice, depending upon Sam's BATNA and Terry's BATNA: What is the best they can expect if they do not deal directly with each other? Sam's BATNA is that Terry will likely continue to think Sam is spreading rumors and will remain angry at Sam for the shoving incident. Their friendship will be damaged. Terry's BATNA is that Sam will likely be mad at Terry and blame Terry for causing the argument that resulted in Sam's suspension. Their friendship will be damaged.

If the mutual friendship is important to Sam and Terry, their BATNAs suggest that a negotiated agreement is advisable since their best alternative to doing so is very likely a damaged relationship. Through mediation, they can develop options to address relationship concerns (such as confidentiality and trust) and can thus continue as best friends. If the friendship is not important to one or both of them, or if they believe they can continue to coexist in the school without future problems, they will have little motivation to negotiate an agreement.[5]

Principles of Conflict Resolution

The ideas in the book *Getting to Yes* (Fisher, Ury, and Patton, 1991) provide the foundation for teaching students and adults the problem-solving strategies of conflict resolution. The conflict resolution principles, or in other words, the principled negotiation elements described in *Getting To Yes,* are requisite for any program of conflict resolution. The following discussion illustrates how the four principles in that work are applied in programs to teach conflict resolution strategies to young people.

Separate People from the Problem

The first principle, *separate people from the problem,* concerns people's strong emotions, differing perceptions, and difficulty in communicating. When dealing with a problem, it is common for people to misunderstand each other, to get upset, and to take things personally. Every problem has both substantive issues and relationship issues. Unfortunately, the relationship of the parties tends to become involved in the substance of the problem. Fisher, Ury, and Patton (1991) assert that "before working on the substantive problem, the 'people problem' should be disentangled from it and dealt with separately. Figuratively, if not literally, the participants should come to see themselves as working side by side, attacking the problem, not each other."[6]

People problems fall into three categories: *perception, emotion,* and *communication.* These problems must be dealt with directly; they cannot be resolved indirectly with substantive concessions. As Fisher, Ury, and Patton (1991) maintain: "Where perceptions are inaccurate, you can look for ways to educate. If emotions run high, you can find ways for each person involved to let off steam. Where misunderstanding exists, you can work to improve communication."[7]

Perceptions. When dealing with problems of perception, it is important to remember that conflict does not lie in objective reality but in how people perceive reality. As the authors of *Getting to Yes* point out, "Truth is simply one more argument—perhaps a good one, perhaps not—for dealing with the difference. The difference itself exists because it exists in their thinking. Facts, even if established, may do nothing to solve the problem."[8] Every conflict involves differing points of view; thus, every conflict involves differing notions of what is true, what is false, or the degree to which facts are important. Therefore, the "truth" and its importance are relative.[9]

Emotions. When dealing with problems of emotion, it is important to remember that the parties may be more ready to fight it out than to work together cooperatively to solve the problem. As Fisher, Ury, and Patton (1991) state, "People often come to a negotiation realizing that the stakes are high and feeling threatened. Emotions on one side will generate emotions on the other. Fear may breed anger; and anger, fear. Emotions may quickly bring a negotiation to an impasse or an end."[10] In conflict resolution, sharing feelings and emotions is as important as sharing perceptions.[11]

Communication.   Given the diversity of background and values among individuals, poor communication is not surprising. Simply put, conflict resolution strategies are processes of communication between disputing parties for the purpose of reaching a joint decision. As Fisher and colleagues claim, "Communication is never an easy thing even between people who have an enormous background of shared values and experience. . . . It is not surprising, then, to find poor communication between people who do not know each other well and who may feel hostile and suspicious of one another. Whatever you say, you should expect that the other side will almost always hear something different."[12]

There are four basic problems in communication:

1. People may not be talking to each other.

2. Even if they are talking to each other, they may not be hearing each other.

3. What one intends to communicate is almost never exactly what one communicates.

4. People misunderstand or misinterpret that which is communicated.

Techniques for dealing with the problems of perception, emotion, and communication are foundation abilities for conflict resolution. These skills work because the behavior of separating the relationship problem from the substantive problem changes people from adversaries in a confrontation to partners in a side-by-side search for a fair agreement, advantageous to each.[13]

Focus on Interests, Not Positions

The second principle, *focus on interests not positions*, holds that the focus of conflict resolution should not be on the positions held by the people in dispute but on what the people really want—in other words, their interests. The objective of conflict resolution is to satisfy the underlying interests of the parties. Understanding the difference between positions and interests is crucial because *interests*—not positions—define the problem. Positions are something that people decide they want; interests are what cause people to decide. Fisher, Ury, and Patton note that "compromising between positions is not likely to produce an agreement which will effectively take care of the human needs that led people to adopt those positions."[14]

Reconciling interests rather than compromising between positions works because for every interest there are usually several possible satisfactory solutions. Furthermore, reconciling interests works because behind opposing positions lie a larger number of shared and compatible interests than conflicting ones. Thus, focusing on interests instead of positions makes it possible to develop solutions. Positions are usually concrete and clearly expressed, often as demands or suggested solutions. But the interests underlying the positions are less tangible and often unexpressed. Asking questions to identify the interests of the parties in a conflict is a foundation ability of conflict resolution.

In almost every conflict there are multiple interests to consider. Only by talking about and acknowledging interests explicitly can people uncover mutual interests and resolve conflicting interests. In searching for the interests behind people's positions, it is prudent to look particularly for the basic human needs that motivate all people. If these basic needs can be identified as shared or compatible interests, options can be developed that address these basic psychological needs. Shared interests and compatible interests both serve as the building blocks for a wise agreement. Unless interests are identified, people in conflict will likely not make a wise agreement. A temporary agreement may be reached, but such agreements typically do not last because the real interests have not been addressed. For lasting agreements, interests—not positions—must be the focus.

Invent Options for Mutual Gain

The third principle, *invent options for mutual gain,* allows parties the opportunity to design options that may be potential solutions without the pressure of deciding. Before trying to reach agreement, the parties brainstorm a wide range of possible options that advance shared interests and creatively reconcile differing interests. Fisher and colleagues say that "in most negotiations there are four major obstacles that inhibit the inventing of an abundance of options: (1) premature judgment; (2) searching for the single answer; (3) the assumptions of a fixed pie; and (4) thinking that 'solving their problem is their problem.' In order to overcome these constraints, you need to understand them."[15]

The problem with premature judgment is that such judgment hinders the process of creating options by limiting imagination. When searching for the single answer, people see their job as narrowing the gap between positions, not broadening the options available. Looking from the outset for the single best answer impedes the wiser decision-making process in which people select from a large number of possible answers. When people make the assumption that resources are finite (that is, a "fixed pie"), they see the situation as essentially either-or: one person or the other gets what is in dispute. If options are obvious, why bother to invent them? Thinking that solving their problem is the problem presents an obstacle to inventing options because each side's concern is only with its own immediate interests. This shortsighted self-concern leads people to develop only partisan positions, partisan arguments, and one-sided solutions.

The foundation ability of brainstorming is used to separate the inventing from the deciding. Brainstorming is designed to produce possible ideas to solve the problem; the key ground rule is to postpone criticism and evaluation of those ideas. In order to broaden options, those in a dispute should think about the problem in different ways and use ideas to generate other ideas. Inventing options for mutual gain is done by developing notions that address the shared interests and the compatible interests of the parties in dispute. The final decision on a solution is easier when there are options that appeal to the interests of both parties.

Use Objective Criteria

The fourth principle, *use objective criteria*, ensures that the agreement reflects some fair standard instead of the arbitrary will of either side. Using objective criteria means that neither party needs to give in to the other; rather, they can defer to a fair solution.

Objective criteria are developed based on fair standards and fair procedures. Objective criteria are independent of will, they are legitimate, and they are practical. Theoretically, they can be applied to both sides. In *Getting to Yes,* the authors use the example of the age-old way to divide a piece of cake between two children to illustrate the use of fair standards and procedures: one cuts and the other chooses. Neither complains about an unfair division. It is important to frame each issue as a joint search for objective criteria, to reason and be open to reason regarding which standards are most appropriate and how they should be applied, and to yield only to principle, not pressure of will (which takes such forms as bribes, threats, manipulative appeals to trust, or simple refusal to budge).

One standard of justification does not exclude the existence of others. When what one side believes to be fair is not what the other believes to be fair, this does not automatically exclude fairness as a criterion or mean that one notion of fairness must be accepted over the other. It does require both parties to explain what that criterion means to them and to respond to reasons for applying another standard or for applying a standard differently. When people advance different standards, the key is to look for an objective basis for deciding between them, such as which standard has been used by the parties in the past or which standard is more widely applied. The principle response is to invite the parties to state their reasoning, suggest objective criteria that apply, and refuse to budge except on the basis of these principles. Plainly, refusal to yield except in response to sound reasons is an easier position to defend—publicly and privately—than is refusal to yield combined with refusal to advance sound reasons. One who insists that problem solving be based on merits can bring others around to adopting that tactic once it becomes clear that to do so is the only way to advance substantive interests. The critical-thinking abilities of establishing criteria and evaluating possibilities based on criteria are foundational to conflict resolution.[16]

Foundation Abilities for Conflict Resolution

According to Crawford and Bodine (forthcoming), certain attitudes, understandings, and skills are facilitative or essential in the problem-solving strategies of conflict resolution. For problem solving in conflict situations to be effective, attitudes and understandings ultimately must be translated into behaviors, that is, into foundation abilities. Although there exists considerable overlap and interplay, these foundation abilities involve the following clusters of behaviors.

Orientation Abilities

Orientation abilities encompass the values, beliefs, attitudes, and propensities compatible with effective conflict resolution:

Nonviolence

Compassion and empathy

Fairness

Trust

Justice

Tolerance

Self-respect

Respect for others

Celebration of diversity

Appreciation of controversy

These values, beliefs, attitudes, and propensities can be developed through teaching activities that promote cooperation and reduction of prejudice.

Perception Abilities

Perception abilities encompass the understanding that conflict does not lie in objective reality but in how people perceive that reality:

Empathizing in order to see the situation as the other side sees it

Self-evaluating to recognize personal fears and assumptions

Suspending judgment and blame to facilitate a free exchange of views

Reframing solutions to allow for face saving and to preserve self-respect and self-image

These abilities enable one to develop self-awareness and to assess the limitations of one's own perceptions. They also enable one to work to understand others' points of view.

Emotion Abilities

Emotion abilities encompass behaviors to manage anger, frustration, fear, and other emotions:

Learning the language and developing the courage to make emotions explicit

Expressing emotions in nonaggressive, noninflammatory ways

Exercising self-control in order to control one's reaction to others' emotional outbursts

These abilities enable one to gain the self-confidence and self-control needed to confront and resolve the conflict. The basis for these behaviors is acknowledging that emotions—often strong ones—are present in conflict, that those emotions may not always be expressed, and that emotional responses by one party may trigger emotional responses from another party.

Communication Abilities

Communication abilities encompass behaviors of listening and speaking that allow effective exchange of facts and feelings:

Listening to understand

Speaking to be understood

Reframing emotionally charged statements into neutral, less emotional terms

These abilities include the skills of active listening, which allows one to attend to another person and that person's message, to summarize that message to check out what was heard and advise the other person of the message received, and to ask open-ended, nonleading questions to solicit additional information that might clarify the conflict. Also included are the skills of speaking to be understood rather than to debate or impress, speaking about yourself by describing the problem in terms of its impact upon you, speaking with clarity and concision to convey your purpose, and speaking in a style that makes it as easy as possible for the other party to hear. The skill of reframing, coupled with acknowledging strong emotions, is highly useful in conflict resolution.

Creative-Thinking Abilities

Creative-thinking abilities encompass behaviors that enable people to be innovative in problem definition and decision making:

Contemplating the problem from a variety of perspectives

Approaching the problem-solving task as a mutual pursuit of possibilities

Brainstorming to create, elaborate, and enhance a variety of options

Included is the skill of uncovering the interests of the parties involved in a conflict through questioning to identify what the parties want, as well as probing deeper by seeking to understand why they want what they want. The skill of problem definition involves stating the problem, and thus the problem-solving task, as a pursuit of options to satisfy the interests of each party. Flexibility in responding to situations and in accepting a variety of choices and potential solutions is an essential skill in decision making. The behavior is brainstorming: separating the process of generating ideas from the act of judging them. Also critical to success is the ability to elaborate potential solutions and to enhance and embellish existing solutions.

Critical-Thinking Abilities

Critical-thinking abilities encompass the behaviors of analyzing, hypothesizing, predicting, strategizing, comparing and contrasting, and evaluating:

Recognizing and making explicit existing criteria

Establishing objective criteria

Applying criteria as the basis for choosing options

Planning future behaviors

These foundation abilities are integral to the facilitation of the four principles of conflict resolution: separating people from the problem; focusing on interests, not positions; inventing options for mutual gain; and using objective criteria as the basis for decision making. Thus, they are necessary in using the problem-solving strategies of conflict resolution. Since most, if not all, are also abilities central to learning in general, they can be developed in schools through a variety of applications, many separate from the issue of conflict. Although these abilities are essential for using the problem-solving strategies of conflict resolution, programs that teach them are not always conflict resolution education programs. Conflict resolution involves developing these abilities and using them to carry out a problem-solving strategy that includes the four principles of conflict resolution. When conflict resolution problem-solving strategies and the abilities necessary to carry out the strategies are learned and practiced, students and adults are better able to resolve their own disputes and assist others in resolving disputes.[17]

Conflict Resolution Problem-Solving Process _____

Genuine conflict resolution education programs employ the four principles of conflict resolution through a structured problem-solving process (negotiation, mediation, or consensus decision making) designed to allow the participants to successfully exhibit the behaviors intrinsic to the foundation abilities. The conflict resolution processes are characterized by a series of steps that enable the disputants to identify their own needs and interests and to work cooperatively to find solutions to meet those needs and interests. The structured process gives support and direction to the cooperative effort, assisting the parties in staying focused on the problem and not each other, and in finding a mutually acceptable resolution. In addition, genuine conflict resolution education programs include extensive training and practice in using the principles and problem-solving processes of conflict resolution.

There are six basic steps in each conflict resolution problem-solving process:

1. Set the stage.
2. Gather perspectives.
3. Identify interests.
4. Create options.
5. Evaluate options.
6. Generate agreement.

Conflict Resolution Problem-Solving Methods

The problem-solving strategies of conflict resolution are negotiation, mediation, and consensus decision making. In each strategy, the parties of the dispute work through a cooperative, collaborative procedure that incorporates the four principles of conflict resolution. By implementing the principles of conflict resolution, the procedure enables the parties to maximize the potential that a resolution will be crafted that satisfies the interests of each party. The three conflict resolution strategies are each based on *negotiation theory*, and although the terms, especially *negotiation* and *mediation*, may be used interchangeably in conflict resolution literature and practice, for the purpose of this publication the processes are defined by Bodine, Crawford, and Schrumpf (1994) as follows:

- *Negotiation* is a problem-solving process in which the two parties, or representatives of the two parties, in the dispute meet face-to-face to work together, unassisted, to resolve the dispute between the parties.

- *Mediation* is a problem-solving process in which the two parties, or representatives of the two parties, in the dispute meet face-to-face to work together, assisted by a neutral third party called the *mediator,* to resolve the dispute.

- *Consensus decision making* is a group problem-solving process in which all of the parties, or a representative of each party, in the dispute meet to collaborate to resolve the dispute by crafting a plan of action that all parties can and will support and embrace. This process may or may not be facilitated by a neutral party.[18]

In summary, authentic conflict resolution programs provide more than the foundation abilities of orientation, perception, emotion, communication, creative thinking, and critical thinking. Conflict resolution programs deliver training in and practice using a process of conflict resolution, incorporating the foundation abilities for effective employment of the set of conflict resolution principles.

The problem-solving processes of conflict resolution are *future* directed. *The disputants craft and commit to a plan of action to behave differently from this point forward.* The idea from control theory that one's behavior is composed not of four different behaviors but of four components of what is always *a total behavior* is especially useful for viewing conflict resolution. These four total behavior components always occur synchronously:

1. Doing (for example, walking, talking)
2. Thinking (reasoning, fantasizing)
3. Feeling (angering, depressing)
4. Physiology (sweating, head aching)[19]

The feeling component of behavior is typically the most obvious, especially in stressful situations such as conflict. In terms of total behavior, the way to change a behavior is to change the behavior's doing or thinking components. One has almost total control over the doing component of behavior, and some control over the thinking component; less control over the feeling component, and almost no control over physiological phenomena. When one changes what one is doing, one notices that thoughts, feelings, and physiological responses change as well. To get their needs met effectively, people must realize that they always have control over the doing component and can choose to do something that is more effective than their presently elected behavior. *Every individual, in every situation, has a choice to behave differently.* One can always choose a new behavior; although doing so is not always easy. The essential quality of conflict resolution is the development of a plan to *take a different action in the future*, that is, to change the doing component. Thus the problem-solving strategies of conflict resolution are action-oriented. A program of conflict resolution education is by definition a program of action strategies that utilizes the four principles of conflict resolution to plan future behaviors. A conflict resolution education program in schools deals with behavior in its totality by emphasizing planning to act (doing) and affording sufficient practice in both planning and trying out those plans.[20]

CHAPTER 5

An Overview of Exemplary Programs

There are four basic approaches to conflict resolution education in operation in schools. The lines dividing the four approaches are sometimes difficult to draw in practice, but the categories are useful in describing the focus of each approach. Some of the best programs in schools have evolved when the implementation of the principles and problem-solving processes of conflict resolution allowed for gradual expansion from one approach to another.

The *process curriculum approach* is an entrée to conflict resolution education characterized by devoting a specific time to teaching the foundation abilities, principles, and one or more of the problem-solving processes of conflict resolution as a separate course, distinct curriculum, or daily or weekly lesson plan. The *mediation program approach* to conflict resolution education program trains selected individuals (adults or students) in the principles and foundation abilities of conflict resolution and in the mediation process in order to provide neutral third-party facilitation services to help those in conflict reach a resolution. The *peaceable classroom approach* is a whole-classroom methodology that includes teaching students the foundation abilities, principles, and one or more of the three problem-solving processes of conflict resolution. Conflict resolution education is incorporated into the core subjects of the curriculum and into classroom management strategies. Finally, peaceable classrooms are the building blocks of the peaceable school. The *peaceable school approach* is a comprehensive whole-school methodology that builds on the peaceable classroom approach by using conflict resolution as a system of operation for managing the school as well as the classroom. Conflict resolution principles and processes are learned and used by every member of the school community: librarians, teachers, counselors, students, principals, and parents.

We offer operational examples of each approach to illustrate the variety of options for program implementation.

Process Curriculum Approach

Process curriculum approaches teach the conflict resolution principles and processes through a time-limited course or through daily (or at least weekly) lessons. Typically, time-limited courses include teaching negotiation or mediation over a semester course period or in a series of workshops in secondary schools. The daily (or weekly) lessons are most typically taught as part of a unified scope and sequence of both the content and the skills of the conflict resolution processes. Process curriculum approaches are designed to help students better understand and resolve the conflicts they encounter in their lives at school, at home, and in the community.

Most of the learning through process curriculum takes place by way of structured activities, such as simulations, role plays, group discussions, and cooperative learning activities. The processing and debate embedded in these structured experiences is an important component of learning. By using training that the teacher has received or user-friendly materials, or both, the teacher implements the program in short time segments throughout the semester or the school year. Although portions of the process curriculum could be integrated into existing curricula, prevailing practice is to adopt this curriculum as a separate entity in the total curricular offering to students.

Program for Young Negotiators

Founded in 1993, the Program for Young Negotiators (PYN) aims to build the capacity of young people, their teachers, and other mentors to use negotiation skills as a powerful means of achieving their goals. A youth-oriented adaptation of the Harvard Negotiation Project, PYN uses the principles espoused by Fisher, Ury, and Patton in *Getting to Yes.*

Although PYN's theories and concepts initially were drawn from negotiation curricula intended for adults, they have since been adapted and improved by students, teachers, and PYN staff to be developmentally appropriate and enjoyable for primary and secondary school students. PYN's negotiation curriculum was first piloted in the Boston area during the fall of 1993. Since then, the Program for Young Negotiators has trained over two hundred teachers and twenty-five hundred students in the Boston area, earning honorable mention from the Boston Plan for Excellence in the Public Schools. In addition to the work in Boston, PYN's programs have spread to California, New York, and Toronto. PYN offers comprehensive curriculum materials, Life Negotiations training seminars, and ongoing support to schools and other youth-service providers throughout the United States and Canada.

PYN believes that teaching people how to achieve their goals without violence is the best means of violence prevention. PYN's philosophy is based not on a do-good perspective but on a pragmatic self-empowerment perspective. Participating students, teachers, and administrators are taught the same powerful means of goal achievement and dispute resolution that have proven to be effective in a wide range of situations over the past fifteen years.

PYN's approach to principled negotiation challenges the notion that disputes are resolved only when one side wins at the other's expense. It enables students to envision scenarios and generate options in which both sides are satisfied with the outcome, and both are able to achieve their goals. The perspective-taking skills and critical-thinking skills taught in negotiation courses help students learn that in order to satisfy their own interests, they must empathize with the interests of others.

The PYN Program has four primary components:

1. Teacher training and community involvement
2. Negotiation curricula
3. Follow-up opportunities
4. Ongoing curriculum development and innovation

Teacher training and parent and community involvement. PYN first trains school teachers, administrators, and other youth-service providers to negotiate their own issues. During intensive training seminars, participants learn negotiation from professors who teach negotiation and by practicing negotiators. Subsequently, when teachers involved in PYN's programs begin teaching negotiation concepts to their students, they continue to attend regular curriculum implementation meetings and are provided with ongoing technical support.

Upon request, each teacher participating in PYN programs is assigned one to three community volunteers, recruited by PYN to help implement his or her first negotiation course. PYN's diverse corps of volunteer teaching assistants has included professional negotiators, graduate students, parents, and community leaders. Volunteer teaching assistants commit to attending the training seminars and to learning and teaching negotiation techniques alongside their partner teachers.

To reinforce the concepts learned in the classroom, PYN provides materials and workshops for parents to encourage use of negotiation at home. PYN is also developing a school-to-community initiative linking the teaching of negotiation in schools with the teaching of negotiation in the community. This initiative involves designing an urban, community-based program, drawing upon the PYN curriculum currently in use in area schools. Other aspects of the curriculum are developed in cooperation with youth leaders from the schools and community.

Negotiation curricula in schools. The PYN curriculum presents negotiation skills not simply as an alternative to violence but as a necessary condition for attaining a high-quality life. Like successful adult negotiation courses, the curriculum relies heavily on experiential learning. Courses begin with cases that highlight basic principles, but as the curriculum unfolds, examples are increasingly drawn from the lives of teenagers. In a typical session, through creative games and role-play exercises, students actively participate in mock negotiations and experience firsthand empowerment through careful communication, collaboration, and win-win thinking.

Like the Harvard Negotiation Project and *Getting to Yes*, the PYN curriculum emphasizes seven basic elements. PYN's seven elements are based on those espoused by the Harvard Negotiation Project:

Harvard Negotiation Project's Seven Elements of Negotiation	**PYN's Seven Elements of Negotiation**
Communicate unconditionally both ways.	Understand the other party's perceptions and communicate your own.
Build a relationship in which you work together side by side.	Be trustworthy at all times, especially over the long term.
Clarify everyone's underlying interests.	Find out the other party's real interests, as well as your own.
Without commitment, generate options to meet the interests.	Brainstorm options without critisizing each other.
Find external standards of legitimacy by which to evaluate and improve options.	Search for good reasons on both sides.

Think about the walk-away alternatives if no agreement is reached.	Only settle for something that's better than your backup plan.
Carefully draft terms that are better than the best alternatives. Then make commitments.	Find your shared interests, and package options based on those interests.

Follow-up opportunities. Upon a teacher's completion of a basic negotiation curriculum in the classroom, he or she is presented with a number of follow-up opportunities. Each teacher receives PYN's list of supported follow-up options:

- Infusing the negotiation concepts into multiple subject areas, such as social studies, language arts, math, and science

- Developing a whole-school program that integrates negotiation into the entire school community at every level

- Arranging negotiation workshops for parents and other community members

- Developing a Young Negotiators Club

- Training student council members and other peer leaders

- Holding weekly or monthly negotiation periods where students help each other with their personal conflicts

- Organizing student focus groups to develop new teaching cases

Ongoing curriculum development and innovation. As a result of its alliance with the Program on Negotiation at Harvard Law School, PYN is able to provide its teachers with cutting-edge techniques. In addition to working with the Program on Negotiation, PYN constantly collects valuable feedback from teachers and other training participants. New cases are continually being developed, and existing ones are modified as part of PYN's ongoing curriculum development and revision process. Each year, PYN makes available to its teachers any newly submitted cases developed during the previous year. For example, one PYN teacher developed a negotiation case in his social studies class to present the issue of Mayan farmers and landholding; another teacher developed a case from a conflict in a required language arts novel. Both teachers submitted their cases to PYN for use by future PYN social studies and language arts teachers. In this way, teachers and students can use the resources of PYN to have an impact on curriculum development and keep abreast of classroom innovations.

In order to sustain implementation in each school, PYN focuses on training classroom teachers who in turn train students or other classroom teachers. PYN aims to be preventive, empowering entire classes of students to resolve potential conflicts for themselves before escalation to the point of actual conflict. In this way, PYN graduates learn to manage conflicts preemptively, and without the need for an intermediary.

Although PYN believes that violence prevention may be an important benefit of implementing PYN courses, negotiation theory is applicable under a variety of circumstances in which violence is not imminent. From inner-city neighborhoods to small country towns, negotiation skills are not only universally applicable but essential to achieve effective communication. Although values are somewhat implicit in any curriculum, the emphasis of the PYN course is to demonstrate the futility of adversarial aggression and the utility of collaboration. The goal of negotiation, as taught by PYN, is positive attainment of "interests" from a utilitarian perspective, rather than explicit discouragement of violence from a do-good perspective. Thus, PYN demonstrates that negotiation is an effective, pragmatic, and powerful option for goal attainment.

Street Law, Inc.

To promote cooperation instead of competition, Street Law, Inc., formerly the National Institute for Citizen Education in the Law (NICEL), has interwoven strategies for conflict management and mediation into many of its programs and curriculum materials. In 1985, Street Law, in partnership with the National Crime Prevention Council (NCPC), formed the Teens, Crime, and the Community (TCC) program with funding from the U.S. Department of Justice Office of Juvenile Justice and Delinquency Prevention. The TCC program helps teens understand how crime affects them and their families, friends, and communities; it involves them in service focused on making their communities safer. Conflict management lessons are a key student activity. This program includes comprehensive program design, teacher and community resource training and preparation, and development of materials for students and teachers.

Street Law and NCPC produced conflict resolution education curricula designed for specific student audiences: *We Can Work It Out! Problem Solving Through Mediation* (elementary and secondary editions)[1] and *The Conflict Zoo*.[2]

We Can Work It Out! for elementary schools involves a step-by-step design to teach the skills of personal conflict management and the process of mediation. Through these lessons, teachers can impart valuable skills in analytical reasoning, active listening, patience, empathy, and generating options. The curriculum teaches key terms and concepts, with terminology appropriate for elementary school students, and allows them to learn experientially. Students apply the skills they learn in scenarios in which they assume the roles of disputants and mediators. The scenarios often involve fairy tales, cartoons, and interpersonal conflicts.

We Can Work It Out! for secondary schools follows the same format as the elementary school edition, except that the terminology used and the scenarios created in this curriculum are appropriate for secondary school students.

An outgrowth of *We Can Work It Out!* is the Mediation Showcase. In partnership with the National Institute for Dispute Resolution (NIDR), Street Law designed mediation showcases to popularize conflict management skills. At these showcases, students are given conflict scenarios where they role-play the disputants and mediators. Community resource people, including community mediators and other volunteers who use skills involved in conflict management, provide feedback to the students on their ability to resolve the conflicts presented to them. This forum provides an opportunity for students to celebrate their newly learned skills and interact with adults in a constructive and affirming environment. In turn, these events provide an excellent opportunity for authentic assessment.

The Conflict Zoo is a curriculum for the third and fourth grades designed to teach the building blocks of conflict resolution and the concepts of justice and fairness. The lessons are given at the beginning of the school year to help students understand conflict management and develop fair rules to live by. The lessons begin with the story of a junior zoo, where baby animals play together. To do this, the baby animals must resolve their conflicts nonviolently and build a sense of community. The students experience these everyday conflicts through the eyes of the animals. The philosophy, principles, and skills of conflict resolution are interwoven in role plays about junior-zoo conflicts. Students gradually move from helping the animals resolve their conflicts to resolving conflicts in their own lives. Over the course of the lessons, children learn important terms, create journals, and apply these new ideas to their lives. Role plays, art, and journal keeping are used to maintain the children's interest and provide ways for them to internalize and apply the skills they learn in a range of situations.

Street Law programs can be used separately or integrated into existing curricula and programs. Schools that have a peer mediation program can use the *We Can Work It Out!* curriculum to extend the philosophy and skills to the rest of the school population. If a school has not yet developed a conflict resolution education program, a logical first step might be to teach the philosophy and skills of conflict resolution to the entire school community and then to set up a mediation program. Using these programs and curricula can help develop a corps of trained practitioners in the school community who have the skills to handle everyday conflicts.

Mediation Program Approach

Mediation programs give students and adults an opportunity to manage conflict and resolve disputes with the assistance of a neutral third party, using a process that advances reconciliation of both substantive issues and relationships. Mediation is a conflict resolution strategy that can be used within the classroom *and* as a schoolwide artifice for resolving conflicts.

Mediation programs in schools may provide mediation services to manage and resolve conflicts between students, conflicts between students and adults, and conflicts between adults. The role of mediator is a valid one for the teacher, principal, or other adults in the schools to assume in order to help students and adults resolve their disputes. Trained adult mediators may assist disputing adults in resolving conflicts such as work problems between faculty members, disciplinary actions disputed by parents, and development of appropriate programs for children with special needs.

The role of mediator can often be fulfilled by students to help resolve some of the disputes between peers such as those involving jealousies; rumors; misunderstandings; bullying, harassment, threats, or fights; personal property; and damaged friendships.

In addition, students and adults may serve together as co-mediators to resolve disputes between students and teachers that might involve personality clashes, issues of respect, behavior issues, and other conflicts that diminish student-teacher relationships. Student-teacher mediations are often an outgrowth of established peer mediation programs or adult mediation programs.

The Mediation Process

Mediation is a process in which a mediator (or co-mediators) serves as a neutral process facilitator to help disputants negotiate an agreement. In the mediation process, the mediator creates and maintains an environment that fosters mutual problem solving. During the mediation, the mediator involves the disputing parties in a six-step problem-solving process:

1. Set the stage: establish ground rules for problem solving.

2. Gather perspectives: listen to each disputant's point of view.

3. Identify interests contributing to the conflict.

4. Create options that address the interests of both disputants.

5. Evaluate these options according to objective criteria.

6. Generate an agreement.

Although the mediator is responsible for controlling the process, the disputants control the outcome. Participation in mediation is voluntary, and the mediator does not judge, impose an agreement, or force a solution. The power of mediation lies in the recognition that conflicts cannot actually be resolved if the disputants themselves do not choose to do so, that the disputants are the best judges of what will resolve the conflict, and that the disputants are more likely to execute the terms of an agreement if they possess authorship.

Schools establish mediation programs to address a variety of needs:

- Reducing the number of disciplinary actions, such as detentions, suspensions, or expulsions

- Encouraging more effective problem solving

- Reducing the time teachers and administrators spend dealing with conflicts between students

- Improving the school climate

- Providing students an alternative forum for problem solving

- Providing the faculty an alternative forum for problem solving

Peer Mediation

Peer mediation programs have emerged as one of the most widely used types of conflict resolution program in schools. This is because peer mediation programs take the educator out of the time-consuming role of arbitrating sanctions that rarely resolve the real conflicts among students. According to Richard Cohen,[3] young people can become effective mediators because they understand their peers, make the process age-appropriate, empower their peers and command their respect, and normalize the conflict resolution process.

Students are able to connect with their peers in ways that adults cannot. Peer mediators are capable of framing disputes in the perspective, language, and attitudes of youth, making the process age-appropriate. Students perceive peer mediation as a way to talk out problems without fear of an authoritative adult's judging their behavior, thoughts, or feelings. Peer mediators are respected because they honor the problem-solving process and their peers in the dispute by the way they conduct the mediation sessions. The self-empowering aspects of the process appeal to youth and foster self-esteem and self-discipline. When students come up with their own solutions to problems, they feel in control of their lives and are committed to the plan of action they have created to address their problems.

Peer Mediation Training.   In schoolwide peer mediation programs, a cadre of diverse students is selected to participate in intensive training in foundation abilities and the conflict resolution process of mediation. Peer mediation training is flexible in design and accommodates both the requirements of the school schedule and resources as well as the developmental level of the students involved. For example, a training for elementary students might be conducted in two-hour sessions over several weeks, whereas a training for high school students might be done in full-day sessions during a week or weekend. Peer mediation training takes a minimum of twelve to fifteen hours with ongoing follow-up learning opportunities to support the skill development of peer mediators.

Respect for diversity and cultural competency are areas that must be advanced in teaching student mediators. Infusing training activities and simulations with cross-cultural and social-justice issues provides an effective, relevant method to prepare peer mediators to deal with conflicts deriving from diversity.

Gaining expertise in conflict resolution skills and strategies such as mediation must be viewed as a lifelong process. Peer mediators need to overlearn procedures by using them as often as possible in conducting mediation sessions to resolve conflicts between peers and in ongoing training that focuses on mediator development. Recommended follow-up lessons include bias awareness, cultural competency, prejudice reduction, power issues, practice with difficult mediations, support group discussions, and self-evaluation.

Peer Mediation Opportunity.   Although a peer mediation program offers every student constructive means for resolving conflicts, the peer mediators themselves often gain the most from the program. Peer mediators are able to acquire and internalize conflict resolution skills that will benefit them in their present and future lives. For this reason, many experts believe that peer mediation programs should exist not as a solitary entity but as an integral and critical part of a total-school conflict resolution program that affords mediators as well as others the opportunity to develop conflict resolution skills.

Illinois Institute for Dispute Resolution

In 1986, a group of individuals developed a program within the school district where they worked at that time. The Illinois Institute for Dispute Resolution was formed in 1992. Those individuals are now staff members of IIDR, whose peer mediation program was the initial focus of the statewide conflict resolution in schools program professional development program.

IIDR approaches implementation and operation of a peer mediation program through six developmental phases as described in their program guide, *Peer Mediation: Conflict Resolution in Schools.*[4] The first phase involves creating and training the conflict resolution program team, designating program coordinator(s), conducting a needs assessment, and building faculty consensus for program development. IIDR is actively involved with the school or district in this phase. IIDR provides technical assistance in all components of phase one and provides the training for the program team. Following phase one, IIDR continues to provide technical assistance to the program team as they work through the remaining five phases. This assistance may also include providing first-time training to other staff, community members, and parents as well as to the student peer mediators. In all of these trainings conducted by IIDR, the program team members participate with the expectation that the team will conduct training after the initial year of implementation.

Phase one   Develop program team and commitment to program
    A. Create program team
    B. Train program team
    C. Designate program coordinator(s)
    D. Conduct needs assessment
    E. Build faculty consensus for program development

Phase two   Design and plan program
    A. Develop time line for implementation
    B. Establish advisory committee
    C. Develop policies and procedures
    D. Identify and develop funding sources

Phase three Select and train mediators
    A. Conduct student orientation
    B. Select peer mediators
    C. Train mediators
    D. Recognize peer mediators

Phase four   Educate a critical mass of the school population
    A. Conduct staff in-service
    B. Conduct student workshops

    C. Provide family and community orientation

    D. Offer parent workshops

Phase five   Develop and execute promotional campaign

    A. Design and implement initial campaign

    B. Conduct ongoing promotional efforts

Phase six   Operate and maintain the program

    A. Develop process for requesting mediation

    B. Schedule mediations and mediators

    C. Supervise mediation session

    D. Provide mediators with ongoing training and support

    E. Evaluate program

Chapter Eight provides a detailed discussion of these implementation phases.

The IIDR program for student mediation training involves twelve to fifteen hours of basic training as well as the same number of hours of additional advanced training. The basic training activities include understanding conflict, responses to conflict, sources of conflict, communication skills, the role of the mediator, and the mediation process. Advanced training includes bias awareness, social and cultural diversity, advanced communication, uncovering hidden interests, dealing with anger, caucusing, negotiating, and group problem solving.

Students completing the basic training are equipped to mediate most disputes between peers. The advanced training is designed to strengthen their abilities to use the mediation process and to expand their understanding of issues of diversity and how those issues affect conflict resolution.

IIDR views peer mediation as a service to be requested. Mediation requests may originate from a variety of sources: students, teachers, administrators, supervisors, other school staff, parents, and so forth. When it is determined that the disputants are willing to participate, a mediation is scheduled. IIDR encourages using trained peer mediators to promote the mediation program through participation in educational and informational campaigns, but it discourages direct involvement of the trained mediators in solicitation of mediations. Such solicitation, for example, is often the role given mediators when they are assigned to patrol a playground.

The employment of these six developmental phases can be readily adapted to serve the varying needs and interests of almost any school.[5]

The IIDR mediation program is also a capacity-building model that enables both schools and school districts to develop, implement, and sustain programs. During program implementation the entire student body and school faculty are offered workshops that focus on understanding conflict and the principles of conflict resolution. The program builds the conflict resolution skills of both adults and students and challenges everyone in the school community to use conflict resolution processes in their daily lives.

Community Board Program

The Community Board Program (CBP) is a nonprofit conflict resolution organization established in San Francisco in 1976. For more than twenty years, "Community Boards" (as the program is known) has provided free dispute resolution services to every neighborhood in San Francisco. In 1982, CBP's conflict resolution efforts were enhanced and adapted for use in schools with the central goal of infusing the values and philosophy of conflict resolution and putting mechanisms in place that enable conflicts at all levels to be resolved peacefully, positively, and effectively.

Initially, CBP worked with schools to implement student-to-student peer mediation, known as the "Conflict Managers Program." In the mid-1980s, Community Boards' staff developed elementary and secondary classroom curricula as a means of reaching more students and teachers, and shifting from simply reacting to school conflicts (through peer mediation) to preventing them. This approach enabled many more students to be exposed to the philosophy of conflict resolution, and it worked well in conjunction with existing peer mediation programs. Students who learn effective communication and problem-solving skills in the classroom are better prepared to deal constructively with some conflicts and are certainly more likely to make use of peer mediation.

The whole-school conflict resolution approach represents the next evolution of Community Boards' work in schools. By exposing and training as many school-related constituents as possible (that is, students, teachers, staff, administrators, and parents) in conflict resolution concepts and skills, and by encouraging widespread use of the classroom curricula (K–12), a significant impact accrues to Community Boards' goal to change the fundamental beliefs about and system for dealing with conflict.

The following examples illustrate other Community Boards' experiences connecting whole-school and community efforts.

Parent Involvement in Whole-Schools Work. Parent involvement is an integral component of Community Boards' whole-school approach. It is confusing and difficult for students who are encouraged and expected to use conflict resolution skills for handling disputes at school to return home and experience a completely different approach to conflict there. Educators trained by Community Boards express frustration when they hear a student say, "My dad says if somebody hits me, I can hit them back." By incorporating parents into the whole-school project, schools provide effective alternatives for youths (and parents) to deal with conflicts peacefully both on school grounds and at home.

Parents are encouraged to become involved in a variety of ways, beginning with the initial step of creating a "core committee." This committee is a planning and implementation team made up of teachers, counselors, administrators, students, and parents. Based on the needs of a particular school, the committee develops an action plan and time line and oversees the project.

Depending on their time and availability, parents can also participate by helping to do outreach and publicity, training new student mediators, taking referrals, scheduling mediation sessions, keeping records, facilitating biweekly student mediator meetings, doing follow-up on cases, and fundraising. Parents could perform certain functions with limited training, but such duties as training conflict managers and facilitating biweekly meetings require special and intensive training. Parents could join teachers in a two-day mediation training. Or they could be offered a series of workshops over time that would introduce them to basic family communication and problem-solving skills with specific suggestions for use in the home. Some schools elect to create a parent support group to receive ongoing skills training and practice, and to discuss areas of concern.

Parents can be invaluable to schools trying to secure support for a whole-school conflict resolution project by conducting overview presentations at PTA meetings, student or parent assemblies, staff meetings, town meetings, and students' classes. A well-informed parent group also serves as an important referral source. They can refer school-related conflicts to the peer mediation program, and they can also refer family and community-related disputes to a community mediation program. Community Boards provides free outreach presentations to parent groups on how to refer cases to the program.

Partnerships Between School and Community Mediation Programs.   Partnerships between school-based mediation programs and their community-based counterparts serve to strengthen and benefit both programs. Community Boards of San Francisco and the San Francisco Unified School District have developed a very strong relationship through the years. The following strategies are in place:

Sharing mediators. The potential for involving student mediators as young community conflict resolvers is great. Community Boards trains youths as young as fourteen to become community mediators at their free annual training (thirty hours). If a student is already trained as a peer mediator, he or she need only participate in an orientation session to join Community Boards' pool of more than two hundred active volunteers. Such "sharing" of student mediators provides important additional resources for the community mediation program. The young people involved learn valuable lessons about effective citizenry and receive advanced conflict resolution skills development.

Cross-referral system. Whether or not a school has a peer mediation program in place, educators benefit by understanding the sorts of dispute that may be appropriately referred to community mediation programs. These include more serious incidents, involving nonschool youth or a range of issues relating to parents, educators, and the community. Certain complex disputes may benefit from the attention of both school-based and community-based mediation sessions. Outreach efforts to schools include having community volunteer mediators and shared student peer mediators distribute flyers and give presentations.

Parent-child mediation. Youth who may be experiencing attendance or behavior problems can benefit from a parent-child mediation session through the community mediation program. This service is especially useful for youths who are making a transition from a special school intended for dealing with behavioral difficulties into a traditional school setting. School districts who make use of the local community mediation program in this way find these free services a valuable tool to improve or reestablish parent-child communication, and to create understandings within the family about rules, behavior, and other issues. This work can lead to improved social behavior and academic success.

Training youths as trainers. Young people can be trained as trainers to assist with preparation and training of new mediators in both school and community settings. Again, students already trained as peer mediators are a natural source of "talent" for such an undertaking. Students are encouraged to participate in Community Boards' free neighborhood "Training of Trainers" offered each year. Community Boards also found it valuable (and inspiring) to have student mediators demonstrate the school mediation process as part of its annual community mediation training. This reinforces the benefit of conflict resolution in general and underscores the intergenerational communitywide aspect of creating conflict-resolving communities. School and community mediation programs may also want to explore the potential of compensating youth mediators and trainers for their training work by "marketing" training delivery opportunities to youth-serving and other agencies in the local community.

Youth club and youth councils. Where community and school mediation programs wish to develop joint strategies, the development of a youth club or council may be appropriate. Community mediation programs can certainly benefit by forming a youth group to provide a focus for young mediators, helping the program retain youth volunteers, recruiting new youths, and providing opportunities for young people to take leadership roles in directing the program's youth agenda. A youth club also provides a forum for developing and undertaking special youth-initiated projects. Programs may find it helpful to offer stipends to youths participating in the club or council.

Encouraging Youth-Initiated Cases in Community Mediation

There is strong interest in having more youths themselves come forward as "first parties" in the community mediation process. Most programs now involve youth primarily as the second party, the one being "complained about." This represents a failure to recognize and respond to young people's disputing needs. There is an outreach effort by CBP staff and volunteers to youth-serving organizations and schools to alert students as to how they may refer disputes they experience to Community Boards.

Another effort to attract youth-initiated referrals involves developing working relationships with selected youth-serving organizations. Many of these organizations carry out some form of youth organizing efforts. CBP's intent is to use the work of these groups in effect to create collective first parties of young people for mediation. Youth issues may be police harassment, school policies, lack of jobs, etc. The youth organization would be the incubator where the young people would identify their issues, think them through, consider who their "allies" might be, and identify the true second parties to the dispute. This is a unique effort to join youth-organizing efforts with community conflict resolution to better meet the disputing needs of young people.

Forging partnerships between school mediation programs within the San Francisco Unified School District and Community Boards means that the number of youth-related cases referred to our program has increased dramatically. These referrals have come from teachers, administrators, parents, and youth themselves. Community Boards has also seen a significant rise in the number of young people serving as volunteer community mediators.

Peaceable Classroom Approach _____

The peaceable classroom approach is a holistic classroom conflict resolution education program that integrates conflict resolution into the curriculum and into classroom management, as well as using the instructional methods of cooperative learning and academic controversy. Peaceable classrooms are typically initiated teacher by teacher and are the building blocks of the peaceable school.

Curriculum Integration and Classroom Management

Curriculum integration primarily involves teaching the skills and concepts needed to resolve conflict constructively, and infusing the principles of conflict resolution into core subject areas. Teachers who integrate curriculum build peaceable classrooms by creating classroom environments that support conflict resolution and prosocial behavior. William Kreidler, a pioneer of the peaceable classroom, approaches the classroom as a caring and respectful community wherein five qualities are present: *cooperation, communication, emotional expression, appreciation for diversity*, and *conflict resolution*.[6]

Peaceable classrooms contribute learning activities and teachable moments that encourage youth to recognize options in conflict situations and to choose options that are nonviolent, meet the needs of the people involved, and improve relationships. Teachers incorporate conflict resolution strategies and skills into their day-to-day classroom management as well as into the curriculum content of their daily lesson plans.

Cooperative Learning and Academic Controversy

Teachers in peaceable classrooms also extensively use the cooperative learning and academic controversy methods developed by David Johnson and Roger Johnson. Cooperative learning involves students' working in small groups to accomplish shared learning goals. In these cooperative learning groups, students have two responsibilities: to learn the assigned material and to ensure that all other group members also learn it. Academic controversy exists when one student's ideas, information, conclusions, theories, and opinions are incompatible with those of another and the two seek to reach an agreement. Controversies are resolved by engaging in deliberate discourse, discussing the advantages and disadvantages of proposed actions. Such discussion is aimed at synthesizing novel solutions.[7]

In peaceable classrooms, youths learn to take responsibility for their actions and develop a sense of connectedness to others, and to their environment. Peaceable classrooms build the capacity of young people to manage and resolve conflict on their own by learning to:

- Understand and analyze conflict
- Understand peace and peacemaking
- Recognize the role of perceptions and biases
- Identify feelings
- Identify factors that cause escalation
- Handle anger and other feelings appropriately
- Improve listening skills
- Improve verbal communication skills
- Identify common interests
- Brainstorm multiple options that address interests
- Evaluate the consequences of different options
- Create a win-win agreement

The Ohio *Conflict Management Resource Guide for Elementary Schools*[8] provides the following as some suggested ways to infuse learning about conflict and conflict resolution into standard areas of the school curriculum:

Art. Contrast, perspective, feeling, and bias are a few of the foundational concepts that may be reinforced through making or studying art.

Health. Students can learn skills to handle emotions in a healthy manner, assertively resist what is unhealthy, and recognize and evaluate consequences when solving problems and making decisions.

Language arts. The whole-language approach is ideal for weaving conflict management concepts into a wide variety of subjects.

Reading. During discussions about stories, students are asked to analyze and identify the root causes of specific conflicts and to brainstorm other potential options for resolving conflicts that arose in the reading.

Speech. The difficulty and challenge of speaking in such a way that another gains a clear understanding of your perspective is easily reinforced in such activities as presenting a persuasive speech, explaining instructions to a game one has invented, or describing a design in such a way that another can draw it.

Writing. Story starters provide daily opportunities for students to think about and apply conflict management and resolution skills. Starters can range from simple phrases such as, "The good thing about conflict is . . ." to longer introductions that invite students to brainstorm alternative methods of resolving a conflict and to anticipate the possible consequences of each. Students can keep track of their progress in using and improving their skills through logs or journals.

Math. Mathematical problem solving involves the following steps: reading and formulating the problem, analyzing and exploring the problem and selecting strategies to solve it, finding and implementing solutions, and verifying and interpreting solutions to ensure that they are correct. A teacher might ask students to develop a plan for a city park that meets a variety of community interests and budget constraints.

Music. Conflict management concepts can be reinforced through song and taught in principles of harmony and discord.

Physical education. This subject provides opportunities for students to experience and discuss the differences between competitive and cooperative games. It is an ideal setting for students to learn how ground rules can encourage a cooperative or competitive climate.

Science. One could say that the earth, as we know it now, has undergone many conflicts. What have been some of the positive and negative effects of volcanoes, earthquakes, fires, etc.? What are some win-win resolutions in nature? Symbiotic relationships are an example.

Social studies. Teachers ask students to analyze local, state, national, and international conflicts and to discuss potential conflict resolution strategies to resolve those issues. The conflicts may be a current event or a past occurrence.[9]

Here are examples for infusing conflict resolution into primary and supplementary lessons for the secondary level, adapted from the Educators for Social Responsibility curriculum *Making Choices About Conflict, Security, and Peacemaking*:

Literature. Examine the theme of interpersonal conflict and security in a literature unit. Explore the concept of conflict escalation in novels and short stories. Read selections about American and global peacemakers whose life work has made a positive difference for others (examples: Eleanor Roosevelt, Cesar Chavez, Mary McLeod Bethune, Ralph Bunche, Jane Addams, Anwar Sadat, Bishop Desmond Tutu). Read about young people (fictional and biographical) who, through courage and determination to survive, confront conflicts not of their own making (examples: *Farewell to*

Manzanar, Stand Up Lucy, A Frost in the Night, Sadako, and *The Thousand Cranes*).

Math. Manipulate decimals and percentages to create bar and circle graphs that compare and contrast vital statistics on the security of children in various nations.

Science. Introduce the concept of global ecology by examining "transnational" environmental problems that require international cooperation.

Civics. Explore tools of public policy and political pressure that are employed at the local, national, and international levels. Study state and federal legislation or international policies aimed at increasing children's security, at taking a position, and at working for passage or rejection of legislation or recommendations.

Economics. Compare and contrast the strategic value of different countries' natural resources and products in the world marketplace. Examine how that market value affects the economic well-being of each nation's citizens. Investigate the impact of defense spending on local economies.

Introduction to the law. Explore the "tuna fish" controversy (drift net fishing and the law of the seas) as a way to understand the impact of change in the law on local and national economies and international relations. Examine the competing interests between policies that promote and protect national interests and those efforts that increase international security.

World geography. Examine geopolitical factors that contribute to a nation's relative strengths or weaknesses within a region or the world. Compare data profiles of different nations to identify how geographic features influence the economy and quality of life.

American history. Examine the values and competing interests of groups in conflict in the making of the United States in the seventeenth and eighteenth centuries. Study the successes and failures of international peacekeeping in the twentieth century, specifically contrasting the League of Nations and the United Nations. Discuss under what conditions students would "go to war." Compare "just war" criteria with the United States's rationales for various wars and interventions.

World history. Examine the role of military expansion and arms technology in the building of empires and their decline. Explore how the "settler state" mentality and the concept of "manifest destiny" promoted nineteenth-century and twentieth-century American imperialism.[9]

Opportunities for curriculum integration at both the elementary and the secondary levels are abundant. The foundation abilities and the problem-solving processes of conflict resolution are easily infused into any of the social sciences, since each offers an opportunity to explore points of view, interests that underlie positions, and successful and unsuccessful attempts at problem solving. Literature, at every level, is replete with conflict; students can analyze what is presented and create resolutions differing from those advanced by the authors. All aspects of the humanities contain issues between and among people that easily can be related to the reality of the students' lives. Every branch of science is confronted with ethical issues that invite exploration, generation of options, and thoughtful examination of consequences of possible actions. Both science and mathematics provide problem-solving strategies, the efficacy of which can be tested for the animate as well as the inanimate. Interdisciplinary units and project learning in particular provide some of the strongest forums for curriculum infusion. The possibilities to provide experiences with conflict are numerous without establishing conflict and conflict resolution as additional areas of study.

The peaceable classroom approach offers individual classroom teachers access to establishing conflict resolution education programs independently of total-school implementation. Since this approach is designed to enhance teaching methods, the core curriculum, and classroom management, teachers perceive it as working smarter, not harder. Increasingly, teachers are turning to programs that use conflict management skills to handle classroom misbehavior and to enhance the teaching methods and content of core academic subjects.

Cooperative Learning Center, University of Minnesota

The Teaching Students to Be Peacemakers program (TSP) is a twelve-year spiral school program in which each year students learn increasingly sophisticated negotiation and mediation procedures. The program began in the mid-1960s at the University of Minnesota. Educators were trained in how to resolve conflicts constructively and teach students how to do likewise. Building positive relationships among disputants as well as reaching integrative agreements is a major emphasis of the program. TSP's major creator, David Johnson, translated the theory and research on constructive conflict resolution, negotiations, perspective taking, and mediation into a set of practical procedures for students and faculty to use. The TSP program is a central emphasis of the Cooperative Learning Center. Over the past thirty years, thousands of preschool, primary, intermediate, middle school, high school, and college faculty members and administrators have been trained in how to implement the TSP program throughout North America and in countries in Europe, the Middle East, Africa, Asia, and Central and South America.

The Teaching Students to Be Peacemakers program consists of four parts: creating a cooperative environment, teaching peacemaking, implementing the program, and continuing the teaching and upgrading of peacemaking skills.

Creating the Environment.   First, school faculty create a cooperative environment. Cooperative learning creates the context necessary for conflicts to be resolved constructively and reduces the factors that place students at risk of using violence: poor academic performance (with an inability to think through decisions), alienation from schoolmates, and psychological pathology. Compared with competitive or individualistic learning, cooperative learning results in higher achievement and increased use of higher-level reasoning strategies, more caring and supportive relationships, and greater psychological health.

Teaching Peacemaking.   Second, faculty teach all students how to be peacemakers. The TSP program is constructed so that all students receive thirty minutes of training per day for about thirty days and then receive thirty minutes of training on average twice a week for the rest of the school year. The training consists of five parts:

Part one: Understanding the nature of conflict.   Learning is focused on how to recognize when a conflict is and is not occurring. Conflicts can have many positive outcomes. Conflicts focus attention on problems to be solved, clarify disputants' identity and values, reveal how disputants need to change, increase higher-level cognitive and moral reasoning, increase motivation to learn, provide insights into other perspectives and life experiences, strengthen relationships, add fun and drama to life, increase disputants' ability to cope with stress and be resilient in the face of adversity, and increase general psychological health.

Part two: Choosing an appropriate conflict strategy.   Students, faculty, and administrators learn that in conflicts they have two concerns: (1) to achieve their goals and (2) to maintain a good relationship with the other person. The importance of their goals and the importance of the relationship determine whether they should adopt a strategy of *withdrawing* (giving up both the goals and the relationship), *forcing* (achieving the goal at the other person's expense, thereby giving up the relationship, that is, win-lose negotiations), *smoothing* (giving up a goal in order to enhance the relationship), *compromising* (giving up part of a goal but at the cost of some damage to the relationship), or *negotiating* to solve the problem (achieving the goals and maintaining the relationship). Participants are taught that in a long-term relationship, such as with schoolmates and faculty, the most important strategy is problem-solving negotiation.

Part three: Negotiating to solve the problem. It is not enough to tell students to be nice, or talk it out, or "solve your problem." They must be taught a specific procedure to use to resolve conflicts. This part of the peacemaker training teaches students, faculty, and administrators a concrete and specific procedure for negotiating integrative agreements that result in all disputants' achieving their goals while maintaining or even improving the quality of their relationship.

The problem-solving negotiation procedure has six steps:

1. *Describe what you want.* ("I want to use the book now.") This step includes using good communication skills and defining the conflict as a small and specific mutual problem.

2. *Describe how you feel.* ("I'm frustrated.") Disputants must understand how they feel and communicate it accurately and unambiguously.

3. *Describe the reasons for your wants and feelings.* ("You have been using the book for the past hour. If I don't get to use the book soon, my report will not be done on time. It's frustrating to have to wait so long.") This includes expressing cooperative intentions, listening carefully, separating interests from positions, and differentiating before trying to integrate the two sets of interests.

4. *Take the other's perspective and summarize your understanding of what the other person wants, how the other person feels, and the reasons underlying both.* ("My understanding of you is . . .") This includes understanding the perspective of the opposing disputant and being able to see the problem from both perspectives simultaneously.

5. *Invent three optional plans to resolve the conflict that maximize joint benefits.* ("Plan A is . . ., Plan B is . . ., Plan C is . . .") This includes inventing creative optional agreements that maximize the benefits for all disputants and solve the problem.

6. *Choose the wisest course of action to implement and formalize the agreement with a handshake.* ("Let's agree on Plan B!") A wise agreement is fair to all disputants and is based on principles. It maximizes joint benefits and strengthens the disputants' ability to work together cooperatively and resolve

conflicts constructively in the future. It specifies how each disputant should act in the future and how the agreement will be reviewed and renegotiated if it does not work.[10]

Part four: Mediating others' conflicts. The fourth part of the TSP program is to train participants in a concrete and specific four-step mediation procedure:

1. Ending hostilities: mediator ensures that disputants end hostilities and cool off. If disputants are too angry to use problem solving, then they must cool down before mediation begins.

2. Ensuring disputants are committed to the mediation process: mediator introduces the process of mediation and sets the ground rules.

3. Helping disputants successfully negotiate with each other: mediator carefully takes the disputants through the negotiation procedure.

4. Formalizing the agreement: mediator formalizes the agreement by completing a report form and having disputants sign it as a commitment to implement the agreement and abide by its conditions.

Implementing the Program.   Third, once students have completed the initial training, the teachers implement the peacemaker program. Each day the teacher selects two class members to serve as official mediators. Any conflicts students cannot resolve themselves are referred to these class mediators. The mediators work in pairs. They wear official T-shirts, patrol the playground and lunchroom, and are available to mediate any conflicts that occur in the classroom or school. The role of class mediator is rotated throughout the class or school so that all students serve as class mediator for an equal amount of time. If peer mediation fails, the teacher mediates the conflict. If teacher mediation fails, the teacher arbitrates by deciding who is right and who is wrong. If that fails, the principal mediates the conflict. If that fails, the principal arbitrates.

Teaching Students the Skills.   Fourth, faculty continue to teach students negotiation and mediation skills weekly throughout the school year to refine and upgrade students' skills. Gaining real expertise in resolving conflicts constructively takes years of training and practice. The TSP program is aimed at being a twelve-year spiral curriculum in which students receive the training every year from first through twelfth grades. Each year, the training gets more complex and complete. Students need to practice these procedures over and over again until they become an automatic pattern. If students have to stop and think what they should do in a conflict, it may be too late to manage it constructively. Students need to over-learn the problem-solving negotiation and mediation procedures.

Daily practice is ensured (and academic achievement is increased) by integrating the TSP training into academic units. All literature, history, and science involves conflict. Almost any lesson in these subject areas can be modified to include role-playing situations in which negotiation or mediation procedures are used. The TSP program can be extended and enhanced by teachers' using the academic controversy procedure to create intellectual conflicts that increase learning and higher-level reasoning. In these controversies, students practice their conflict skills while studying academic issues.

The Teaching Students to Be Peacemakers program is implemented through a combination of bottom-up and top-down strategies. Committed faculty members are trained in how to implement the program. Their training program consists of thirty to forty hours of training given either in three two-day sessions distributed throughout the school year or else in a five-day intensive summer session. Although any educator is welcome to participate in the training, faculty are typically trained in teams.

After the training, the teams become collegial teaching teams that meet at least once a week to help each other's implementation efforts. Following the training sessions, trainers provide support to the collegial teaching teams by giving demonstration lessons, helping members prepare lessons, observing their implementation efforts, providing feedback, and trying to continuously increase faculty commitment to teaching students to resolve conflicts constructively. Staff developers also assist faculty in integrating the TSP training into ongoing academic curriculum units.

Educators for Social Responsibility

Educators for Social Responsibility (ESR) is a nonprofit organization in Cambridge, Massachusetts, recognized for promoting children's ethical and social development through its national leadership in conflict resolution, violence prevention, intergroup relations, and character education. The primary mission is to help young people develop the convictions and skills to shape a safe, sustainable, and just world. ESR has provided on-site peaceable classroom and peaceable school training to more than six thousand educators at two hundred schools, training institutes to more than four thousand educators, and shorter awareness workshops to thousands of other educators. This training prepares educators to teach conflict resolution, communication, and intergroup relations. ESR has distributed some thirty-five thousand educational resources to support peaceable classrooms across the United States.

ESR provides site-based professional development training with follow-up support for schools nationwide; it also provides institutes that individuals or teams may attend to learn how to create peaceable classrooms and schools. By the term *peaceable,* ESR means learning environments that are safe, caring, respectful, and productive. Workshops, curricula, and ongoing support help educators develop instructional and management practices that foster skillfulness in six interrelated areas: cooperation, caring communication, appreciation of diversity, expression of feelings, responsible decision making, and conflict resolution.

ESR begins work with a school or district by conducting a needs assessment to help the institution define more clearly the problems that it seeks to address, current program strengths, specific needs, and short-term and long-term goals. At this stage, ESR also provides information about the peaceable classroom and school model, the ingredients of successful implementation, and the components of a comprehensive school and community program. ESR recommends creating a program steering committee, multiyear planning, voluntary staff participation in training, and developing local leadership capacity.

The ESR core four-day training model provides theoretical background on key topics such as social and emotional learning, and developmentally appropriate classroom teaching activities. Woven throughout the workshop are direct instruction strategies, ideas on curriculum infusion, and classroom management and discipline applications. This training is participatory and experiential, placing emphasis on building community. A major premise is that adults need to learn and practice using key conflict resolution concepts and skills at the same time that they explore different ways to teach these to young people. In order to be successful, teachers must effectively model the behavior they seek to teach through direct instruction, and schools must reflect the values they seek to nurture among young people throughout all facets of their program.

Participants in workshops develop action plans appropriate to their classroom and school. ESR recommends that students and teachers make decisions about classroom norms and guidelines together at the beginning of the school year, and that teachers provide early instruction in key skill areas so that the skills are used and reinforced throughout the year. The peaceable classroom involves students in problem solving and decision making about classroom issues to a much greater extent than many traditional classrooms do.

Ongoing follow-up and support is an essential feature of successful implementation. ESR recommends a minimum of three on-site follow-up days by a staff development specialist. These days include a range of activities: demonstration teaching, coaching, planning, and problem solving. For many teachers, seeing is believing, and the opportunity to watch a staff development specialist model how to teach conflict resolution with their students is essential. Opportunities for the cohort who trained together to meet, share ideas, and discuss difficulties periodically is important. ESR offers various advanced training options as teachers gain experience. For example, teachers learn how to teach conflict resolution through children's literature, how to diffuse anger and hostility, and how to interrupt expressions of prejudice.

Interviews six to eighteen months following training and follow-up sessions reveal that participants bring new ways of thinking about teaching and learning to their classrooms. Through the use of new teaching and management strategies, teachers transform their classrooms in ways that fundamentally empower young people to help create a caring classroom community in which adults and young people use conflict resolution skills daily. We provide excerpts from interviews with teachers who have created peaceable classrooms at four developmental levels.

(From an Early Childhood Education Report)

Kindergarten teacher Abby Gedstad loves her work at Edward Devotion public school in Brookline, Massachusetts. "I went into teaching as a political act. I wanted to make a difference in the lives of my students so that they could make a difference." She's found the ESR peaceable classroom approach an important part of making that happen.

Gedstad reports change in the climate of her classroom since she has implemented the peaceable classroom. "One of the nicest benefits is that kids are treating each other with a lot of respect. . . . By training the kids to negotiate their own conflicts and solve their own problems," adds Gedstad, "I can spend my time doing what I love to do: teach!"

It was not always this way. "When I first began teaching, I was more concerned about establishing my authority and my power. It was easier to just mete out justice." Then gradually Gedstad started to implement ideas gathered from ESR peaceable classroom training and curricula. "Problem-solving and conflict resolution skills are just a part of this approach," Gedstad emphasizes; "It's a process, not an answer." Developing a caring classroom community can be critical to preventing some conflicts from occurring in the first place.

(From an Elementary School Report)

Second grade teacher Bonnie Lawlor tells one of her favorite stories. "I was out on playground . . . [and] another teacher told me that one of my kids had just interrupted a fight between two kids. She said she wished she had had a video camera. This kid sashayed up to the other kids with her hands on her hips and said, 'Do you know what you're doing to escalate this?' And the two kids were so stunned they stopped. And the peacemaker asked, 'If you use name calling, how do think the other person is going to feel?' It's working," Lawlor exclaims. "It's really working."

Lawlor's work on her peaceable classroom at Thetford Elementary School in Thetford, Vermont, began in the early 1990s, when she attended an ESR institute. She has been at it ever since. "When we began teaching, we solved problems for our students," Lawlor explains, reaching back twenty years to her start in the classroom. "Then I realized, 'I'm not giving them any skills if I'm helping them solve this.'" So Lawlor turned her attention to teaching problem-solving skills, conflict resolution, and community building. "It amazes people that by midyear, if there's a problem, I can say to two second graders, 'What do you think would work here?' And you will get kids who will make suggestions like, 'Should I use the problem puppets? Should I think about a win-win?' Guidance counselors come in and say, 'I don't believe these kids.'"

(From a Middle School Report)

"Kids are kids. They're pretty much dealing with the same issues everywhere," explains Jane Harrison, drawing from twenty years of experience teaching middle school. "I've worked in California and New York. No matter where we go, kids are saying we live in a scary world."

Harrison starts each year by setting class rules along with her kids. "I say, 'This is our community, and we need to think about how we should treat each other. How can we get along? That's an important tool for middle school kids, because then they have buy-in." Harrison uses other ESR curriculum tools as well. "Like the anger thermometer," she explains. "Identifying one's feelings is so important. Oftentimes middle school kids can only say that they are happy, sad, mad, or glad. Unless they can go further with that, then they can't deal with it effectively. We use the conflict escalator lessons from the curriculum. We role-play options. When we talk about deescalating: 'How would that look? Let's go beyond apologizing. What could you do?'"

(From a High School Report)

"We attended two ESR conflict resolution institutes and brought one of their trainers into our school for three days," explains teacher Eva Patterson, an experienced English teacher at Lasalle High School in South Bend, Indiana. She is well aware that change does not come easily, and she brings an openness and patience to her own growth process. "Since we started this work, so many wonderful things have been happening.

"I'm beginning to see that I'm going to have to step back and not be the arbitrator in my classroom. To step back from control. To help students see that they are responsible for their own behavior. I used an activity from the ESR institute, where students cooperatively have to build their ideal house to introduce group dynamics: how to work together, how to develop listening skills, to give the other person a chance before you jump on them. And you know?" Patterson adds with a laugh. "Their houses were better than the ones the teachers built in the institute!"

Though a seemingly simple project, Patterson found the results for her students profound. "The change I saw is when we're working together and the students themselves are coming up with their objectives and the material they will study, they assume personal responsibility. They relied on one another."

Individual teachers can utilize ESR curricula and make a significant difference within their classroom. Curricula and resources are classroom-tested, creative, user-friendly, and immediately applicable. Teachers can naturally integrate conflict resolution and intergroup relations into their classrooms through direct instruction and reinforcement of skills, teacher modeling during "teachable moments," and more systematic classroom management practices and infusion into subject areas. In-depth training, easily used curricula, and follow-up support are all crucial parts of successful implementation. Even more significant change results when a critical mass of teachers creating and sustaining peaceable classrooms are joined by counselors, administrators, parents, and others to forge a peaceable school and to link with other conflict resolution initiatives in the community.

Children's Creative Response to Conflict

Children's Creative Response to Conflict (CCRC) is generally identified as a pioneer organization in the field of conflict resolution in schools. It grew from the Quaker Project on Community Conflict in New York City, a program of the Peace and Social Action Program of the New York yearly meeting of the Religious Society of Friends that provided nonviolence training for individuals participating in civil rights, peace, farm worker, and student demonstrations. Four of the group's nonviolence facilitators, operating on the premise that if children were taught the skills of nonviolence and nonviolent conflict resolution at an early age, they would be less likely to use violence later, developed Children's Creative Response to Conflict. They began using the program in some New York City schools in 1972.

Cooperation, communication, affirmation, and conflict resolution were the four original major themes of CCRC, around which the program staff developed training activities. As the field of conflict resolution in schools grew, several subthemes of CCRC's conflict resolution theme emerged as requisite areas for training. CCRC has developed separate training activities in problem solving, mediation, and bias awareness as part of their advanced workshops.

The CCRC program developed a workshop format (gathering, agenda review, activities, evaluation, closing) that was adopted by a number of other conflict resolution programs. The adopted format also embraced the basic concepts of CCRC workshops:

The circle

Voluntary participation

The right to pass

Belief that everyone has something positive to offer

Agenda setting

Evaluation

Modeling

Experiential learning

Having fun

The training programs provide adults with a variety of activities to use with youth to develop the following themes of the CCRC program:

- Cooperation is defined as working or acting together toward a positive common goal. Many activities for small and large groups are offered so that people become skilled in cooperation in a crowded and increasingly dangerous world.

- Communication is divided into listening, observing, and speaking, with activities designed to develop skills in each aspect of communication. Becoming a good communicator includes the skill of learning to make *I*-statements and learning the skills of active listening.

- Affirmation, viewed as positive affirming of self and others, is seen as requiring a high level of cooperation and communication skills. Also, affirmation activities can present a somewhat higher degree of risk; thus it is important for individuals to feel safe in the group environment. For these reasons, affirmation activities are explored after the development of cooperation and communication abilities.

- The CCRC approach to conflict resolution is based on the ideas that conflict exists and is not going away and that conflict can lead to growth. CCRC takes a problem-solving approach to conflict, that is, developing skills to follow a step-by-step method of solving conflicts and finding win-win solutions.

- Problem solving, viewed as a way to resolve conflict, is a step-by-step process having as a goal solving the problem. CCRC provides activities that emphasize "creativity" in problem solving: developing *fluency* (generating many ideas), increasing *flexibility* (adapting ideas), developing *originality* (thinking of unique responses or seeing our problems in different ways), and practicing the skill of *elaboration* (expanding and adding to ideas). CCRC's training program focuses on learning the component skills of problem solving and providing direct practice in the step-by-step processes.

- CCRC defines mediation as resolving conflict between two or more parties by providing a third party to help disputants solve their problem. CCRC advises establishing a mediation program after the school participates in a conflict resolution program. They believe that such an approach is more likely to be successful over a long period of time and that all students benefit from learning conflict resolution.

- CCRC provides bias awareness training activities for all ages because a number of conflicts seen in schools are directly related to bias incidents: racism, sexism, classism, homophobia, or other "isms" that exist in our society.

As an organization with a long history in conflict resolution in schools, CCRC has evolved with the field. CCRC activities are well tested and time proven for creating peaceable classrooms. CCRC's current goals include movement toward changing the school or community culture by establishing a critical mass of teachers and community members who practice creative conflict resolution, model the skills of active listening, and seek to find solutions that are fair to everyone. This approach spends time and effort in long-term planning, choosing to develop at least a five-year plan to include parent and community education side by side with conflict resolution for all grade levels. The plan integrates conflict resolution and bias awareness into the curriculum and everyday lives of students, parents, staff, and community members.

Peaceable School Approach

The peaceable school approach integrates conflict resolution into the total operation of the school. Conflict resolution concepts and skills are learned and used by every member of the school community. Peaceable school climates reflect caring, honesty, cooperation, and appreciation of diversity. Peaceable school programs are comprehensive whole-school programs that incorporate:

- Cooperative learning environments
- Direct instruction and practice of conflict resolution abilities and processes
- Noncoercive school and classroom management systems
- Integration of conflict resolution concepts and abilities into curriculum

Peaceable school programs challenge youth and adults to believe and act on the understanding that a nonviolent, diverse society is a realistic goal. Peaceable schools create a system in which diversity is valued and encouraged and in which peacemaking is the normative behavior of adults and students alike. In the peaceable school, peacemaking involves applying the conflict resolution foundation abilities and processes to address interpersonal and intergroup problems and issues that confront students, faculty, administrators, and parents. The objectives of peacemaking are to achieve personal, group, and institutional goals and to maintain cooperative relationships.

Peaceable school approaches incorporate process curriculum approaches, mediation programs, and peaceable classroom approaches. In the peaceable school, the classroom is the place where students gain the knowledge base and skills needed to resolve conflicts creatively. The classroom is also the place where the majority of conflicts are addressed. The peaceable classroom is therefore the unit block of the peaceable school.[11]

Peaceable school programs offer training in the foundation abilities and the problem-solving processes of conflict resolution to all members of the school community. Employment of consensus decision making characterizes each classroom, and negotiation is used by all members of the school community to resolve conflicts equitably. Peer mediation is applicable both as a schoolwide conflict resolution strategy and as a service provided in the classroom to assist disputing students to settle their differences constructively. Peaceable school programs infuse conflict resolution into the way the school conducts its business, between students, between students and teachers, between teachers and administrators, and between parents and school personnel. Developing effective conflict resolution behavior requires a relationship of mutual appreciation and trust between the teacher and each learner. The learner's success in achieving quality conflict resolution behaviors depends above all else on the absence of coercion. The most important challenge of an educator in the peaceable school is to relate consistently and noncoercively to each learner.[12] The same notion holds equally true for the interactions between and among adults.

Peaceable School Transformation

Peaceable school approaches typically urge the school community to address specific elements in order to transform the school. The following list of elements for building a peaceable school is not intended to be a developmental sequence. There are multiple entry points to initiating peaceable school programs. The peaceable school materializes in parts and in stages, reaching fruition when all of the transformational elements are operational:

- Instituting conflict resolution training for adults that encompasses all understanding and behavior listed herein for student development

- Designing behavior expectations and management systems supportive of and in concert with conflict resolution theory

- Building a cooperative context through generous infusion of cooperative learning activities and cooperative interaction opportunities

- Developing a scope and sequence plan for teaching the foundation abilities of conflict resolution to all students

- Providing each student with an opportunity for age-appropriate understanding of conflict: definition of conflict; its origins in basic needs, resources, and values; choices for responding to conflicts; outcomes of different choices; and opportunities within conflicts

- Providing each student with an opportunity for age-appropriate understanding of peace and peacemaking behavior

- Providing each student with an opportunity for age-appropriate understanding of the principles of conflict resolution based on integrative negotiation theory: separating the people from the problem; focusing on interests, not positions; inventing options for mutual gain; using fair criteria

- Providing opportunities for each student to learn, practice, and use the problem-solving strategies of negotiation and consensus decision making within the classroom

- Providing opportunities for students to serve as mediators within their classrooms to help peers resolve issues of the classroom that they choose not to resolve or cannot resolve through negotiation or consensus decision making

- Providing mediation training for those who will serve as mediators in the schoolwide program

- Developing a formative evaluation process for continuous improvement and continuing growth toward becoming a peaceable school

Systemic Change

Peaceable school approaches recognize that policies and practices inherent in the operation of schools often provide powerful contradictory messages to peaceful resolution of conflicts. For comprehensive conflict resolution programs to realize maximum potential, rethinking those operations is inescapable. Unless the operational expectations of the system correspond to desired behavioral expectations for the individuals within the system, the contradictory messages are likely to result in a continuation of current behavior. Two overarching areas addressed in this list of elements of transformation are the degree of competition promoted or demanded within the system and the manner in which behavioral expectations are enforced.

Conflict resolution is problem solving for mutual benefit; thus cooperation is an operational value of conflict resolution. In competitive systems, individuals focus on the short-term and self-interests and engage in problem solving to maximize their own outcomes at the expense of the other disputant (win-lose negotiations). In cooperative systems, individuals focus on the long-term, on mutual interests, and engage in problem solving to maximize joint outcomes (win-win negotiations). The more cooperation is promoted and valued in the overall operation of the school, the more the problem-solving strategies of conflict resolution seem natural, logical, and desirable. Cooperative systems create the context necessary for conflicts to be resolved constructively and reduce the factors that place individuals at risk of using violence.

Much of the dysfunctional behavior in conflict occurs when one party coerces the other. Typically, coercion intends to control another's behavior or force the other person to behave differently. The message of conflict resolution is to choose problem solving, not choose to coerce.

Peaceable school programs address this transformation by developing a sense-based behavior management system that ends reliance on punishments and rewards to gain student compliance with the school's behavioral expectations, in favor of a discipline plan that provides positive learning experiences based on the learner's self-evaluation and choice. Both self-evaluation of behavior and generation and evaluation of alternative behavioral choices are fundamental to success in conflict resolution.[13]

A sense-based system for defining and managing behavior is foundational to such a discipline plan. Each student must fully understand the behavioral expectations of the school and the classroom. Such understanding is simplified when expectations make sense to the learner. Expectations make sense when there is a logical, age-appropriate explanation for their existence; when rules are few and simple; when expectations are predictable and can be applied in new situations; and when the consequences for inappropriate behavior are known, nonpunitive, and consistently applied. Students can use such a logical and fundamentally simple framework without adult intervention to determine what is and what is not acceptable behavior. This type of independent assessment is crucial to the schoolwide implementation of a conflict resolution education program.[14]

The goal of peaceable school approaches is to create a schoolwide discipline program focused on empowering students to regulate and control their own behavior. The program must allow educators to model an orderly, productive system accomplished through cooperation and persistent pursuit of constructive behavior. Also, students must be provided with alternative ways to behave—not just told to not behave in a particular manner. Thus the behavior management program becomes an educational program; the problem-solving strategies of conflict resolution are presented as tools to enable individuals to plan for new, effective future behavior.

Resolving Conflict Creatively Program

Resolving Conflict Creatively Program (RCCP) is a peaceable school program disseminated nationally by Educators for Social Responsibility (ESR). This comprehensive, K–12 approach to conflict resolution and intercultural understanding aims to reduce violence and promote caring and cooperative schools and communities. RCCP began in 1985 as a collaboration of the New York City Board of Education and the ESR New York City chapter (ESR Metro). In 1993, ESR established the RCCP National Center to replicate the program across the nation. Replication efforts are under way within school systems in New York, Louisiana, Alaska, New Jersey, California, Georgia, Oregon, and Massachusetts.

RCCP focuses on reaching young people through the adults who relate to them daily at home, in school, and in their communities. RCCP requires support at the highest levels within the school system before program implementation. A participating school district must make RCCP part of its vision for school change and commit to multiyear involvement in order to ensure proper institutionalization of the program.

The RCCP approach incorporates the following components:

RCCP introductory training and staff development component. A twenty-five-hour introductory course is provided for teachers who express interest in implementing RCCP in their classrooms. This training presents the theory behind, and a hands-on experience of, the concepts and skills of conflict resolution, intercultural understanding, and emotional and social literacy; prepares participants to model and teach these skills in their classrooms; illustrates ways to infuse conflict resolution strategies and skills into academic subjects; and demonstrates creative teaching techniques such as role playing, interviewing, brainstorming, small-group sharing, and cooperative learning teams.

The staff development component lets teachers receive feedback on lessons that they teach, and see skilled practitioners give demonstration lessons within the classroom. There is also opportunity to plan classroom activities and find resources in collaboration with an RCCP consultant. RCCP staff developers visit newly trained teachers from six to ten times during their first year, and numerous times during subsequent years. The staff developer conducts bimonthly follow-up meetings after school so that teachers can receive additional training, share their experiences and concerns, problem solve, and plan schoolwide events.

RCCP curriculum component. Teachers utilize the K–12 curricula to demonstrate that there are many choices for dealing with conflict other than passivity or aggression, to develop skills to make those choices real in life situations, to increase understanding and appreciation of different cultures, and to empower youth to play a significant role in creating a more peaceful world.

RCCP developed the curricula in close collaboration with participating teachers. They provide effective teaching strategies on the elementary, middle school, and high school levels. Curriculum themes include peace and conflict, communication, affirmation, fostering cooperation, working with feelings, negotiation and mediation, appreciating diversity, bias awareness, countering bias, peacemakers, and envisioning a positive future. Some of the individual skills integrated into the curriculum themes are active listening, perspective taking, dealing with anger, assertiveness, win-win negotiation, understanding cultures, and interrupting expressions of bias.

RCCP encourages teachers to set aside a thirty-to-forty-five-minute period at least once a week throughout the school year for a specific workshop in conflict resolution prepared from the curriculum guide. Teachers also integrate conflict resolution lessons, strategies, and skills into the regular academic program.

RCCP peer mediation component. Peer mediation reinforces the emerging problem-solving skills students learn through the curriculum component. The curriculum component must be implemented for at least a year prior to initiating peer mediation. A cadre of students, representative of the diverse cultures and backgrounds in the school, are selected by their classmates and teachers to be peer mediators. Once trained, elementary students take turns being "on-duty" on the playground during recess. Wearing special mediator T-shirts and working in teams with their adult advisors nearby, they help students talk out their disputes. Middle school and high school peer mediators do not work on the playground but listen to disputes in a room designated for mediation.

RCCP administrator component. Training is provided for administrators in order to introduce the concepts of conflict resolution and bias awareness and to encourage them to embrace and model the humane and creative approaches to dealing with conflict that teachers are implementing through the classroom curriculum. Administrative support is needed to make RCCP work at the school level.

RCCP parent involvement component. Parents participate in a twelve-hour training in the skills and concepts of conflict resolution and intergroup relations so they can help make their homes more peaceful and their children adept at using conflict resolution skills learned at school. Parents learn ways of dealing with conflict and prejudice at home and become more effective leaders in their schools and communities. Parents may become trainers for other parents by participating in a district-level sixty-hour training-for-trainers program.

RCCP develops an ongoing, long-term commitment with the school district. The close and equal partnership between the ESR nonprofit organization and the participating school district builds strong support and voluntary participation of the school community: students, teachers, administrators, support staff, and parents. The developmentally appropriate curricula for young people from kindergarten through twelfth grade, developed in collaboration with teachers, gives equal emphasis to issues of diversity and bias awareness on the one hand and conflict resolution on the other. Conflict resolution and issues of diversity are upheld as basic to youth education, not an add-on.

Illinois Institute for Dispute Resolution

Creating the Peaceable School is a comprehensive conflict resolution program initiated in 1993 by the Illinois Institute for Dispute Resolution (IIDR). This peaceable school approach is designed to help schools develop the internal capacity to improve the learning environment and develop a generation of responsible citizens with a commitment to social justice and the ability to express and resolve conflicts peacefully. In addition to facilitating the development of peaceable school programs throughout the state of Illinois, IIDR staff have conducted peaceable school workshops in the District of Columbia, Arkansas, Washington, Michigan, Indiana, Texas, Georgia, California, Missouri, Canada, and Australia.

The Creating the Peaceable School program focuses on making enduring systemic changes through applying conflict resolution principles to management of schools and classrooms. The program may be implemented within a school or school district. IIDR helps schools and school districts develop a comprehensive plan for program development based on identified needs and resources.

Fundamental Skill Areas

There are six skill areas fundamental to achieving a peaceable school. The curriculum gives the educator a theoretical overview of the skill area, and then a number of activities and strategies to engage students in developing a knowledge base and acquiring critical skills for each of the six skill areas. Each activity contains step-by-step procedures to be followed with the students, and each can be offered in a variety of learning formats: class workshop, team project, learning center, cooperative learning, and class meeting.

Building a peaceable climate. Responsibility and cooperation are the foundation on which all other skills in the peaceable school are built. In order to manage student behavior without coercion, the adults—operating from the perspective that effective behavior is the responsibility of each student—strive to develop each student's self-responsibility. Rights and corresponding responsibilities guide students in making responsible choices. As students and teachers together build the peaceable climate, they define and experience cooperation in ways that make that idea come alive in the school and the classroom.

Understanding conflict. A shared understanding of the nature of conflict is a prerequisite for students to engage in successful conflict resolution. The program provides information and activities designed to instill a shared understanding of the nature and causes of conflict, as well as of the possible responses to conflict and potential benefits of it. The idea that psychological needs are the underlying cause of conflict is particularly useful to students as they seek common interests to resolve disputes.

Understanding peace and peacemaking. Activities are designed to help students understand the concept of peace and put this concept into practice. Students are taught to observe peacemaking and peacebreaking behaviors within the school and classroom. Students learn the specific behaviors associated with peacemaking: appreciating diversity, understanding perceptions, empathizing, dealing with emotions, managing anger, countering bias, and communicating. The principles of conflict resolution are taught as the behaviors of peacemaking.

Mediation. Mediation is defined as assisted conflict resolution between disputants for use within the classroom and as a schoolwide vehicle for resolving conflicts. Training activities cover a six-step mediation process designed to allow students to gain the skills to act as neutral third parties in facilitating conflict resolution between disputants.

Negotiation. The concept of negotiation is defined as unassisted conflict resolution between two disputants. Disputants learn to state their individual needs, focus on their interests rather than their positions, and generate options for mutual gain. Training activities focus on a six-step negotiation process paralleling that presented for mediation.

Group problem solving. Group problem solving is presented as a creative strategy to deal with conflicts that involve a number of students within the classroom, within groups, and between groups in the school. The group is responsible for working to achieve a consensus decision that is implemented to resolve the conflict.

The Creating the Peaceable School program includes intensive professional development: training, coaching, and technical assistance for administrators, teachers, and support staff; parent education; and community initiatives.

Professional development is an intensive program of school change. IIDR approaches professional development as the opportunity to create a learning community among school staff (teachers, administrators, and support staff). As a learning community, educators help and support each other in the processes of learning. Part of this process includes examining how they handle conflict in their private and public lives, and particularly in their relationships with students.

IIDR delivers two-day and three-day introductory workshops along with follow-up technical support and strategic planning support. The introductory workshops provide learning experiences focused on developing abilities in the six fundamental skill areas. After the introductory workshops, IIDR consultants work on site in schools to support school staff (again, teachers, administrators, and support staff) as they implement the peaceable program. This support may include demonstration teaching in classrooms, helping teachers plan, observing classes, providing feedback, and coaching. During the on-site days, consultants use after-school meetings to conduct advanced training, discuss concerns, do problem solving, and offer opportunities for sharing experiences. IIDR also facilitates strategic planning for further program development.

Regarding parent education, Creating the Peaceable Home workshops may be initiated on site in elementary schools, middle schools, high schools, alternative education sites, public housing projects, community centers, etc. These workshops focus on teaching parents the skills and concepts of conflict resolution. Parents learn ways of applying these concepts within the home and their association with others in the school and community.

Community initiatives in creating peaceable schools demand that school administrators and teachers play a critical role in reaching out to the leaders of the community and to families to engage them in conflict resolution strategies. The peaceable school expands into the "peaceable neighborhood" through work with parents, police, churches, and neighborhood coalitions. The following is a list of three types of youth and community activities that may be established to mobilize the involvement of youth, parents, community activists, agencies, and organizations in creating peaceable schools:

1. *Peer education:* high school youths are recruited to form a Youth Peace Corps. This core group is trained to teach conflict resolution strategies, including anger management, to their peers and to middle and elementary school students. These highly trained youths provide strong role models for younger students as they teach these skills in the school setting and further serve as models by using their skills in various neighborhood settings. Representation of a cross-section of the entire student body is an important requisite.

2. *Community training:* partnerships are developed with those who encounter youth in conflict and with youth-serving organizations so as to support positive youth development. Conflict resolution training may be provided for police, park district personnel, the Boys Club/Girls Club, Urban League, and other interested agencies and organizations who work with youth. Personnel from the various agencies and organizations are specifically recruited to attend community training

3. *Police, youth, and community dialogues:* after-school sessions on site and Saturday retreats in a peaceful country setting bring youth, police, and community members together to learn about one another and to practice the conflict resolution skills needed to solve problems. In working sessions, participants engage in a series of game activities designed to demonstrate how teams of people working together solve problems. These lead to the development of a common vision and offer a chance for the participants to confront not just their differences but also their interdependency.

IIDR builds a shared vision among faculty through implementing Creating the Peaceable School. The curricula are designed to guide schools toward a system transformation that creates an active climate of peace. IIDR is committed to helping the school build the capacity to manage conflict and change in the process of developing a peaceable school program. In collaboration with IIDR consultants, individual schools determine where and how to begin the implementation process. Each school is encouraged to assess its needs and resources and develop commitment among staff through a strategic planning process focused on building a comprehensive conflict resolution program.

CHAPTER 6

Research Findings on What Works

Research conducted on conflict within schools and on the impact of conflict resolution education programs provides strong support for establishing conflict resolution programs in schools. One of the most comprehensive studies on conflict within schools was conducted by DeCecco and Richards[1] almost twenty years ago. They interviewed more than eight thousand students and five hundred faculty members in more than sixty junior and senior high schools in areas of New York City, Philadelphia, and San Francisco. They found that over 90 percent of the conflicts reported by students were perceived either to be unresolved or resolved destructively. Negotiation of conflicts was practically nonexistent.

The Johnson and Johnson Studies

More recently, David Johnson and Roger Johnson have conducted eleven research studies examining the effectiveness of the Teaching Students to Be Peacemakers program.[2] This program is directly based on the research and theory of integrative negotiation, perspective reversal, and constructive conflict resolution.

The Johnson and Johnson research is significant, because Teaching Students to Be Peacemakers[3] is based on the integrative negotiation theory that has provided the substructure for a number of school programs of conflict resolution that are in operation today. Results of these studies afford educators valuable quality information indicating the need for conflict resolution programs and the impact of conflict resolution training programs on students' ability to manage their conflicts constructively. A summary of the Johnson and Johnson research follows.

Students involved were from kindergarten through tenth grades. The studies were conducted in inner-city and suburban school districts in the United States and Canada. In most of the studies, students were randomly assigned to conditions—one group received peacemaker training, one group did not—and teachers were rotated across conditions. These carefully controlled field-experimental studies addressed a series of nine questions.

1. *How often do conflicts among students occur, and what are the most commonly occurring conflicts?* The findings indicate that students engage in conflicts daily. In the suburban schools studied, the majority of conflicts reported were over possession of and access to resources, preferences about what to do, playground issues, and taking turns. Some conflicts involved physical and verbal aggression. In the urban elementary school studied, the vast majority of conflicts referred to mediation involved physical and verbal violence.

2. *Before training, what strategies did students use to manage their conflicts?* Before training, students generally managed their conflicts through trying to win by forcing the other to concede (either by overpowering the other disputant or by asking the teacher to force the other to give in) or withdrawing from the conflict and the other person. In her log, one of the teachers stated, "Before training, students viewed conflict as fights that always resulted in a winner and a loser. To avoid such an unpleasant situation, they usually placed the responsibility for resolving conflicts on me, the teacher." Students all seem to lack knowledge of how to engage in problem-solving, integrative negotiations.

3. *Was the peacemaker training successful in teaching students the negotiation and mediation procedures?* After the peacemaker training, the students knew the negotiation and mediation procedures and retained their knowledge after the training ended.

4. *Could students apply the negotiation and mediation procedures to conflicts?* For all three types of measures used, students were able to apply the negotiation and mediation procedures to a variety of conflicts.

5. *Do students transfer the negotiation and mediation procedures to nonclassroom and nonschool situations?* The studies demonstrated that students did in fact use the negotiation and mediation procedures in the hallways, lunchroom, and playground. In addition, students used the procedures in family settings.

6. *When given the option, would students engage in "win-lose" or problem-solving negotiations?* Following the peacemaker training, students were placed in a negotiation situation in which they could either try to win or maximize joint outcomes. Whereas untrained students almost always strive to win, the majority of trained students focused on maximizing joint outcomes.

7. *Does the peacemaker training increase students' academic achievement?* In three of the studies the peacemaker training was integrated into English literature units. While studying a novel, students also learned the negotiation and mediation procedures and used them to understand the dynamics among the major characters. Following the end of the unit, students were given an achievement test; they were tested again several months later. The results indicated that students who received the integrated training scored significantly higher on the achievement and retention tests than did students who spent all their time studying the novel without learning the conflict resolution procedures.

8. *Does the peacemaker training result in fewer discipline problems that have to be managed by the teacher and the administration?* In the studies, the number of discipline problems the teacher had to deal with decreased by about 60 percent, and referrals to the principal dropped by 95 percent.

9. *Does the peacemaker training result in more positive attitudes toward conflict?* Untrained students uniformly had negative attitudes toward conflict. After training, students had more positive attitudes toward conflict. Teachers, administrators, and parents perceived the peacemaker program to be constructive and helpful. Many parents whose children were not part of the project requested that their children receive the training the next year, and a number of parents requested that they receive the training so they could use the procedures to improve conflict management within the family.

Analysis of the Johnson and Johnson research supports the need for conflict resolution education programs as the results indicate that before training most students were found to be involved in conflicts daily, indicating that conflicts are pervasive within classroom and schools. The conflicts most frequently reported were:

Put-downs and teasing

Playground conflicts

Access or possession conflicts

Physical aggression and fights

Academic work conflicts

Turn taking

Before training, students referred the majority of these conflicts to the teacher, used destructive strategies that tended to escalate the conflict rather than resolve it, and lacked knowledge of how to negotiate. Results indicated that after the negotiation and mediation training, the student-student conflicts that did occur were by and large managed by the students themselves without the involvement of adults. *The frequency of student-student conflicts that teachers had to manage dropped 80 percent after the training, and the number of conflicts referred to the principal was reduced to nearly zero.* Such a dramatic reduction of referrals of conflict to adult authorities changed the adult role in the discipline programs of the participating schools from arbitrating conflicts to maintaining and supporting the conflict resolution program.

This research also supports the importance of teaching the integrative negotiation strategy; the investigation of how students would manage conflicts in which they could use either a win-lose strategy or integrative negotiation strategy (win-win) found that (1) all untrained students used the win-lose strategy and (2) trained students primarily used the integrative negotiation strategy.

Conflict Resolution Education: Assessment Highlights from the Field

Other assessments from the conflict resolution education field support the need for conflict resolution programs and legitimize the contention that effective conflict resolution education programs must be based on proven negotiation theory operationalized into instructional procedures that educators can be trained to use. Brief highlights of other research from the field follow:

• The Ohio School Conflict Management Demonstration Project conducted in seventeen schools between 1990 and 1993 indicated that most students improved their attitudes toward conflict, increased their understanding of nonviolent problem-solving methods, and enhanced their communication skills.[4]

• The Clark County Social Service School Mediation Program in Nevada reported for the 1992–93 school year that the amount of conflict among students in the two participating elementary schools was reduced and that the existence of the program helped prevent fights among students. Peer mediators mediated 163 conflicts and resolved 138 (85 percent). Peer mediators demonstrated a significant increase in conflict management skills, self-esteem, and assertiveness. In addition, the number of teachers who spent less than one-fifth of their time on discipline increased by 18 percent after the program. Similar findings occurred in the reported results for the 1993–94 school year.[5]

• Evaluation of a mediation program in a suburban Chicago high school indicated positive results. Researchers testing the hypothesis that mediation is an effective alternative to traditional discipline found that mediation was more effective than traditional discipline in reducing the number of interpersonal conflicts and that the majority of both the disputants and student mediators were highly satisfied with all aspects of the mediation.[6]

• Evaluation of the impact of the Resolving Conflict Creatively Program in four multiracial, multiethnic school districts in New York City showed that in response to a survey 84 percent of teachers reported noticing positive changes in classroom climate. Seventy-one percent of teachers involved in the RCCP evaluation reported moderate or great decreases in physical violence in the classroom, while 66 percent observed less name calling and fewer verbal put-downs. Similar percentages said that students were showing better perspective-taking skills, a greater willingness to cooperate, and more "caring behavior." In addition, over 98 percent of respondents said that the mediation component gave children an important tool for dealing with conflicts. Other changes reported by teachers and administrators in the evaluation are spontaneous use of conflict resolution skills on the part of children, increased self-esteem and sense of empowerment, increased awareness of feelings and verbalizing of those feelings, and more acceptance of differences.[7]

• Project S.M.A.R.T. (School Mediator Alternative Resolution Team), ongoing in six New York City high schools, reported that suspensions for fighting decreased by 46 percent, 45 percent, 70 percent, 60 percent, and 65 percent at five of the high schools during the first year of operation.[8]

• An evaluation report for the New Mexico Center for Dispute Resolution Mediation in Schools program summarizes that teachers in program schools perceived less violence and hurtful behavior among students, and teachers in nonprogram schools reported more violence. Program teachers were likely to use positive, noncoercive conflict resolution strategies—especially mediation—in response to "hurtful" behavior among students. Nonprogram teachers, on the other hand, were more likely to use coercive, win-lose, adult-authored strategies—especially detention and sending students to the principal's office—in response to problem behavior.

The peer mediation process clearly "belongs to the students." In a total of more than 2,300 hundred mediations, only 250 required some sort of adult intervention. Students trained as mediators had clearer definitions of mediation and conflict resolution strategies and skills than their untrained peers. Untrained students did not fully grasp the benefits of win-win situations and more specific and creative conflict resolution strategies. Also, untrained students did not show the levels of self-esteem and confidence demonstrated by trained students, nor did they feel as good about school.

The amount of time staff members in program schools spent in dealing with conflicts was reduced, as was the number of violent incidents among students.[9]

The International Center for Cooperation and Conflict Resolution (ICCR) at Columbia Teachers College in New York initiated a conflict resolution research project at one of the New York city alternative high schools. Results indicated positive effects on the students trained in conflict resolution. These students improved in managing their conflicts, and they experienced increased social support and less victimization from others. This improvement in their relations with others led to increased self-esteem as well as a decrease in feelings of anxiety and depression and more frequent positive feelings of well-being. The higher self-esteem, in turn, produced a greater sense of personal control over their own fates. The increases in their sense of personal control and in their positive feelings of well-being led to higher academic performance. There is also indirect evidence that the work readiness and work performance of students were improved by their exposure to the training.[10]

• The Harvard Graduate School of Education is undertaking a systematic evaluation of the impact of the Program for Young Negotiators. Preliminary findings from the evaluation team suggest that the majority of students participating in PYN are learning the basic messages taught by the program and are using them, at least in certain situations. Most interviewees were able to discuss in depth the importance of talking it out to avoid fights and to accomplish one's goals. And most interviewees reported experiencing the program as "fun," because of its use of games and role plays. This latter point is important in that the fun experience keeps the students engaged in the training process and facilitates their recall of the basic messages. The interviews also revealed that most students could cite concrete examples of using their negotiation skills with peers and, perhaps more unexpectedly, with parents. Several students reported that their parents were caught off guard by their practice of negotiation at home. The shift from arguing, complaining, and resisting to negotiating was generally met positively by parents, according to many PYN graduates. In addition, parents too have shared information related to their children's negotiation strategies; the general parent feedback is that the use of negotiation opens up avenues for parent-child discussion. Teachers who taught the curriculum evaluated the training as useful to their work both in PYN and in their other classes. They reported that the curriculum content and structure, particularly the role plays and negotiation games, promoted important discussion of topics such as decision making, planning for the future, and conflict resolution. Teachers also reported seeing changes in the communication and conflict resolution styles of many of the students participating in the program. The benefits cited by the six principals interviewed included improvement in the students' ability to talk through disagreements and the opportunity for teachers to think through their own conflict management style.[11]

• In 1991, the Peace Education Foundation Conflict Resolution and Peer Mediation programs were initiated throughout Dade County (Florida) Region II public schools. Training for school staff was provided in order to establish both classroom-based and schoolwide student mediation programs and infuse school curricula with conflict resolution instruction. A review of mediator reports showed that 86 percent of conflicts mediated were resolved. Student case management systems, a method of incident reporting, showed a statistically significant reduction in the rate of referrals for general disruptive behavior in the elementary schools with the highest levels of implementation. Conflict resolution affected student attitudes toward resolving conflicts positively. Results from student surveys indicated that those who received training were more willing to respond to conflict situations with actions other than threats and violence.[12]

In 1994, staff teams from seven alternative and two middle schools with a high percentage of at-risk students received training in the PEF conflict resolution model. Postintervention surveys showed that student attitudes toward conflict changed significantly after learning the PEF model. Students were more inclined to explain, reason, compromise, or share in order to resolve their conflicts; they were less likely to appeal to authority figures or use aggression and threats when in conflict. Teachers surveyed indicated that they felt more respected and less frustrated as a result of implementing the PEF model.[13]

Evaluations of the Palm Beach County Schools initiative include a considerable reduction in student referrals and suspensions. For example, the number of referrals at Spady Elementary dropped to 5 between September and December 1994 from 124 during the same period in 1992. Parents who attended a Fighting Fair for Families workshop sponsored by the Safe School Center reported favorable results. According to two-month follow-up surveys from 163 participants, 79 percent reported improvement with the way conflicts are handled at home, 76 percent with how feelings are treated at home, and 70 percent with how people listen to each other at home; 80 percent reported that their "Rules for Fighting Fair" poster is still displayed in their homes.[14]

• The Mediation Project of the Public Justice Department of St. Mary's University of San Antonio, Texas, has provided conflict resolution training for middle and high schools through a school-university-community project. Preliminary studies of some of the first schools trained have shown significant decreases in disciplinary problems and student violence on school campuses. Smithson Valley Middle School recorded a 57 percent drop in disciplinary actions in the first year of operation of its peer-based mediation program.[15]

• Through the Lawyers Adopt-a-School Program of the American Bar Association (Section of Dispute Resolution), lawyers have successfully adopted several schools in Montgomery County, Maryland. After one year of operation, the program reported the following middle school results: office referrals were reduced from 384 to 67, suspensions for disruptive behavior were reduced from 54 to 14, and fights were reduced from 52 to 9. The disputes were usually mediated during lunch break, with the average mediation lasting twenty-two minutes. As a result of the program's success, the program is being replicated in sites across the country.[16]

Research results clearly support the efficacy of conflict resolution education for youth. Because mediation programs are distinctive and perhaps more prevalent in schools, many studies of the mediation approach have been conducted. Since mediation is often a central component of the other approaches, the results from these studies can be extrapolated. The evidence of the success of the peaceable classroom and process curriculum approaches is difficult to separate from the general research into effective classrooms since conflict resolution is either integrated into other curricula or offered as a part of the total classroom curriculum. The two peaceable school approaches highlighted in Chapter Five are each currently involved in comprehensive evaluation studies.

In summary, further research and evaluation of conflict resolution education is anticipated, but it is unlikely to alter the impression of the efficacy of conflict resolution education. What further research and evaluation promises is information concerned with strengthening, expanding, and sustaining conflict resolution education. Further research and evaluation of conflict resolution education programs can provide information that delineates strengths and weaknesses of program elements and strategies. Research should also address cultural issues and developmentally appropriate practices in conflict resolution education. This type of information is invaluable in strengthening the rationale for adopting and implementing conflict resolution education in schools programs. Additionally, data from future studies may illuminate lessons learned from successful use of conflict resolution by young people in all aspects of their lives.

Implications for Conflict Resolution Education from the Research on Risk Factors and Resilience

Research on social development indirectly supports the value of conflict resolution education, especially for at-risk youth. Some youths whose social or economic circumstances place them at risk for violent or self-destructive behavior are able to avoid outcomes such as dropping out of school, using drugs, getting pregnant, or participating in gang activities. These young people have been identified as possessing "resilience" derived from such factors as a sense of belonging, the ability to communicate effectively, flexibility, and good problem-solving skills. Resilience is characterized as the ability to overcome the effects of a high-risk environment and to develop social competence despite exposure to severe stress. Resilient youth are able to overcome such risk factors as inadequate bonding or caring, low expectations, a negative school climate, academic failure, and economic or social deprivation. To develop strategies to prevent violent and other antisocial behavior, it is important to understand what factors increase the risk of youths' developing those behaviors. Research indicates that many interrelated conditions place young people at risk, with no single factor having greater impact than any other.

Risk Factors for Predicting Violent and Other Antisocial Behavior

David Hawkins and Richard Catalano, researchers at the University of Washington, identify nineteen specific risk factors for which research is consistent in predicting youth delinquency or other antisocial behavior. Here is a composite summary of these factors:

- Alienation and lack of bonding to family, school, and community
- Early, persistent antisocial behavior
- Family history of high-risk behavior
- Poor family management practices
- Exposure to media portrayals of violence
- Family conflict
- Economic and social deprivation
- School failure
- Lack of commitment to education
- Association with delinquent peers
- Community disorganization (little sense of community, high crime, low surveillance, availability of drugs, availability of firearms, etc.)[17]

Although the presence of these risk factors does not guarantee development of violent or other antisocial behavior, presence does represent an increased probability of such behavior occurring. Awareness of risk factors can alert teachers, counselors, social workers, and others to the need for early intervention. For example, since it is known that peer harassment, or bullying, is an early indicator of lifelong antisocial problems, then it makes sense to target preschool and early elementary school as a time to intervene to reduce this factor.

Resilience to the Effects of High-Risk Factors

Research also shows that some children exposed to multiple risk factors manage to avoid behavior problems later even though they are exposed to the same risks as children who do develop behavior problems. These children appear to be resilient. They are able to bounce back and withstand the inevitable stresses in life. Resilient children have the following characteristics:[18]

Social Competence	Problem-Solving Skills	Sense of Autonomy
Responsiveness to others	Ability to apply abstract thinking	Positive sense of independence
Conceptual and intellectual flexibility	Engagement in reflective thought	Emerging feelings of efficacy
Caring for others	Critical reasoning skills	High self-esteem
Good communication skills	Development of alternative solutions in frustrating situations	Impulse control
Sense of humor		Planning and goal setting
		Belief in the future

Resiliency allows students to rise above the underlying risk factors already mentioned (lack of bonding or caring, low expectations, negative school climate, academic failure, economic or social deprivation).

Protective Factors That Ameliorate Risk Factors

Protective factors are those conditions or influences that ameliorate the risk factors and promote the characteristics of resilience. In their social development strategy, Hawkins and Catalano organize evidence about protective factors into a theory for addressing risk factors and promoting resilience. This theory identifies bonding—the feeling of being connected to others—as the overarching protective factor in the development of healthy behaviors. Early on, resilient children tend to establish positive adult and peer relationships that help them bond to their family, school, and community.

Hawkins and Catalano outline three protective processes necessary for developing strong bonds:

1. *Opportunities.* Children must have the opportunity to contribute to their family, school, and community. The task is to provide all children with meaningful, challenging, developmentally appropriate opportunities that help them feel responsible and significant. Research shows that bonding to school increases when instructional methods emphasize proactive classroom management, interactive teaching, and cooperative learning.

2. *Skills.* Opportunities for involvement are of little value if students lack the skills that enable them to participate. If children do not have the cognitive and social skills necessary for solving problems and getting along with others,

they experience frustration and failure. Lack of skill denies the opportunity to bond.

3. *Recognition.* Children feel potent and powerful when their contributions are valued by their peers, teachers, and families. Children must be recognized and acknowledged for their capabilities and for their participation.[19]

In summary, risk factors identified by researchers explain why some youth are prone to engage in violent or self-destructive behaviors, while the identified resiliency factors seem to protect otherwise at-risk youth from engaging in dangerous or violent behavior. It is not a coincidence that these protective factors of resiliency (such as belonging, effective communication, flexibility, and good problem-solving skills) and the foundation abilities for conflict resolution are nearly mirror images.

Relationship Between Resiliency and Conflict Resolution

The relationship between resiliency and conflict resolution is clear and significant. In developing conflict resolution education programs, schools can create environments that support the development of resilient characteristics in children in three ways. First, resolving conflicts in principled ways promotes and preserves relationships, thereby facilitating the bonding that is essential to the development of resilience. Continuing and improving relationships is a prime outcome when conflicts are resolved peacefully, and bonding is the overarching protective factor in developing healthy behaviors. Second, conflict resolution education fosters resiliency by conveying to youth that they have the power to control their own behavior by making choices that satisfy their needs. Finally, in giving youths the opportunity to resolve their conflicts peacefully, a conflict resolution education program sends to involved youth a powerful enabling message of trust and perceived capability. Thus an environment in which the characteristics of resilience can emerge and thrive is created. The foundation abilities of conflict resolution—orientation, perception, emotion, communication, creative-thinking, and critical-thinking abilities—are the same abilities and skills that form the foundation for developing and strengthening resiliency in youth.[20]

PART THREE

Establishing Programs in Schools

CHAPTER 7

Ensuring Developmentally Appropriate Practices

Conflict resolution viewed as a curriculum to be learned is no different than any other subject matter. This chapter presents a developmental sequence of behavioral expectations associated with the foundation abilities and the problem-solving processes of conflict resolution. The expectations are reasonable for the various general age groupings only if learning opportunities and ample practice have been provided. This developmental sequence is based on examination of the literature in the field of conflict resolution and examination of school practices in delivering conflict resolution training to students.

Any general developmental sequencing of expectations should be held subordinate to consideration of the individual. Because of the pervasiveness of conflict, every individual experiences it. Everyone enters and exits those experiences differently. Thus, the concept of age appropriateness is illogical unless tempered by attention to the individual's prior experiences, or lack of same.

Best practice suggests that developing proficiency for each of the various age levels requires development of proficiency at all the earlier age levels. Although assessment of proficiency for an earlier stage of development is valid only for each individual, the developmental continuum does at least suggest *what* to assess.

Assessment is important; it is unfair to expect students to behave in any manner if those behaviors have not specifically been taught. It is foolish to assume that a behavior has been learned simply because a student is "old enough to know that." Thus, when developing a program for students of high school age, the program must address more than the high school portion of the continuum provided here. If students have not had the opportunity to develop proficiency in the foundation abilities and the problem-solving processes through prior experience, the program for these older students must provide those learning opportunities through age-appropriate experiences.

Circle of Learning

It is not intended that the developmental continuum provided here ascribe to the "vaccination theory" of learning, that is, once you have had something, you will not need to have it again. Learning to employ all of the abilities and strategies of conflict resolution is a lifelong pursuit. There is always more to learn and internalize. Learning to perform is circular, moving through four stages (Figure 7.1):

1. Unconsciously unskilled: being unaware of what one does not know

2. Consciously unskilled: being aware of what is not known; recognizing the need to be able to do something

3. Consciously skilled: being able to perform in a prescribed manner by paying close attention to the sequential, component steps of a procedure

4. Unconsciously skilled: performing competently and almost automatically

Learning is not only circular, as the figure illustrates. It is cyclic: one evolves through the circle of learning with each refinement and improvement one learns in the employment of a strategy.

The pedagogy of a conflict resolution education program includes practice in building foundation abilities as well as actual practice using the problem-solving processes of conflict resolution. The operative notion is *practice.* Transferring what is learned about the processes of conflict resolution in simulated or practice settings to using those processes in real-life situations requires overlearning the processes. Students need to be taught the intellectual framework, provided the tools to think systematically about conflict, and given the opportunity to practice these skills and employ these tools within a real-life context. Sufficient and diverse age-appropriate practice in the "laboratory" setting of the school—trial, evaluation, and retrial—is an absolute condition for a successful conflict resolution education program.

Figure 7.1.   Circle of Learning

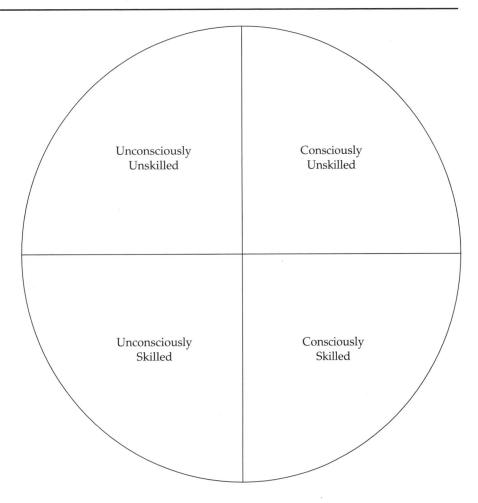

Effective Learning Activities

Early Childhood Education

Effective learning activities for preschool through grade two include stories, role playing, games that promote cooperation, classroom projects, "going out" activities involving the greater community, activity cards, posters, puppets, activities including older children, skits, and demonstrations.

Elementary School

Additional effective activities for grades three to five are integration of problem-solving analysis into areas of the standard curriculum, role playing, classroom projects and meetings, establishing a school-based peer-mediation program, videos, games, school assemblies, classroom demonstrations, and student presentations to parent and community groups.

Middle School

Additional learning and practice activities particularly appropriate for grades six to eight include training children to be trainers of younger students in the use of the problem solving strategies of conflict resolution (by assisting them to negotiate or by facilitating consensus decision making sessions), integrating conflict resolution into the regular school curriculum, school assembly demonstrations, videos, having students create their own role-playing exercises, and interaction with the greater community by providing informational demonstrations or skits or by providing actual conflict resolution services to community organizations.

High School

Learning and practice activities for the high school age group include peer mediation programs, training students to train other students to serve as peer mediators, school assemblies and demonstrations, creating role-play exercises, producing videos, having students and school professionals offer conflict resolution training and services to the greater community, letting students assist schools for younger children in developing conflict resolution programs, students' serving as mediators or facilitators for community programs for younger children and senior citizens or other community based groups, and asking students to serve as mediators in neighborhood disputes (all types of school and community disputes). In the departmental framework of most secondary schools, conflict resolution education can be offered as a specific course(s) in the general curriculum, integrated into all other courses offered, or organized as special units of instruction within appropriate subject matter courses.

Learning and practice activities for any age level should be designed to reach all learning channels and all learning styles. Students need to be actively involved in activities that reinforce lessons learned. Teachers and other professionals must be alert and sensitive to "teachable moments" and respond to those moments. These very real incidents have the potential to stimulate and make relevant the learning of conflict resolution abilities and use of conflict resolution processes. It cannot be overemphasized that students also learn what they live. Adults communicate much by the behavior they model. Modeling appropriate and desired behavior does not replace the need to provide learning and practice opportunities for students, but inappropriate modeling by adults easily negates even the most rigorous practice schedule.

Conflict Resolution Developmental Sequence

A conflict resolution program, like any other educational program, provides optimal outcomes when engineered to meet the specific needs of the population of students it serves. The developmental sequence in Table 7.1 is intended only to provide guideposts for the journey of learning about and developing proficiency in conflict resolution. It is not intended to be all-inclusive of conflict resolution education.

In summary, this developmental sequence is valid for educating youth regardless of the setting for that education. The crucial consideration is not the age of the student, but the developmental stage of the student. If the student has not developed the proficiencies expected for someone younger, the development of those proficiencies must be addressed through age-appropriate learning opportunities.

Table 7.1.   Conflict Resolution Developmental Sequence

	Early Childhood–Grade 2	Grades 3–5	Grades 6–8	Grades 9–12
Orientation Abilities	■ Understands that having conflicts is natural; knows that involvement in conflicts is all right	■ Understands that conflict is inevitable and that it can be a positive force for growth	■ Recognizes that the sources of conflict and the problem-solving processes of conflict resolution are applicable to all types of conflicts: interpersonal, intergroup, and international	■ Maintains a variety of good working relationships with parents, family, siblings, boyfriends, girlfriends, teachers, acquaintances, bosses, etc.
	■ Knows conflicts can be solved through cooperation	■ Understands that conflicts can become better or worse, depending upon the chosen response	■ Diagnoses conflicts appropriately and selects resolution strategies for conflicts in various settings (school, home, neighborhood, etc.)	■ Analyzes conflict in the context of a present relationship and uses an appropriate problem-solving strategy
	■ Differentiates between prejudice and a dislike	■ Understands and recognizes soft, hard, and principled responses to conflicts	■ Exhibits effective responses to another who, in a shared conflict, chooses a soft or hard response	■ Recognizes patterns in his or her responses to conflict and strives for positive growth and change in those patterns
	■ Views peace as a desired condition and can identify several peacemaking and peacebreaking behaviors	■ Participates in cooperative endeavors	■ Takes action to inform when prejudice is displayed	■ Understands that conflict resolution skills are life skills
		■ Recognizes prejudice in self and in the actions of others	■ Suggests a peacemaking action as an alternative to a displayed peacebreaking action	■ Confronts prejudice effectively in self and others and in the school as an institution
		■ Understands own behavior in terms of the needs of belonging, power, freedom, and fun		■ Promotes equal access and opportunity on many fronts
		■ Understands peace as a personal action; differentiates between peacemaking and		

peacebreaking behaviors in self and others

- Seeks diverse and multicultural experiences and relationships
- Works actively to promote peace in the school and in the community

Perception Abilities

- Accepts that he or she is not always "right"
- Accepts that others may see things differently
- Describes a conflict from own perspective and from the point of view of others
- Withholds blame

- Identifies and checks own assumptions about a situation
- Understands how others perceive words and actions
- Empathizes and accepts the feelings and perceptions of others
- Analyzes a conflict from the perspective of unmet basic psychological needs
- Understands friendships and good working relationships and strives to build and maintain them
- Understands the effects of blaming and accusing behaviors; chooses not to act in that manner

- Recognizes the limitations of own perceptions and understands that selective filters affect seeing and hearing
- Identifies and checks assumptions that self and others make about a situation
- Possesses a rudimentary understanding of how problem-solving strategies can be influenced
- Recognizes the prevalence and glamorization of violence in society
- Recognizes that conflict can escalate into violence

- Critically analyzes own perceptions and modifies understanding as new information emerges
- Articulates how own words, actions, and emotions are perceived by others
- Analyzes how perceptions of others relate to probable intent or purpose
- Understands how problem-solving strategies can be influenced and regularly chooses to exercise positive influence
- Prevents escalation of conflicts, even with adults
- Helps others recognize the potential for vio-

Emotion Abilities

• Knows that feeling anger, frustration, and fear is all right	• Understands own emotions	• Takes responsibility for emotions	lence and for nonviolent conflict resolution
• Controls anger	• Understands that others have emotional responses and that those responses may be different from his or her own	• Accepts and validates emotions and perceptions of others	• Remains calm and focused on problem solving when confronted with a strong emotional display from another person, including an adult
• Expresses feelings in language that expands beyond happy, sad, glad, or mad	• Expresses emotions effectively and appropriately	• Possesses effective strategies for "cool down" and uses them at appropriate times	• Prevents conflict escalation and violence effectively by using communication-based conflict resolution strategies
• Hears and acknowledges the feelings of others	• Disagrees without being disagreeable		
• Does not react to emotional outbursts of others by elevating own emotional response			

Communication Abilities

• Listens without interruption while another describes an incident or defines the problem and summarizes what that person has said	• Summarizes the facts and feelings of another person's point of view	• Uses summarizing and clarifying to diffuse anger and otherwise deescalate conflict	• Summarizes position and interests of others in conflict situations efficiently and accurately
• Tells what happened by speaking to be understood, using "I" language	• Asks specific clarifying questions to gather more information	• Withholds judgment and is open to persuasion	• Acknowledges the validity of emotions and perspectives of others
• Uses questions "How did that make you	• Uses appropriate problem-solving phraseology (e.g., using "and" rather than "but" and "we" instead of "I" or "you")	• Is productively persuasive	• Reframes statements of others, removing biased or inflammatory messages to capture
		• Tests understanding, listens to understand, and speaks to be	

- the underlying meaning
- Expresses interests explicitly
- Uses clarifying questions to uncover "hidden" interests of others
- Possesses a conflict resolution vocabulary (e.g., "position," "interests," "options," "alternatives," "consensus," "commitment," "legitimacy," "brainstorm," etc.) and uses it appropriately

- Evaluates and reconciles positions and interests of self and others in most situations
- Prioritizes interests and develops a strategy for working toward agreement, focusing on easier issues first (those of mutual concern) and most difficult issues last (those of conflicting concerns)
- Articulates mutual interests and reconciles

- understood
- Reframes own statements using unbiased and less inflammatory language

- Understands that underlying interests, not positions, define the problem in conflict situations
- Understands that there are often multiple, unclear, or conflicting interests
- Understands and begins to use analytical tools to diagnose problems
- Uses problem solving for conflicting as well as common or compatible interests

---

- Makes *I*-statements rather than *you*-statements in expressing point of view
- Shows awareness of nonverbal communication by self and by others, especially related to feelings
- Communicates desire for cooperative working relationships

- Distinguishes between positions and interests
- Identifies interests beyond own position in any situation
- Separates inventing options from making decisions
- Identifies mutual and compatible interests and creates behavioral options to satisfy those interests

---

- feel?" and "What happened next?"
- Answers questions about a conflict
- Uses a conflict resolution vocabulary (such as "interests," "options," "brainstorm," "negotiate," "point of view," etc.)

Creative-Thinking Abilities

- Describes what is wanted and why it is wanted
- Generates ideas for solving a problem
- Improves a simple idea

Critical-Thinking Abilities				
- Chooses from multiple ideas - Understands when something is fair to self and fair to another person - Explains why something is not fair	- Evaluates realistically the risks and consequences of "flight or fight" in conflict - Identifies best self-help alternative in a conflict situation - Chooses to work	- Challenges assumptions about what is possible - Thinks about both short- and long-term consequences of proposed options - Negotiates without	conflicting interests - Switches perspectives to generate new options - Manages brainstorming effectively, separating inventing from deciding, and focuses on advocates for options for mutual gain - Brainstorms multiple options in any situation: improving, refining, embellishing, and expanding on existing options - Using various analytical tools to diagnose problems, formulate new approaches, and evaluate the likely effectiveness of those approaches	- Uses problem-solving processes when engaging in difficult conversations - Speculates on best alternatives to negotiated agreement for self and others

Negotiation Abilities

- Participates unassisted with a peer in simplified problem solving: each cools off, tells what happened, imagines ways to solve problem, chooses one of the ways
- Participates in a negotiation session when giving in

- Expresses a realistic and workable plan for resolving a conflict
- Understands what it means to commit to a plan and be trustworthy

- Manages the negotiation process without assistance

- toward mutual fairness in resolving a dispute rather than to accomplish self-imposed will
- Evaluates interests of self and others according to fairness standards
- Crafts win-win resolutions
- Specifies clear agreement by stating who, what, when, and how

- Identifies outside standards and criteria for fairness (such as legal standards or school rules) when evaluating interests and solutions
- Recognizes the efficacy of committing only to solutions that are fair, realistic, and workable
- Endeavors to fulfill commitments

- Performs principled negotiation with peers and adults
- Involves a peer who has little or no conflict resolution training in negotiation of a conflict
- Understands that nearly every interaction is a negotiation

- Analyzes ways to improve best alternatives to negotiated agreement
- Analyzes willingness and ability of self and other person to honor a plan of action in any situation
- Identifies uncontrollable factors that might have an impact on the ability of the parties to fulfill an agreement
- Identifies external standards of fairness and use them in resolving conflicts
- Honors commitments and encourages others to do the same

- Negotiates with difficult parties effectively
- Teaches negotiation process to peers and adults
- Enjoys negotiation process

Mediation Abilities	• coached by an adult or older child • Participates in a mediation facilitated by an adult or older student mediator	• Teaches younger students the negotiation process • Participates in mediation process facilitated by another student(s) or an adult • Serves as a peer mediator in a classroom program or a schoolwide program	• Mediates a wide assortment of disputes involving various disputants • Trains others in the mediation process • Mediates disputes among peers • Co-mediates disputes between peers and adults • Coaches younger students and peers as they learn to mediate
Consensus Decision-Making Abilities	• Engages in group problem-solving discussions and processes facilitated by a teacher or other adult	• Participates in classroom sessions endeavoring to resolve group conflicts and problems • Manages consensus problem-solving sessions for classroom groups of younger students • Manages consensus decision making in a small group of peers (such as classroom work group or student council committee)	• Manages consensus problem solving in various groups • Facilitates consensus decision making as a member of a group

CHAPTER 8

Developing and Implementing Programs

Since conflict is inevitable and conflict resolution is entirely consistent with the mission of every school in America to develop an effective, responsible citizenry, the question to be addressed is *not* "Does our school need a conflict resolution program?" The answer to that question, supported by the content of this book, is clearly yes. But this will not be the answer obtained from school personnel in the collective until and unless opportunities are provided for individual staff members to gain awareness of the need for and the potential of conflict resolution programs for students. Once awareness is created, the real question becomes "Where does one start in developing a conflict resolution program?" The answer to that question is to *start somewhere.* Where the school actually chooses to start is less important than for the school to begin to provide opportunities for students to become peacemakers.[1]

The initial opportunities should reflect efforts that the school leaders believe can be sustained and eventually expanded. An individual classroom teacher may provide conflict resolution training for the students of that classroom. A group of teachers could combine their resources and offer a conflict resolution program to a larger group of students. A few staff members, supported by the other staff members who at least accept that a conflict resolution program is desirable, may develop and orchestrate a school wide peer mediation program. Or all staff members could agree to implement one of the problem-solving strategies of conflict resolution, perhaps negotiation or consensus decision making, in every classroom of the building, or the entire school-community could commit to long-term development of a peaceable school. Various combinations of implementation initiatives may occur simultaneously.

Program Development Continuum

A primary purpose of this book is to provide information and delineate resources that are available to assist schools in initiating a conflict resolution education program for students and subsequently in developing a comprehensive conflict resolution education program. Implementation of such a program is likely to be a journey of achievements along a program development continuum involving discernible stages:

1. Assess needs and resources
2. Develop awareness of program and training possibilities
3. Develop a strategic plan for implementation
4. Implement initial staff training
5. Implement (initial) student training and pilot (initial) program
6. Evaluate pilot program
7. Develop continuing staff training program
8. Extend (initial) student training program to additional students
9. Extend pilot (initial) program to additional students
10. Implement additional program components
11. Implement total-school program

Program Implementation Phases

To develop, implement, and sustain a successful conflict resolution program, participants must embrace the belief that conflicts can be resolved peacefully. Many adults in schools are familiar with and most comfortable with using means of resolving conflict that are grounded in such methods as exercise of adult authority, reliance on school rules, discipline hearings, and other administrative procedures. Moving from these methods to ones that encourage people to talk about their interests and needs and to work collaboratively to come up with solutions requires a major paradigm shift.

It is important to realize that student's success in developing awareness of the positive potential of conflict resolution is an outgrowth of the endeavors and commitment exhibited by the adults in the school to approach conflict positively. Educators who bring positive ways of resolving conflict into their classrooms see results that have a powerful effect on their lives and work, as well as on the lives and work of their students.

Designing, implementing, and operating a comprehensive conflict resolution education program can be approached through five developmental phases (Exhibit 8.1).

The first phase involves creating and training the conflict resolution education program team, designating program coordinator(s), conducting a needs assessment, and building faculty consensus for program development.

The second phase establishes an advisory committee, develops policies and procedures including the role of conflict resolution within the school discipline program, selects a strategy for implementation, develops time lines for implementation, and identifies and develops funding sources.

Phase three is the program implementation phase; it differs depending on the implementation strategy selected: a peer mediation schoolwide approach or an approach based in each classroom. If the peer mediation schoolwide approach is selected, the third phase encompasses recruiting peer mediator applications and nominations and then selecting and training student mediators. It focuses on educating a critical mass about conflict, peacemaking, and conflict resolution processes via workshops for faculty, students, parents, and community. It also involves developing and executing a promotion campaign and every aspect of program operation and maintenance (request for mediation, scheduling mediations and mediators, supervising mediators, recording mediation data, providing ongoing training and support, to evaluating programs). If peer mediation is selected as the initial program thrust, phase four then involves moving the program into each classroom. When an approach based in each classroom is selected to initiate the program, phase three involves training all classroom staff and developing a staff consensus about the student training and program to be implemented in each classroom.

Phase four involves implementing the other strategy (the classroom-based approach if schoolwide peer mediation was selected for phase three, or vice versa).

Phase five is to create the peaceable climate.

These five developmental phases can be readily adapted to serve the varying needs and interests of almost any school. Phases

Exhibit 8.1.   Five Phases of a Comprehensive Conflict Resolution Education Program

Phase One: Develop Program Team and Commitment
    Create program team
    Train program team
    Designate program coordinator(s)
    Conduct needs assessment
    Build faculty consensus for program development

Phase Two: Design and Plan Program

    Develop time line for implementation
    Establish advisory committee
    Develop policies and procedures
    Identify and develop funding sources

Phase Three: Implementing the Peer Mediation Approach

    Conduct student orientation
    Select peer mediators
    Train mediators
    Recognize peer mediators
    Conduct faculty in-service
    Conduct student workshops
    Provide family and community orientation
    Offer parent workshops
    Develop and execute promotion campaign
    Carry out program operation and maintenance
        Receive requests for mediation process
        Schedule mediations and mediators
        Supervise mediation session
        Provide ongoing training for mediators
        Evaluate program
OR

Phase Three: Implementing Classroom-Based Approach
    Conduct staff training
    Develop staff consensus regarding classroom program
    Provide classroom program to students

Phase Four: Classroom-Based Approach OR Peer Mediation Approach

Phase Five: Create Climate of Peace

    Develop rights and responsibilities
    Develop program to educate about behavioral expectations

Source: Adapted from Schrumpf, F., Crawford, D., and Bodine, R. *Peer Mediation: Conflict Resolution in Schools.* (Rev. ed.). Champaign, Ill.: Research Press (1997), p. 71.

three, four, or five can occur in any order, since creating the climate for peace could precede implementation of either of the approaches discussed here.

Phase One: Develop Program Team

Create Program Team.   A conflict resolution education program will be a success only if faculty and students alike perceive it to be a need-fulfilling program. Formulating a leadership group comprising representatives from among administrators, classroom teachers, special educators, counselors, social workers, psychologists, etc. who have an interest in developing a conflict resolution program within the school provides the broad-based coalition necessary for building a need-fulfilling program. Further options for team membership include parents, students, or community members. The program team becomes the initiator of the conflict resolution program and is eventually charged with eliciting the support of the entire school staff for program development. That charge includes:

- Designating program coordinators (especially crucial when only some staff are to be responsible for the student program, as is usually the case in a peer mediation schoolwide approach)
- Conducting a needs assessment
- Building faculty consensus for program development and support
- Developing policies and procedures
- Determining the role of conflict resolution within the school discipline program
- Developing awareness and support for the program among students, families, and community
- Conducting training (selecting and training peer mediators if the initial program effort is establishment of a schoolwide peer mediation program; training staff so that each can in turn train students if the initial program effort is classroom-based)

Train Program Team.   Once the program team is formed, the next step is to build their capacity to develop a quality conflict resolution program. In order to become informed decision makers, effective implementers, and strong advocates for the program, training is required. It is beneficial to train the team using the same model and resources that are appropriate for in-school training of students and other faculty. Since the program team is usually responsible for supervision and training of other staff and of student mediators for the schoolwide mediation program, they need training in content areas such as the principles of conflict resolution and conflict resolution processes as well as in techniques or methods for conflict resolution training. Basic training typically ranges from two to four days. Content for such training includes:

- Understanding conflict
- Principles of conflict resolution
- Social and cultural diversity and conflict resolution
- Mediation, negotiation, and consensus decision-making processes and skills
- Program organization and operation
- Role of conflict resolution in the school
- Rationale for student-based conflict resolution

It is important for those training students to have actual conflict resolution process experience, preferably in mediation or negotiation. Mediation and negotiation processes cannot be learned by reading a book or following a curriculum guide step-by-step. Skilled mediators and negotiators make a number of astute and consequential decisions during the course of the mediation or negotiation process based on their ability to apply the principles of conflict resolution. Unskilled mediators and negotiators mimic the six-step process without much discretion. Becoming a skilled mediator or negotiator requires simulated and real mediation and negotiation experiences, with the guided feedback of skilled trainers. Therefore, it is important for the team to be involved in mediation and negotiation training and to continue to seek opportunities to increase their skill level.

Designate Program Coordinator(s).   Let us assume that a schoolwide peer mediation program is the initial programmatic effort of the school toward developing a comprehensive conflict resolution education program. If all staff are involved from the outset, designating program coordinators may be inappropriate, although the leadership of the program team continues to be crucial. The effectiveness of the peer mediation program is strongly linked to the quality of the program coordinator(s). Coordinators are responsible for the ongoing organization and operation of the peer mediation program; most importantly, they must personify the conflict resolution principles that they promote. Program coordinators may be designated on the basis of interest, flexibility, commitment, and ability to lead both faculty and students. There are many approaches to coordinating peer mediation programs, ranging from an individual coordinator to various staff combinations of co-coordinators. Some options for consideration in designating a peer mediation coordinator include:

- Having a school social worker and a school counselor co-coordinate

- Having a suspension room supervisor and a teacher co-coordinate

- Sharing coordination responsibilities among several teachers

- Having the principal or assistant principal coordinate with various teachers assigned to specific supervision times

- Designating a peer mediation coordinator with no other assignments

Programs can function effectively whether people are employed for the sole purpose of being peer mediation program coordinators or existing faculty assume coordination of peer mediation integrated with their other professional responsibilities within the school.

Responsibilities of the program coordinator include facilitating the program team in their efforts to design and plan the peer mediation program; planning and conducting orientation sessions for faculty, students, families, and community; coordinating selection of peer mediators; establishing and facilitating the advisory council; coordinating training of students; promoting the program; receiving requests for mediation; scheduling mediators and mediations; arranging for supervision of mediators; collecting mediation data; providing for ongoing mediator training and support; facilitating ongoing communication with program team; developing parent and community participation; and evaluating the program.

Assess Needs and Resources. To move beyond the individual efforts of staff members toward a school-community effort for a school conflict resolution program, it is judicious to conduct an assessment to determine the specific nature of the needs for conflict resolution in the school and the resources present in or available to the school to address those needs. Support for introduction of any new program depends to a large extent on (1) the degree to which the school staff sees that the new program addresses current needs and (2) the degree to which the new program draws upon existing efforts, extending or embellishing the school mission. A well-designed needs assessment can evoke support by employing questions to elicit information regarding these two points.

Here are some suggested issues to probe in a needs assessment:

1. To what extent are conflicts interfering with the teaching and learning processes within the school?

2. What percentage of these conflicts are attributable to:

    The competitive atmosphere of the school or classroom?

    An intolerant atmosphere in the school or classroom?

    Poor communication?

    Inappropriate expression of emotions?

    Lack of conflict resolution skills?

    Adult misuse of power in the school or classroom?[2]

3. To what extent are diversity issues manifested as conflicts in the school-community?

4. To what extent is representation (or lack of it) in decision making an issue manifested in the conflicts observed in the school?

5. What percentage of the conflicts arising in the school are:

    Between students?

    Between teachers and students?

    Between teachers?

    Between students and school expectations or rules or policies?

    Between teachers and administrators?

    Between school staff and parents?

    Between various other combinations specific to the school?

6. What procedures are followed when conflicts cause disruption of the teaching-and-learning process?

7. Who administers which procedures? Who are the sources of referrals to these procedures?

8. Regarding the effectiveness of these procedures, what are the perceptions of students? Parents? Teachers? Administrators? Others?

9. What attitudes or behaviors exist that facilitate implementation of a conflict resolution program in the school? Who exhibits these?

10. What attitudes or behaviors exist that impede implementation of a conflict resolution program in the school? Who exhibits these?

11. Which foundation abilities for conflict resolution are now included in the school curriculum? When are they developed? Who provides the training in the skills? Which students receive the training?

12. To what extent have staff members received training in conflict resolution?

13. What staff development opportunities in conflict resolution are available? What opportunities are desired?

14. What conflict resolution processes currently exist within the school? Within the school-community?

15. What community resources exist to assist the school in designing and implementing a conflict resolution program in the school?

16. What present and future monetary resources are available to support implementation of a conflict resolution program?[3]

Some of these probes may not be applicable to a specific school, and not all are required of any school. The probes are provided to assist the stakeholder group in thinking about information to gather that might help them develop an action plan for implementing a conflict resolution program for the school. Exhibit 8.2 is an example of an assessment instrument.

Build Faculty Consensus for Program Development.   The process of building faculty consensus for conflict resolution education program development may be initiated by the program team's sharing the results of the needs assessment and the comprehensive conflict resolution program strategic plan, especially the belief statement and the shared vision. (See Chapter Nine on strategic plan development for an expanded discussion.) Involving the staff in an open discussion of these matters provides the opportunity to develop broad-based commitment to conflict resolution education. It may not be required that each faculty member commit initially to direct involvement in the program, but nearly all must agree to at least minimally support the program. Minimal support means the staff member believes providing conflict resolution opportunities to students is acceptable and he or she will encourage students to take advantage of such opportunities.

Phase Two: Design and Plan Program

Determine Implementation Strategy.   Creating a comprehensive conflict resolution education program ultimately requires that the program be incorporated into every classroom. Initially, a

Exhibit 8.2.   Conflict Resolution in Schools: Needs Assessment Form

Answer each question by providing the response that most accurately reflects your personal view of your school.

(1) I am a: ☐ student   ☐ staff member   ☐ parent   ☐ other

(2) Conflicts interfere with the teaching and learning process:

☐ often   ☐ sometimes   ☐ rarely

(3) Problems between people at this school are caused by:

	often	sometimes	rarely
(a) expectation to be competitive	☐	☐	☐
(b) intolerance between adults and students	☐	☐	☐
(c) intolerance between students	☐	☐	☐
(d) poor communication	☐	☐	☐
(e) anger and/or frustration	☐	☐	☐
(f) rumors	☐	☐	☐
(g) problems brought to school from somewhere else	☐	☐	☐

(4) Without exceeding 100% as the total, what percentage of the problems referred for disciplinary action are problems:

(a) between students   _____ %
(b) between student and classroom teachers   _____ %
(c) between student and other staff members   _____ %
(d) between student and school rules   _____ %
(e) other: _____   _____ %

Total   100%

(5) Indicate the types and frequency of conflicts experienced by students in this school:

	often	sometimes	rarely
(a) put-downs/insults/teasing	☐	☐	☐
(b) threats	☐	☐	☐
(c) intolerance of differences	☐	☐	☐
(d) loss of property	☐	☐	☐
(e) access to groups	☐	☐	☐
(f) rumors	☐	☐	☐
(g) physical fighting	☐	☐	☐
(h) verbal fighting/assaults	☐	☐	☐
(i) schoolwork	☐	☐	☐
(j) other: _____	☐	☐	☐

(6) Indicate the effectiveness of each of the following actions in causing a student to change a problem behavior

	very effective	somewhat effective	not effective
(a) time-out	☐	☐	☐
(b) detention	☐	☐	☐
(c) conference with an adult	☐	☐	☐
(d) suspension	☐	☐	☐
(e) contacting parent(s)	☐	☐	☐
(f) expulsion	☐	☐	☐

(7) Without exceeding 100% as the total, what percentage of influence do the following groups have in the way the school operates?

(a) students _____ %
(b) teachers _____ %
(c) parents _____ %
(d) principals and school administrators _____ %
(e) superintendent and district administrators _____ %
(f) board of education _____ %
(g) other: _____ _____ %

Total 100%

(8) In this school, I am generally:

	most of the time	about half the time	not very often
(a) treated fairly	☐	☐	☐
(b) treated with respect	☐	☐	☐
(c) given equal opportunity	☐	☐	☐
(d) treated with compassion	☐	☐	☐
(e) accepted	☐	☐	☐

(9) I am allowed to solve problems that affect me:

☐ nearly always   ☐ sometimes   ☐ hardly ever

(10) This school should do a better job teaching students to:

	definitely yes	maybe	definitely no
(a) tell another person how you feel	☐	☐	☐
(b) disagree without making the other person angry	☐	☐	☐
(c) respect authority	☐	☐	☐
(d) control anger	☐	☐	☐
(e) ignore someone who is bothersome	☐	☐	☐
(f) solve problems with other students	☐	☐	☐

(11) When I need help, I usually ask for it:

☐ nearly always   ☐ sometimes   ☐ almost never

(12) If I needed help, I think I could get it from:

	definitely yes	maybe	definitely no
(a) a parent	☐	☐	☐
(b) a brother or sister	☐	☐	☐
(c) another family member	☐	☐	☐
(d) a teacher	☐	☐	☐
(e) a counselor	☐	☐	☐
(f) another school staff member	☐	☐	☐
(g) another adult	☐	☐	☐
(h) another student	☐	☐	☐

(13) I think this school has:

☐ more problems than most other schools

☐ about the same amount of problems as most other schools

☐ less problems than most other schools

Source: Schrumpf, Crawford, and Bodine (1997), pp. 65–67.

fundamental judgment required of the program team is which strategy for starting the program will offer the best assurances for realizing that goal. Initial implementation efforts generally fit into one of two categories: a peer mediation schoolwide approach or an approach whereby each classroom participates. (It is possible to undertake both approaches simultaneously.)

Develop Time Line for Implementation.   Implementing a successful conflict resolution education program requires planning. Developing a time line for program execution is one of the first responsibilities of the program team after participating in the training outlined in phase one. The time line form in Exhibit 8.3 is designed to guide the program team through this crucial step in program development.

Establish Advisory Committee.   The advisory committee, consisting of ten to twelve members, has an important role in program development and support. In order to effectively address the varied interests of the school-community, the committee should include parents, teachers, building administrators, district administrators,

Exhibit 8.3.   Implementation Time Line

	Target Date

Phase One: Develop Program Team and Commitment
Create program team _____
Train program team _____
Designate program coordinator(s) _____
Conduct needs assessment _____
Build faculty consensus for program development _____

Phase Two: Design and Plan Program
Develop time line for implementation _____
Establish advisory committee _____
Develop policies and procedures _____
Identify and develop funding sources _____

Phase Three: Implementing the Peer Mediation Approach
Conduct student orientation _____
Select peer mediators _____
Train mediators _____
Recognize peer mediators _____
Conduct faculty in-service _____
Conduct student workshops _____
Provide family and community orientation _____
Offer parent workshops _____
Develop and execute promotion campaign _____
Carry out program operation and maintenance _____
   Receive requests for mediation process _____
   Schedule mediations and mediators _____
   Supervise mediation session _____
   Provide ongoing training for mediators _____
   Evaluate program _____

OR

Phase Three: Implementing Classroom-Based Approach
Conduct staff training _____
Develop staff consensus regarding classroom program _____
Provide classroom program to students _____

Phase Four: Classroom-Based Approach OR Peer Mediation Approach

Phase Five: Create Climate of Peace
Develop rights and responsibilities _____
Develop program to educate about behavioral expectations _____

Source: Adapted from Schrumpf, Crawford, and Bodine (1997), p. 71.

students, support staff, community representatives, and corporate sponsors. The overall responsibility of this committee is to provide consultation and recommendations to the program team and program coordinators regarding policy and program development. In addition, the advisory committee may assist with program activities such as promotion, evaluation, training, orientation, and building financial support. The advisory committee is likely to meet frequently during the initial stages of program development. As the program becomes more established, the committee may only need to have quarterly meetings. It is important to keep the advisory committee involved in ongoing program evaluation efforts and program design changes.

Establish Policies and Procedures.   Policies and procedures for the conflict resolution education program are determined by the program team in collaboration with the advisory committee. The following are major areas for consideration, including suggested questions to address.

Role of conflict resolution processes within the school discipline program. Conflicts characterized as illegal acts or serious violations of the rules and policies of the school (fighting, property destruction, stealing, harassment, abuse, drug use or sale, weapons possession, etc.) generally should not be submitted to mediation or negotiation. However, there may exist related issues between the disputants that are suitable for mediation or negotiation—issues usually related to the disputants' need to continue to relate to one another. Mediation and negotiation are not procedures for initial response to a violent incident. Mediation and negotiation are not processes for assigning blame or determining punishment. Mediation and negotiation are best viewed as processes for planning for future acceptable behavior.
Suggested questions:

- What is the role of mediation or negotiation, if any, when illegal acts or serious rule violations occur?

- What is the role of mediation or negotiation when students are referred by a third party because of the need to plan a future acceptable behavior?

- May those students, in these circumstances, return to the class or activity once they have a mediated or negotiated agreement? If not then, when?

Types of conflicts to mediate or negotiate. If a dispute is referred to peer mediation and the disputants agree to the mediation process, the conflict is worth trying to mediate. When disputants are expected to or desire to have a continuing relationship, conflict resolution provides a process to plan to relate in a manner that is satisfying for each disputant and also acceptable to others within the environment. Typically, conflicts that are characterized by put-downs or teasing, rumors or gossip, access or possession, turn taking or fairness, harassment or extortion or bullying, physical or verbal aggression or fighting, invasions of privacy or turf, and academic work issues are candidates for conflict resolution.

Suggested questions:

- Must the conflicts between students submitted for conflict resolution be school-based?
- May student-teacher disputes, disputes between a student and school rules or policy, teacher-teacher disputes, etc., be submitted to mediation?

Voluntary participation. For any conflict to be mediated or negotiated, the disputants must voluntarily agree to participate.

Suggested questions:

- Who will be responsible for obtaining this agreement from the disputants?
- How will this be done? When?

Privacy. Mediators are trained to keep the content of the mediation private. Generally, knowledge of illegal behavior or plans or threats to harm others or oneself are not covered under privacy restrictions.

Suggested questions:

- What are the limitations on privacy?
- What is the mediator's responsibility for reporting information not covered under privacy provisions?
- To whom is this knowledge to be reported? When and how?

Place of operation. Ideally, a specific location is established as a mediation center. The center provides a private space for the mediations to occur but is located such that an adult is either present or always easily accessible to the mediators. The privacy and adult-availability concerns outweigh the concern for a single designated space. Thus mediations may occur at different locations depending on the time of day, with each location providing privacy and access to an adult program coordinator. The center is equipped with a table and seating for the participants and mediators. A flipchart or chalkboard is useful.

Suggested questions:

- Where will the mediation center be located?
- Are there time limitations on the use of center space?

Hours of operation. The more the mediation or negotiation is accessible during the school day, the stronger is the message that conflict resolution is endorsed by the school as a viable problem-solving process and that the school acknowledges that students' problems are important.

Suggested questions:

- When are program coordinators available to supervise mediations?
- May mediators be called out of class to conduct mediations?
- Will disputants be excused from class to participate in mediations or negotiations?
- If mediations are provided before or after school, is transportation available?

Request procedures. Mediation request forms should be readily available to students and staff. Forms may be available in the classrooms, school office, offices of counselors and other support staff, etc.

Suggested questions:

- Where may completed forms be deposited?
- How often will these depositories be checked?
- Once a mediation is requested, how soon will it be scheduled?

Identify and Develop Funding Sources. Funding for development and ongoing support of a conflict resolution education program often influences program design. Staff training costs and funding for student materials are the largest expenditures when the implementation strategy involves all classrooms. If the implementation strategy is schoolwide peer mediation, costs associated with training the mediators may also involved released-time expenditures for the adult trainers and costs associated with finding off-campus space to do the training. Budgets for peer mediation programs can range from under five thousand dollars to over forty thousand dollars (see the sample budgets in Exhibits 8.4 and 8.5).

The decision to hire a program coordinator or to designate existing staff to coordinate the program is the major discrepancy between the two budget examples in the exhibits. The next significant discrepancy in expenses relates to contracting professional trainers to conduct the peer mediation training. If a school chooses

Exhibit 8.4.   Sample Peer Mediation Budget, Under $5,000

Program team training	
7 people @ $400 ea.	$2,800
Coordinator	
Faculty extracurricular pay	1,000
Student training (conducted by program team)	
materials: 30 manuals @ $10 ea.	300
food, T-shirts, certificates	400
Operating expenses	
promotional materials: posters, brochures	200
forms and printing for ongoing training	200
Total	$4,900

Source: Schrumpf, Crawford, and Bodine (1997), p. 75.

Exhibit 8.5.   Sample Peer Mediation Budget, Over $50,000

Program team training	
7 people @ $400 ea.	$ 2,800
Coordinator salary	40,000
Student training (conducted by professional trainer in collaboration with program team)	
trainer consultation fee (2 days)	2,500
materials: 30 manuals @ $10 ea.	300
food, T-shirts, certificates	400
Operating expenses	
promotional materials: posters, brochures	200
forms and printing for ongoing training	200
Total	$46,400

Source: Schrumpf, Crawford, and Bodine (1997), p. 75.

to contract with a professional trainer to train the student peer mediators, it is typically a one-time expense, since most program teams are able to assume this responsibility after working in collaboration with the professional trainer for the first year. Even though money tends to be an issue for implementing a peer mediation program, it is important to remember money is not a correlative factor to program success. An enthusiastic, well-informed program team and the involvement and education of the school community are more significant factors than money. An effective program can be designed within a limited budget.[4]

Many schools have existing funds or grants for professional development, student leadership development, safe and drug-free schools, school improvement, drop-out prevention, and attendance improvement. These existing funds and grants can be targeted toward conflict resolution because the outcomes of conflict resolution programs closely correlate with the priorities of these grant programs.

Community service organizations such as the Rotary Club, the Optimist Club, Urban League, and the business community are other potential sources of support for peer mediation programs. This support may come in the form of in-kind service such as printing brochures and posters, donating lunch during training, or grants. Businesses often fund projects that help prepare students to be an effective member of the future workforce. Teamwork and problem-solving ability are skills required to effectively work in most companies today. Conflict resolution training certainly contributes to the development of these abilities. In addition, businesses benefit from tax deductions and public relations for supporting such programs.

Phase Three: Implementing the Peer Mediation Approach

Conduct Student Orientation.   Prior to selection of the peer mediators, peer mediation should be introduced to the students who are age-eligible to become mediators. The purpose of student orientation is to provide an overview of the program, generate student interest and support, describe the role of peer mediators, and recruit peer mediator nominations and applications.

Student orientations may be conducted by members of the program team as an all-school or grade-level assembly, or throughout the day in classrooms. The orientation begins with a peer mediation video or live demonstration. Members of the program team then provide an overview of the peer mediation program and describe the role and responsibilities of peer mediators. Include time for questions. At the end of the orientation, any student who is interested may apply to be a peer mediator or nominate another student. Applications (Exhibit 8.6) and nomination forms (Exhibit 8.7) are distributed during student orientation.

Select Peer Mediators.   The group of mediators should represent the diversity of the student population in terms of race, gender, varying degrees of school achievement, behavior, extracurricular

Exhibit 8.6.   Peer Mediator Application Form

Peer Mediator Application

Name _____ Grade _____

Address _____

1. I want to be a peer mediator because . . .

2. List your personal qualities that will help you be a good mediator.

If selected, I agree to the following terms:

1. To complete all required training sessions

2. To serve as a mediator as scheduled

3. Request mediation for personal conflicts

4. Make up class assignments missed due to mediation training or duty

Student signature _____ Date _____

Source: Adapted from Schrumpf, Crawford, and Bodine (1997), p. 77.

Exhibit 8.7.   Peer Mediator Student Nomination Form

Peer Mediator Student Nomination

I would like to nominate the following students to be peer mediators because I would respect and trust them to help me resolve a conflict.

1. _____

2. _____

Signature _____ Date _____

Source: Schrumpf, Crawford, and Bodine (1997), p. 78.

interests, group memberships, and residential neighborhoods. When only those with exemplary school behavior and high academic achievement are selected, many of the students do not see the program as representing their peer group and therefore do not choose to participate in mediation. Personal qualifications of student mediators include:

Respect of peers

Skill in communication

Leadership ability

Sense of responsibility

Trustworthiness and fairness

Empathy

Staff members may nominate peer mediators by completing a peer mediator faculty nomination form (Exhibit 8.8). The most efficient way to gather staff nominations is to explain the criteria and distribute forms at the faculty in-service meeting. Particular faculty, such as social workers, counselors, and disciplinarians, are especially helpful in focusing their nominations to ensure representation of a cross section of students.

At the student orientation, all students learn about the role and expectations of peer mediators. Students then have the opportunity to complete a peer mediator application form or peer mediator nomination student form. The value of student input in the selection of mediators is twofold. First, students feel ownership of the program from the outset. Second, it is likely that peers will

Exhibit 8.8.   Peer Mediator Faculty Nomination Form

Peer Mediator Faculty Nomination

I would like to nominate the following students to be peer mediators because they show leadership potential within their peer group.

1. _____

2. _____

Signature _____ Date _____

Source: Schrumpf, Crawford, and Bodine (1997), p. 78.

name some students who would not otherwise be identified. Students who are nominated by their peers or by faculty are encouraged to complete a peer mediator application form if they have not done so prior to nomination.

Once application forms are complete, student mediators are selected. A variety of processes may be utilized to select mediators. One of the most effective selection processes is a lottery. The advantages to selection by lottery are that, first, more interested students risk applying to become mediators because they do not fear rejection. Second, with this approach the first experience a student has with the peer mediation program is not one of rejection. Not being selected in a lottery is generally perceived differently than not being selected in a criterion-driven selection process. Being rejected as a peer mediator can cause students to reject participation in the mediation process when later on they experience conflict. This rejection can potentially spread from individuals to groups of peers' refusing to participate in the mediation. The lottery process is typically perceived as an opportunity and not a personal risk.

In order for the lottery process to work appropriately, it must include a system that ensures proper representation of the diversity of the school. This system is a "controlled lottery," or actually several lotteries. For example:

1. To generate gender balance, separate the candidates into male and female groups and draw an equal number.

2. To reflect the school's racial composition, first draw from the minority pool the minimum number of candidates to guarantee a representative group.

3. Place all remaining minority candidates in the general pool, and continue to draw until the total number of mediators is determined.

If desired, the pool may be separated by grade level or other desired criteria to ensure other types of diversity.

Selection may also be done by the program team or the program team in conjunction with the advisory committee. With this method, the nomination and application forms are reviewed and evaluated. Prospective mediators may also be interviewed by the program team or program coordinators before making final selections.

Depending on the size of the school, it is recommended that between twenty and forty students be selected to be peer mediators. The key to the number of mediators is to have enough so that it will not be a burden for the mediators to miss class and other school activities, and not to have so many that the peer mediators have only infrequent opportunities to mediate, thus reducing their opportunities to gain skill through practice. Also, the number of mediators should be manageable to allow the program coordinators to supervise and monitor skill development. Sixteen to thirty-six mediators can handle several hundred mediation requests per school year.

After mediators have been selected, the principal may officially notify and congratulate them. The program coordinator (or coordinators) then notifies the students' parents and obtains parental permission for their participation.

Train Mediators.   Basic training for peer mediators requires twelve to fifteen hours and includes considerable directed practice in the mediation process using simulations of problems typical of the age group participating in the training. Basic training activities relate to the following areas:

Understanding conflict

Responses to conflict

Origins of conflict

Communication skills

Role of the mediator

Mediation process[5]

Recognize Peer Mediators.   Peer mediator training certificates may be distributed at the end of the training as part of an award ceremony to which parents and school officials are invited. Certificates may also be presented at a ceremony during a school assembly as a way to announce the opening of the mediation program.

Conduct Staff In-Service.   Staff in-service requires a minimum of six hours. This six-hour workshop may be conducted in one session or divided into three two-hour sessions. The purposes of the staff in-service are to develop among faculty a common understanding of conflict, learn the principles of conflict resolution, develop an understanding of the mediation process, learn how to support development of the peer mediation program through curriculum integration and referral of conflicts to mediation, and prepare to conduct the student workshops.

The agenda for staff in-service includes:

Understanding conflict

Responses to conflict

Origins of conflict

Principles of conflict resolution

Negotiation and mediation process

Curriculum integration ideas

Referral process

Preparation for student workshops

Conduct Student Workshops. Student workshops require a minimum of five hours. The five-hour workshop may be conducted in one session or divided into five sessions over a period of a week. Program team members may team up with other faculty to conduct these workshops. The student workshops are to develop an understanding of conflict, peace, and peacemaking; develop communication skills and negotiation skills; and learn about peer mediation and how to request peer mediation services.

The agenda for student workshops includes:

Understanding conflict

Responses to conflict

Sources of conflict

Peace and peacemaking

Communication skills

Negotiation skills

Mediation process

Request for peer mediation

Provide Family and Community Orientation. Parent and community involvement is a necessary and important part of program development. It is often a parent fundraiser, community organization, service club, or the police department that has formed a partnership with the school to sponsor peer mediation. An evening or lunch meeting can include an overview of the program and discussion of the benefits of peaceful problem solving. Parents or other community members often want to learn more about mediation after such an informational meeting. Offering an educational series for interested community members broadens program support and develops volunteers who might help with the training and supervision of student mediators. Trained student peer mediators can play an integral part in these orientation efforts.

Offer Parent Workshops. Workshops for parents who are interested in conflict resolution training support the potential for students to apply conflict resolution strategies in the home. A four-hour workshop may be conducted in one session or divided into two two-hour sessions. The purposes of the parent workshop are to develop a common understanding of conflict, learn the principles of conflict resolution, and learn how to apply the principles of conflict resolution in the home. Trained student peer mediators can assist in such training, and their participation may help ensure parental involvement.

Agenda items for parent workshops include:

Understanding conflict

Responses to conflict

Sources of conflict

Principles of conflict resolution

Conflict resolution strategies in the home

Develop and Execute Promotion Campaign.   Like many new ideas, peer mediation can be greeted with skepticism. Students may be reluctant to try the approach because it is new. Many students might think talking problems through is like backing down and losing face. Quality promotion among the student population is crucial to the success of the program.

Peer mediation promotion goals include:

Informing everyone in the school that peer mediation services are available

Advancing the benefits of conflict resolution and peer mediation

Encouraging students to request mediation as a normal process for resolving conflicts

Informing everyone about the procedures for requesting mediation and the types of conflict that can be mediated

Promotional campaigns may be planned by a committee of student mediators in conjunction with the program team, perhaps with the involvement of the advisory committee. Peer mediation program promotion campaigns may also be developed through a school-and-business partnership. School faculty members, parents, and community members as well as students are all potential promoters of the mediation program. Here are some promotion campaign ideas:

Conduct demonstration presentations. Groups of mediators may either present at schoolwide or grade-level assemblies or else schedule visits to all classes or homerooms. Peer mediators are highly capable of conducting presentations that include mediation session simulations, the process for requesting mediation, and encouragement for students to seek help in dealing with their conflicts. These demonstrations may also be presented at administrative meetings, faculty meetings, school board meetings, and PTA or PTO meetings.

Create a program name. Student mediators brainstorm a name for the peer program that gives it an identity that youths connect with. Some names that schools have used are Peace Corps, Common Ground, and RESOLVE.

Produce buttons, bumper stickers, T-shirts, sweatshirts, caps. Students might create a graphic design, including the program name, logo, and slogan that can be reproduced on a variety of items. Sales of these items could become a fundraising project for the mediation program. Mediators may want to select a day once a week when they all wear their own mediation T-shirt or sweatshirt.

Poster campaign. Covering the entire school with a series of 8½ × 11 inch posters at regular intervals captures the attention of everyone in the school environment. Posters with messages about mediation may be placed in strategic areas: near cafeteria lines, vending machines, bathrooms, drinking fountains, lockers, classroom and office doors, ceilings, floors, hallways, phone booths, gyms, locker rooms, faculty lounge, etc. Some sample poster messages:

Think Peace: Mediate

Talk It Out—Shift Happens

Caution: Work-It-Out Zone

Have You Made Peace Today?

Got a Conflict? ME-D-8!

Poster projects. Art classes or clubs may develop conflict resolution murals and large posters to display throughout the school and community.

Peer mediator business cards. Print generic peer mediation business cards with information about mediation and how to request service. Student mediators may distribute these cards to students throughout the school.

Brochures. Develop a community brochure and a student brochure about the peer mediation program. These brochures may be mailed to parents and community agencies along with a letter announcing the opening of the peer mediation program. Brochures may also be distributed to students and faculty and become a part of the orientation information distributed to new students and faculty.

Program Operation and Maintenance.   *Requests for mediation process.* All members of the school community are encouraged to make referrals to peer mediation. Mediation request forms are placed in display pocket folders in all classrooms, the main school office, offices of support staff, the mediation bulletin board, the mediation center, and any other location that provides easy access for students and faculty. Students or faculty may complete the form to request a mediation and deposit it in a drop box in the main office or the mediation center. Program coordinators gather requests from each location at least twice per day.

Schedule mediations and mediators. Mediations are scheduled as soon as possible after the request has been deposited. Disputants should not be required to wait more than twenty-four hours after they request mediation. Depending on the program team's decisions about hours of operation, the peer mediation center may be open for mediations during school hours as well as before and after school. Some schools try to schedule mediations for disputants during study times, recesses, or lunch in order to address concerns that students not miss classwork. Since some conflicts seem to interfere with the disputing student's ability to engage productively in classroom activities, it seems appropriate to schedule these disputes during class if necessary.

Two options for scheduling mediators are *case by case assignments* and *period team assignments.* Assigning mediators case by case allows coordinators to choose mediators who are most appropriate for particular cases, taking into consideration issues of race, gender, and social diversity. With this process, mediators co-mediate with a number of different peers, learning from each other and building on their respective experiences. With each new request, the coordinator selects and locates appropriate mediators. An alternative to case-by-case assignment is to assign teams of co-mediators to particular time periods each day or each week. Teams then mediate whatever is scheduled during their time slots. Even though this process does not allow the flexibility to select the mediators for each case, it facilitates the scheduling process. Mediators report to the mediation center at their designated time, receive their cases, and mediate. Other considerations in assigning mediators include their relationship to the disputants, frequency of mediation experience, and the age or grade level of the mediators and the disputants.

Mediators are required to withdraw from a case whenever they feel that their prior relationship with a disputant interferes with their ability to conduct an effective mediation. It usually works best to assign mediators only to those cases in which they do not know the disputants. In situations where this is not practical, the mediators should carefully assess whether or not they can maintain impartiality when mediating the dispute. Disputants often speak more openly about their conflict when they do not have an ongoing relationship with the mediator. Restraining biases, loyalty to friends, and perceptions of partiality are difficult challenges for student mediators when they have ongoing relationships with one or both parties.

It is important that mediators have frequent experiences mediating. The confidence and skill of mediators increase with experience. Coordinators need to monitor the number of cases assigned to each mediator to ensure equal opportunity for growth and development.

Mediators should be assigned to mediate with disputants who are at their age or grade level, or younger. It typically does not work for the mediators to be younger than the disputants. If disputants are different ages, assign a co-mediation team that reflects the ages or grade levels of both disputants.

Supervise mediation sessions. Coordinators may provide brief background information to peer mediators before the session begins. Since the mediators learn the things that they need to know about the dispute from the disputants during the session, this briefing only needs to include the information gathered from the mediation request form.

The disputants may be assembled in the mediation room by delivering passes that designate the scheduled time of mediation. Students present passes to the teacher for the period when the mediation is assigned in order to leave their classroom. Disputants may also be summoned by the mediators and escorted to the mediation center.

At the close of the mediation session, the mediators have the disputants sign an agreement form if they have reached an agreement. If they have not reached an agreement, the mediators consult with the program coordinator prior to closing the session.

Provide mediators with ongoing training. It is recommended that peer mediators meet regularly as a group with program coordinators. Ideally, meetings are held twice monthly for about two hours. A portion of the time is used for the peer mediators to share experiences and take turns presenting cases that illustrate challenges and issues that need discussion. The remainder of the time is used to extend the training of the peer mediators. This training might be a review of those aspects of the basic training that the mediators or the coordinators think need further refinement and practice.

Evaluate the program. Program evaluation provides the information needed to plan for continuous improvement in program quality. In addition, evaluation can build substantive evidence of program efficacy. Evaluations of peer mediation programs may either be uncomplicated designs that program coordinators assimilate into their responsibilities or more complex experimental designs that are conducted by researchers. Since schools typically do not have the financial or human resources to conduct an elaborate program evaluation, a simple program evaluation is included in this book (Exhibit C.1 of Appendix C).

With the assistance of student mediators, the program coordinators monitor the number of mediations, length of mediation sessions, types of conflict, source of requests, location where conflicts materialized, attributes of disputants, outcomes of the mediations, and the durability of the agreements. The primary goal of the mediation program is to bring about changes in students' and educators' attitudes and behavior concerning conflict and approaches to resolution.

Phase Three: Implementing the Classroom Approach

Conduct Staff Training.   The program team provides, or arranges to have provided, training for all staff responsible for the classroom implementation of the conflict resolution program. This training, which requires at least two days, includes:

Understanding conflict

Principles of conflict resolution

Social and cultural diversity and conflict resolution

Mediation, negotiation, and group problem-solving processes and skills

Classroom management

Curriculum integration ideas

This training, a mirror of the training received by the program team (refer to phase one: train program team), is designed to equip staff members with the experience and information needed to provide conflict resolution education to students.

Develop Staff Consensus Regarding Classroom Program.   Initially, the consensus probably involves the nature of the classroom training program: which of the conflict resolution processes (mediation, negotiation, or group problem solving) is the focus of the classroom program? It is likely that in the initial stages of program development, each classroom in the school provides student training in the same strategy, although it is feasible to allow variation for different age levels.

As the program develops, staff consensus regarding a scope and sequence for teaching understanding of conflict and understanding of peace and peacemaking provides for effective and efficient internalization of the program into the curriculum of the school.

Provide Classroom Program to Students.   The staff consensus might be to initially focus the classroom program on mediation, in which case training of all students is the same as training for the peer mediators cited previously.

If the staff consensus is to initially focus the classroom program on negotiation, one option is to train students as mediators, then show students how negotiation differs from mediation, and provide practice in the negotiation process. The other option is to train students directly in the negotiation process. Basic negotiation training involves:

Understanding conflict

Responses to conflict

Origins of conflict

Communication skills

Conflict resolution principles

Role of the negotiator

Negotiation process

If the staff consensus is to implement the consensus decision-making strategy, one student training option is to provide training experience in the foundation skills of orientation and communication, establish the ground rules for problem solving in a group, and then proceed with a trained adult acting as the group facilitator. The other needed understandings and skills can be developed as ongoing training while also using the consensus decision-making strategy in the classroom.[6]

The educational and promotional suggestions for parent and community audiences presented for peer mediation (in this chapter) are equally appropriate for the classroom approach.

Phase Four: Implementing the Classroom or the Peer Mediation Approach

The next developmental stage is to implement the other approach, the one *not* selected in phase three. A schoolwide peer mediation program is a starting point for creating a comprehensive conflict resolution education program, but a comprehensive school program is not realized until the conflict resolution education program becomes part of all classrooms in the school and each member of the school community is afforded the opportunity to learn and use conflict resolution day-to-day in the classroom and in the school.

Even if every classroom participates in the conflict resolution education program, a schoolwide peer mediation program is still a viable option for conflict resolution within the school. There are many conflicts that are not classroom-based, and there are conflicts between individuals in the same classroom that might best be resolved in an atmosphere removed from the classroom that affords privacy to the disputing parties.

When the schoolwide peer mediation option is developed as phase four, the staff in-service and student workshops are unnecessary since staff and students all participate in the classroom program.

Phase Five: Create the Climate of Peace

Develop Rights and Responsibilities.   Rights and responsibilities provide the foundation for establishing behavioral expectations and creating a sense-based system for managing behavior that eliminates coercion in the management process. See Chapter Two for discussion about, and an example of, a rights-and-responsibility approach.

Develop a Program to Educate About Behavioral Expectations. Developing an effective behavior management program that is in concert with the philosophy and the principles of the conflict resolution program involves more than creating a rights-and-responsibilities document. The program also provides a plan to educate about expectations and about the processes available for choosing appropriate behaviors.

CHAPTER 9

Conducting a Strategic Plan

Ideally, a school develops a strategic plan, based on assessment of its needs and resources, for a conflict resolution education program that addresses the unique needs and resources of the particular school. Preferably, a school-community stakeholder group with broad-based representation generates the strategic plan. The strategic planning process suggested here for planning a conflict resolution program has four basic components: a belief statement, a mission statement or shared vision statement, a statement of program goals, and a specific action plan.

Formulating a Strategic Plan

Formulation of a strategic plan involves the stakeholder group in a practical exercise in conflict resolution. The six-step conflict resolution process of consensus decision making is recommended in developing a strategic plan. Each component of the strategic plan may, in fact, involve the group in all or most of the six steps of the conflict resolution process.

To begin formulating the strategic plan, the group first establishes ground rules for discussion and input:

- All group members have equal status; each is accorded full opportunity to participate. Forming a circle for discussions usually helps emphasize this notion.

159

- Every member of the group is responsible for communication (listening and speaking). This means that each person is responsible for sharing his or her point of view if that point of view has not already been shared in the group; each person works to inform others rather than to impress or overpower (speak concisely); and each person is responsible for working to understand the other's point of view (attend, summarize, and seek clarification whenever needed).

- A speaker is allowed to talk without interruption.

- Sarcasm and destructive criticism do not contribute to constructive examination and refinement of ideas or plans. Each member of the group deserves respect, just as his or her ideas merit full examination.

- Each time someone in the group presents a point of view, a group member summarizes that point of view before anyone else can present another point of view.[1]

Two basic principles always govern consensus decision making: (1) discussion is always directed toward solving the problem (in this case, developing a strategic plan) and (2) the solution never includes fixing blame or punitive action[2] because the strategic plan is a strategy to move forward from the current state of affairs.

The facilitators of each of the groups in the strategic planning process help the group focus on these basic principles by insisting that the ground rules be followed during all discussion and input sessions.

Once the ground rules have been set and agreed to, points of view are collected. Brainstorming is a viable process for collecting ideas in specific categories, that is, beliefs, goals, etc.

The next step is to identify interests in the group. This provides the common ground required for the stakeholders to reach a consensus decision regarding the list of belief statements, the list of goals, or a single mission or shared vision statement.

Applying objective criteria in formulating a consensus list or consensus statement is critical. At any stage of the planning process, consensus is highly unlikely if deliberations focus on positions and if an individual's behavior within the group is designed to influence or force other group members to capitulate to that individual's will. The quality of the group product is evident in the end result of the deliberations at each stage. Use of the conflict resolution process allows the group to go beyond a lowest-common-denominator agreement to visionary common goals. The action plan that is developed also reflects the application of criteria and represents a commitment to take action.

Belief Statements

Beliefs are a comprehensive collection of statements expressing fundamental convictions and tenets related to conflict, conflict resolution, and conflict resolution education. The belief statements provide a basis for achieving consensus within the school-community concerned with providing a conflict resolution education program in the school. Beliefs are the basis for obtaining a school's commitment to such a program. Here are some sample belief statements:

Conflict is a natural part of everyday life.

Conflict is an opportunity to grow and learn.

Neither avoidance nor violence is a healthy response to conflict.

Through awareness of cultural differences, we grow to respect others and to cherish diversity.

Everyone deserves respect; the school environment should allow everyone to live together with respect for differences (racial, cultural, social, and behavioral).

There are many influences in the lives of youth (families, school, community, etc.) that share in the responsibility for educating youth to be effective citizens.

All people have basic needs (belonging, power, freedom, fun, and security), and each wants his or her needs met.

Discipline is a learning process for developing responsible behavior.

Adults provide powerful behavior models for students; this is especially true in dealing with conflict.

Individuals—students and adults—can learn to solve problems peaceably through conflict resolution education.

Students can learn to resolve some of their conflicts without adult involvement.

To develop the listing of beliefs, the stakeholder group begins by brainstorming in small subgroups to produce six to eight belief statements that everyone in the small group can support. There are two phases to the brainstorming process (a foundation ability of conflict resolution): the first involves generating the list of beliefs, and the second involves selecting from the list. It is important to separate the two parts of the process. Each phase has simple but explicit rules:

Phase one   Generate belief statement.
- A. Designate one person to record ideas.
- B. Expect controversial or far-fetched ideas.
- C. Say any idea that comes to mind.
- D. Record every idea.
- E. Do not evaluate ideas.

Phase two   Select beliefs.
- A. Evaluate the statements generated.
  1. Combine those that are similar.
  2. Circle those that nearly everyone agrees are significant.
  3. Eliminate those that do not represent strong convictions among group members.
- B. Improve upon the resulting belief statements.
- C. By consensus, choose six to eight belief statements to bring to the larger group. Establish and employ objective criteria to achieve consensus.
- D. Record the selected belief statements on newsprint and post them.

Each subgroup then presents its listing of beliefs to the large group, which applies the selection phase (phase two) of the brainstorming process to select the belief statements for the conflict resolution education program.[3]

Mission Statement

Mission is the broad statement of purpose of a conflict resolution education program for the school. It is literally the keystone upon with the entire plan for the program is built. Often expressed as a single, general statement, the mission expresses the primary focus of the program, emphasizes the distinctiveness of the program, and represents the commitment of resources to the program. The mission statement is a brief for focusing commitment to and understanding of the program by all factions of the school-community. Here is a sample mission statement:

> The mission of the conflict resolution education program is to allow each person to develop the capacity to resolve his or her conflicts peacefully, to promote mutual understanding of individuals and groups throughout the school, and to enhance the climate of the school by providing each person with opportunities to learn that conflict is natural and that it offers the potential for growth when resolved through the problem-solving strategies of conflict resolution.

Shared Vision Statement

Shared vision is a verbal representation of what is observable within the school when a critical mass of the adults and students are using conflict resolution day-to-day in the school environment. Shared vision paints a picture of how the school will look when the mission is operational. Here is a shared vision statement:

We see our school as:

- A learning environment exemplified by happy, friendly, busy, caring individuals who are sharing, communicating, creating, helping, and encouraging
- A friendly, orderly, inviting, and comfortable place characterized by mutual respect, acceptance of differences, and cooperation
- A peaceable, harmonious community with a welcoming, inviting environment that is educationally enriching and challenging, where all students are reaching their potential

We see each person taking ownership for his or her learning and developing a sense of belonging to, and pride in, our school community.

Along with the belief statement, shared vision provides a relatively clear way to communicate to all school constituencies. Whereas the mission statement is often in language specific to educators, the belief statement and the shared vision statement communicate in a more general fashion and may be more meaningful to students and to those not directly involved in the management of the day-to-day functioning of the school.

The mission statement or shared vision is developed through the process outlined for the belief statements, with the stakeholders first working in small groups to develop a statement and then coming together in the large group to determine a final consensus statement for the total group.[4]

Statement of Program Goals

Goals are expressions of the desired outcomes of a conflict resolution program in the school. The goals are manifestations of the mission (or the shared vision); they give direction to implementation planning. They guide the setting of priorities and allocation of resources, plus providing a framework for evaluation of the program. Goals are aspirations and intentions. The mission (or the shared vision) frames the program's destination; the goals are the map for reaching that destination. Sample goals are:

- To enable students to take responsibility for peacefully resolving their own disputes

- To provide all individuals in the school with the problem-solving skills of conflict resolution (negotiation, mediation, and consensus decision making)

- To allow all individuals to learn to respect, cherish, and celebrate diversity with respect to differences in race, culture, gender, etc.

- To integrate conflict resolution and the foundation abilities of conflict resolution into the existing curriculum at all grade levels

- To design a discipline program and a behavior management plan with reasonable and clear behavioral expectations that is consistent with and promotes the conflict resolution education program and that is accepted as fair and effective by all constituencies of the school

- To provide a school climate characterized by cooperation and collaboration

Goals are developed by the stakeholder group using the same process as for belief, mission, or shared vision statements: first working in small groups to generate supported possibilities and then reaching a consensus list in the total group.

Action Plan

The action plan is an explicit statement of the tasks required to implement the program, the person responsible, the time line for completion, and identification of the resources necessary to implement the program. The action plan provides specific direction to those responsible relative to who is to do what, by when, and how. It provides for coordination of activities among individuals with different responsibilities. Components—in effect, action plans for specific areas of implementation—of the comprehensive plan might address tasks or developments in any of the following:

- An information campaign to inform constituents and to generate support

- Staff development program: initial and ongoing, multidimensional, focusing on more than one area of staff training and education

- Funding for the program: internal and community sponsorships

- The discipline program framework design
- Program to teach students: assigning responsibility, developing curriculum, determining developmental appropriateness, etc.
- Management plan for the program: designate coordination responsibilities, establish procedures and forms, etc.
- Data collection and evaluation
- Implementation stages and time lines

The decision regarding the overall action plan for implementation might best be accomplished using the same small-group, large-group process. This process could yield a decision regarding what the component tasks are to be performed; the details of each component task would be the responsibilities of the action plan committee for each specific task.

Exhibits 9.1, 9.2, and 9.3 are examples of detailed action plans.

Exhibit 9.1.   Sample Staff Development Action Plan

Goal: to provide all individuals in the school with the problem-solving strategies of conflict resolution: negotiation, mediation, and consensus decision making. Subgoal: to provide conflict resolution training for all staff.

Activities	Responsibility	Target Date
Design a survey to assess level of staff interest and expertise in conflict and conflict resolution programs.	Staff development committee	August 15
Conduct survey and compile results.	Staff development committee	September 15
Conduct follow-up interviews with any staff member who reports that he or she has had conflict resolution training in order to assess effectiveness of potential training sources and programs.	Staff development committee; distribute number of staff to be interviewed equally	Interviews completed by September 30
Determine school and district funds available for staff development.	Principal	September 30
Determine other funding sources and assign responsibility for seeking funding support for staff training. Coordinate with program committee in seeking funding.	Staff development committee; finance subcommittee	October 15
Determine off-site training opportunities and costs.	Staff development committee; off-site training subcommittee	October 15
Determine on-site training possibilities and costs.	Staff development committee; on-site training subcommittee	October 15
Select initial training program.	Staff development committee	November 1
Determine participants for initial training.	Staff development committee and principal	November 15
Participate in initial training program.	Staff development committee members and other selected participants	December
Debrief on initial training.	Staff development committee and other training program participants	Within one week of training
Develop a two-year training plan and time line to provide training for all staff.	Staff development committee and principal	January 15
Implement the training program.	Staff development committee; implementation subcommittee	March 1
Develop continuous training program to extend opportunity beyond initial training for interested staff and to provide for a continuous initial training program for training staff new to the school.	Staff development committee	May 1

Exhibit 9.2.   Sample Discipline Policy Action Plan

Goal: to design a discipline program and a behavior management plan with reasonable and clear behavioral expectations that is consistent with and promotes the conflict resolution education program and that is accepted as fair and effective by all constituencies of the school.

Activities	Responsibility	Target Date
Collect all district and school discipline policy statements, behavior or conduct codes and rules, handbook information, promised disciplinary actions, etc.	Chair of discipline policy committee and principal	September 1
Survey staff, students, and parents to determine perceptions of present discipline plan and to determine which behaviors are expected to become the focus for elimination through the behavior management plan.	Discipline policy committee: survey subcommittee	September 15
Categorize behavior management practices in use currently as punishment or discipline according to the chart "Punishment Versus Discipline" from Chapter Two	Discipline policy committee; current practices subcommittee	October 1
Reconstruct present discipline policy into a single rights-and-responsibilities format that addresses the behavioral expectation for all segments of the school population, adults and students.	Discipline policy committee; rights-and-responsibilities subcommittee	November 1
Determine the five or six target behaviors for extinction (as determined from previous survey of constituencies) and assign behavioral consequences that can be consistently administered whenever any of those behaviors is chosen.	Discipline policy committee and principle	December 15
Submit general plan—rights and responsibilities, additional rules (if any), and target behaviors and consequences—to school staff. Obtain consensus commitment to general plan.	Principal	January 15
Create a plan to educate staff and parents about the bahavioral expectations of the plan.	Discipline policy committee; educating-adults subcommittee	February 1
Create a comprehensive program to educate students about the behavior expectations and to teach desired behaviors to students.	Discipline policy committee; developing-responsible-student-behavior subcommittee	March 1
Provide staff training to implement student education program.	Discipline policy committee; developing-responsible-student-behavior subcommittee	March 15
Establish a consistent plan that is noncoercive and uses questioning strategies to promote behavior change, for use by any staff member intervening with students who are displaying unacceptable behavior.	Discipline policy committee and principal or designee	April 15

Activities	Responsibility	Target Date
Survey staff to determine training needs for implementing day-to-day interactions in the behavioral intervention plan.	Discipline policy committee; implementation-training sub-committee	May 1
Develop training program.	Discipline policy committee; implementation-training sub-committee	May 15
Conduct training for all staff members.	Contracted trainers and implementation-training subcommittee	June 15
Implement new discipline program.	All staff	August

Exhibit 9.3.   Sample Development of a Cooperative Context Action Plan

Goal: to provide a school climate characterized by cooperation and collaboration.

Activities	Responsibility	Target Date
Develop a question format for use in conducting focus groups.	Committee to advance cooperation	August 15
Review school policies and handbooks to determine expectations of competition within the system.	Committee to advance cooperation	September 1
Conduct focus groups (two each for parents, for students, for staff) to gather impressions of (1) the degree to which competition is recognized as an expectation of the school program, and (2) how information provided by the evaluation/grading system is viewed.	Committee to advance cooperation; focus group subcommittee	October 15
Design and administer a staff survey to determine (1) degree of prior training in cooperative learning strategies, and (2) use of cooperative learning strategies in delivery of the curriculum.	Committee to advance cooperation; current-practices subcommittee	November 30
Collect information on current evaluation/grading policy and practices and report to the committee to advance cooperation.	Principal or designee	December 15
Conduct three open forums (invite parents, students—current and former—and staff) on the topics: (1) Grades: what do they tell us? (2) Evaluation: what do we want to know?	Principal and committee to advance cooperation	February 15
Develop an evaluation and parent-student reporting system plan of action.	Principal and chairperson of committee to advance cooperation	March 15
Present plan of action developed on evaluation to policy boards for reaction and approval: ▪ parent advisory board ▪ staff ▪ student council ▪ school board	Principal and chairperson of committee to advance cooperation	April 1
Determine school and district funds available for staff development.	Principal	April 5
Determine other funding sources and assign responsibility for seeking funding support for staff training. Coordinate with program committee in seeking funding.	Staff development committee; finance subcommittee	April 15
Select cooperative learning trainers and establish cooperative learning staff development schedule of training.	Committee to advance cooperation	May 15

Activities	Responsibility	Target Date
Provide initial training.	Contracted consultants	June/July
Inform all staff regarding the action plan for evaluation and for promoting cooperation.	Principal and chairperson of committee to advance cooperation	August 30
Establish continuous training for new staff using in-house staff members trained during the initial training program.	Committee to advance cooperation	September 30

Consultation and Training Organizations

Appendix A supplies contact information for a number of organizations that provide national leadership in the field of conflict resolution education through their efforts to promote, develop, implement, and institutionalize conflict resolution education programs.

Children's Creative Response to Conflict
P.O. Box 271
Nyack, NY 10960
(914) 353–1796
(914) 358–4924 (fax)

Community Board Program, Inc.
1540 Market Street, Ste. 490
San Francisco, CA 94102
(415) 552–1250
(415) 626–0595 (fax)

Conflict Resolution and Cooperative Learning Center
Teaching Students to Be Peacemakers Program
University of Minnesota
College of Education and Human Development
60 Peik Hall
159 Pillsbury Drive SE
Minneapolis, MN 55455
(612) 624–7031
(612) 626–1395 (fax)

Educators for Social Responsibility
23 Garden Street
Cambridge, MA 02138
(617) 492–1764
(617) 864–5164 (fax)

Harvard Negotiation Project
500 Pound Hall
Harvard Law School
Cambridge, MA 02138
(617) 495–1684
(617) 495–7818 (fax)

Illinois Institute for Dispute Resolution
National Center for Conflict Resolution Education
110 West Main Street
Urbana, IL 61801
(217) 384–4118
(217) 384–8280 (fax)

International Center for Cooperation and Conflict Resolution
Teachers College at Columbia University
525 West 120th Street
Box 53
New York, NY 10027
(212) 678–3402
(212) 678–4048 (fax)

Iowa Peace Institute
917 10th Avenue
P.O. Box 480
Grinnell, IA 50112
(515) 236–4880
(515) 236–6905 (fax)

National Institute for Dispute Resolution
Conflict Resolution Education Network
1726 M Street NW, Ste. 500
Washington, DC 20036–4502
(202) 466–4764
(202) 466–4769 (fax)

New Mexico Center for Dispute Resolution
National Resource Center for Youth Mediation
620 Roma NW, Ste. B
Albuquerque, NM 87102
(800) 249–6884 (publications)
(505) 247–0571 (information)
(505) 242–5966 (fax)

Ohio Commission on Dispute Resolution
and Conflict Management
77 South High Street, 24th Floor
Columbus, OH 43266
(614) 752–9595
(614) 752–9682 (fax)

Program for Young Negotiators, Inc.
20 University Road
Cambridge, MA 02138
(888) 832–2479 [888-TEACH-PYN, (toll free)]
(617) 354–8467 (fax)

Resolving Conflict Creatively Program
163 Third Avenue
P.O. Box 103
New York, NY 10003
(212) 387–0225
(212) 387–0510 (fax)

Street Law, Inc. (formerly National Institute
for Citizen Education in the Law)
711 G Street SE
Washington, DC 20003
(202) 546–6644
(202) 546–6649 (fax)

Curriculum Resources

This appendix illustrates some of the most current and readily available conflict resolution curriculum resources. The materials have been categorized into five groups: foundation abilities, process curriculum, mediation, peaceable classroom, and peaceable school.

Note that costs are included as general guidelines and are subject to change; contact the supplier for up-to-date price information.

Foundation Abilities

Aggressors, Victims, and Bystanders: Thinking and Acting to Prevent Violence. 1994. Ronald Slaby, Renee Wilson-Brewer, and Kimberly Dash, Education Development Center, 55 Chapel Street, Newton, MA 02160. Phone: (800) 225–4276.

> Audience: grades 6–9.
> Focus: to develop skills in solving social problems nonviolently and in evaluating beliefs regarding violence.
> Key teaching strategies: full-class and small-group discussions, games, role-playing, and skill-building exercises.
> Type of material: teacher's guide and handouts.
> Cost: $45.

Anti-Bias Curriculum: Tools for Empowering Young Children. 1989. Louise Derman-Sparks and the ABC Task Force, National Association for the Education of Young Children, 1509 16th Street NW, Washington, DC 20036–1426. Phone: (202) 232–8777.

> Audience: ages 2–5.
> Focus: to promote critical thinking regarding cultural bias and diversity and problem-solving processes to resolve conflict.
> Key teaching strategies: activities and discussions.
> Type of material: teacher's guide.
> Cost: $17.

Circles of Learning: Cooperation in the Classroom. 1984, 1986, 1990, 1993. David W. Johnson, Robert T. Johnson, and Edythe Holuhec, Interaction Book Co., 7208 Cornelia Drive, Edina, MN 55435. Phone: (612) 831–9500.

> Audience: grades K–8.
> Focus: to teach students to work cooperatively to achieve mutual learning goals. Program is research-based and theory-based.
> Key teaching strategies: experiential/cooperative learning, simulations, role playing, and perspective taking.
> Type of material: book, videos, student manual, and audiocassettes.
> Cost: book, $10; video, $25; audiocassette, $10.

Dealing with Anger: Givin' It, Takin' It, Workin' It Out. A Violence Prevention Program for African American Youth (female and male versions). 1991. Research Press, Inc., P.O. Box 9177, Champaign, IL 61821. Phone: (217) 352–3273.

> Audience: African American youth in grades 6–12. (Each set is specific for males or females.)
> Focus: to teach students ways to express angry feelings, accept criticism, and negotiate a solution.
> Key teaching strategies: videos, discussion, and role playing.
> Type of material: video and discussion guide.
> Cost: each set of videos, $495; both sets, $740.

Discover the World: Empowering Children to Value Themselves, Others, and the Earth. 1990. Susan Hopkins and Jeffery Winters, New Society Publishers, 4527 Springfield Avenue, Philadelphia, PA 19143. Phone: (800) 333–9093.

> Audience: infants, toddlers, and grades pre-K through 5; especially geared toward young children.
> Focus: to teach respect for oneself and others.
> Key teaching strategies: activities and lesson plans that include art, music, movement, and language.
> Type of material: teacher's guide.
> Cost: $14.95.

Everyone Wins! Cooperative Games and Activities. 1990. Sambhava and Josette Luvmour, New Society Publishers, 4527 Springfield Avenue, Philadelphia, PA 19143. Phone: (800) 333–9093.

> Audience: grades pre-K through 4.
>
> Focus: to increase self-esteem and interconnectedness with others through the interaction of game playing.
>
> Key teaching strategies: playing games.
>
> Type of material: teacher's guide.
>
> Cost: $8.95.

The Giraffe Classroom. 1990. Nancy Sokol Green, Center for Non-Violent Communication, 3468 Meadowbrook Boulevard, Cleveland Heights, OH 44118–3660. Phone: (216) 371–1123.

> Audience: grades 1–8.
>
> Focus: to promote caring, cooperative, and safe schools through teaching nonviolent communication skills that empower children and others to get their needs met in mutually satisfying ways.
>
> Key teaching strategies: cooperative pairs and small-group work integrated into language, social studies, art, and music.
>
> Type of material: teacher's manual.
>
> Cost: $14.

Keeping the Peace: Practicing Cooperation and Conflict Resolution with Preschoolers. 1989. Susanne Wichert, New Society Publishers, 4527 Springfield Avenue, Philadelphia, PA 19143. Phone: (800) 333–9093.

> Audience: preschool children and adults who live and work with preschool children.
>
> Focus: to increase altruistic behavior, decrease aggressive behavior, and enhance a greater tolerance among children for the differences in others.
>
> Key teaching strategies: activities and games.
>
> Type of material: teacher's guide.
>
> Cost: paperback, $12.95; hardcover, $34.95.

The PATHS Curriculum: Promoting Alternative Thinking Strategies. 1994. Carol A. Kusche and Mark T. Greenberg, Developmental Research and Programs, 130 Nickerson Street, Suite 107, Seattle, WA 98109. Phone: (800) 736–2630.

> Audience: grades K–5.
>
> Focus: to improve the social and emotional competence and behavior of children, reduce peer and classroom conflict, and improve both student thinking skills and classroom climate.
>
> Key teaching strategies: role playing, stories, and other language arts activities; problem-solving meetings; peer discussions;

cooperative learning; and artistic and other creative activities.

Type of material: scope and sequence instructional manual, lessons, pictures, and photographs.

Cost: PATHS basic kit, $550 (includes curriculum, instruction manual, materials, photographs, and posters).

Productive Conflict Resolution. 1996. Colorado School Mediation Project, 3970 Broadway, Suite B3, Boulder, CO 80304. Phone: (303) 444–7671.

Audience: grades K–2, 2–5, 5–8, and high school.

Focus: To reduce violence and antisocial behavior; develop long-term change in students' and teachers' attitudes and behavior toward conflict, diversity, and decision making; promote greater academic achievement and emotional intelligence; and promote a caring, cooperative, disciplined school environment where learning and creativity take place.

Key teaching strategies: Role playing, discussion, brainstorming, journaling, and other experiential learning.

Type of material: curriculums for grades K–12, videos, and mediation training manuals.

Cost: grades K–2, $20; grades 2–5, 5–8, and high school, $25; manuals, $9.95.

Saturday Institute for Manhood, Brotherhood Actualization (SIMBA) Replication Manual. 1996. Jennie C. Trotter and SIMBA Coalition Members, WSCI-C/O SIMBA Project, 3480 Greenbriar Parkway, Ste. 310 B, Atlanta, GA 30331. Phone: (404) 699–6891.

Audience: ages 8–18.

Focus: to teach conflict resolution through the Saturday school program for juveniles. Manual includes program overview, curriculum on African American history, program implementation steps, procedures, and schedules. The model is adaptable for community settings.

Key teaching strategies: art, music, group discussions, drama, role playing, photography, and video production.

Type of material: curriculum, training manuals, and videos.

Cost: manual, $50; videos, $25.

Second Step: A Violence Prevention Curriculum, Grades Pre-K–K; Grades 1–3; Grades 4–5; Grades 6–8. 1992. Kathy Beland, Committee for Children, 172 20th Avenue, Seattle, WA 98122. Phone: (800) 634–4449.

Audience: grades pre-K through 8.

Focus: to reduce impulsive and aggressive behavior by teaching students foundational skills in empathy, impulse control, problem solving, and anger management.

Key teaching strategies: stories and discussions, teacher modeling of behaviors and skills, activities, and role playing.

Type of material: 11 × 17 inch photo lesson cards, teacher's guide, posters, filmstrip, puppets, and song tape.

Cost: grades pre-K–K, $245; grades 1–3, $255; grades 4–5, $235; grades 6–8, $285.

Violence: Dealing with Anger. 1994. Thomas Crum, Centre Communication, 1800 30th Street, No. 207, Boulder, CO 80301. Phone: (303) 444–1166.

Audience: grades 4–6.

Focus: to teach new skills to replace violent reactions in problem situations through student role playing.

Key teaching strategies: role playing interspersed with teaching exercises.

Type of material: twenty-five–minute video with teaching guide included.

Cost: $69.95.

Violence in the Schools: Developing Prevention Plans. 1994. Center for Civic Education, 5146 Douglas Fir Road, Calabasas, CA 91302–1467. Phone: (800) 350–4223.

Audience: grades 6–9.

Focus: to develop students' commitment to active citizenship and governance by teaching the knowledge and skills required for effective participation.

Key teaching strategies: Reading, directed discussions, writing, role playing, small-group problem solving, cooperative learning techniques, and critical thinking exercises.

Type of material: teacher's guide, student text, and staff development training manual.

Cost: teacher's guide, $10; student text, $5.50 ($5 each for orders of ten or more); set comprising a teacher's guide and thirty student texts, $150.

Violence Prevention Curriculum for Adolescents. 1987. Deborah Prothrow-Stith, Education Development Center, Inc., 55 Chapel Street, Newton, MA 02160. Phone: (617) 969–7100.

Audience: grades 9–12.

Focus: to increase students' awareness of the causes and effects of violence; illustrate that violence is preventable; teach that anger is a normal part of life that can be expressed and channeled in healthy, constructive ways; and encourage students to think about alternatives to violence in conflict situations.

Key teaching strategies: minilectures, facilitated class discussions, role playing, and observation and analysis.

Type of material: 110–page teacher's guide, student handouts, and video.

Cost: teacher's guide, $30 ($25 each for orders of ten or more); video rental, $60; teacher's guide and video, $150.

Process Curriculum

Conflict Resolution: An Elementary School Curriculum. 1990. Gail Sadalla, Meg Holmberg, and Jim Halligan. *Conflict Resolution: A Secondary School Curriculum.* 1987. Gail Sadalla, Meg Holmberg, and Jim Halligan. Community Board Program, Inc., 1540 Market Street, Ste. 490, San Francisco, CA 94102. Phone: (415) 552–1250.

Audience: grades K–7 and 7–12.

Focus: to help students become aware of their choices in conflict situations. Elementary curriculum includes more than eighty activities focusing on building effective communication and problem-solving skills. Secondary curriculum focuses on enabling students to reduce the tensions and hostilities associated with conflict.

Key teaching strategies: role playing, recordkeeping, group discussions, brainstorming, demonstrations, small-group and large-group work, and experiential practice of skills.

Type of material: classroom curriculum of more than three hundred pages in a three-ring binder for easy copying of handout materials.

Cost: $44 each.

Conflict Resolution for Kindergarten Through Grade 3. 1995. Linda Dunn, Pat Lewis, Lynda Hall, Eileen McAvoy, and Cynthia Pitts, Mediation Network of North Carolina, P.O. Box 241, Chapel Hill, NC 27514–0241. Phone: (919) 929–6333.

Audience: grades K–3.

Focus: to teach the basics of listening skills, "I" messages, anger management, choice and consequences, feelings, perception, diversity, and negotiation. Includes a section on how to make conflict resolution part of regular classroom activities.

Key teaching strategies: discussion and dialogue, simulation games, role playing, and interactive activities.

Type of material: 191–page teaching curriculum, scoped and sequenced.

Cost: $20.

Conflict Resolution in the Schools: A Manual for Educators. 1996. National Institute for Dispute Resolution, 1726 M Street NW, Ste. 500, Washington, DC 20036. Phone: (202) 466–4764.

Audience: educators.

Focus: to show educators how to diagnose conflicts, handle difficult confrontations, and implement appropriate mediation and problem-solving strategies for classroom conflicts, violence, and community divisiveness.

Key teaching strategies: introduces the concepts and skills of conflict resolution that can be practiced in the classroom and throughout the school community.

Type of material: book.

Cost: $35.

Conflict Resolution: Strategies for Collaborative Problem Solving. 1992. Ellen Raider and Susan Coleman, International Center for Cooperation and Conflict Resolution, Teacher's College, Columbia University, Box 53, New York, NY 10027. Phone: (212) 678–3402.

Audience: educators, parents, and youth leaders.

Focus: to teach adults conflict resolution skills that enable them to work collaboratively to resolve disputes within their homes, communities, and workplaces, so that they can become role models for their children and colleagues.

Key teaching strategies: experiential exercises and role playing with audio and video feedback geared for the adult reader.

Type of material: participant manuals and train-the-trainer guide.

Cost: not available for purchase without training within school system or at a teacher's college.

The Conflict Zoo. 1996. Suzin Glickman, Natalie Johnson, Gina Sirianni, and Judith Zimmer, National Institute for Citizen Education in the Law, 711 G Street SE, Washington, DC 20003. Phone: (202) 546–6644.

Audience: grades 3 and 4.

Focus: to teach students to identify words and actions that can lead to conflict, to understand the perspectives of all parties involved in a conflict, and to develop skills for conflict management.

Key teaching strategies: critical thinking, problem solving, cooperative learning, role playing, interviews, group dialogue, brainstorming, and other experiential learning strategies.

Type of material: elementary curriculums.

Cost: not available.

Life Negotiations: The PYN Curriculum for Middle Schools. 1996. Jared R. Curhan. Program for Young Negotiators, 20 University Road, Cambridge, MA 02138. Phone: (888) 832–2479.

Audience: grades 6–9.

Focus: to promote the use of collaboration, communication, and empathy, and foster an environment in which individuals can learn to cope with differences in a productive manner.

Key teaching strategies: role playing, case studies, games, performances, reading and writing assignments, videos, and classroom discussions.

Type of material: teacher's manual, $50; student activity book, $4.50; and video of negotiation vignettes, $35.

Time Out to Resolve It! A School-Based Conflict Resolution Program. 1994. Citizenship and Law-Related Education Center, 9738 Lincoln Village Drive, Sacramento, CA 95827. Phone: (916) 228–2322.

Audience: grades K–12.

Focus: to teach decision-making, problem-solving, and communication skills that help students resolve their own conflicts peacefully.

Key teaching strategies: individual, small-group and large-group work, practice, and discussions; role playing; active, cooperative learning activities; performance-based assessment.

Type of material: Student and adult training manuals, implementation manual, classroom lesson plans linked to middle and high school subject matter, and videotapes.

Cost: currently available only in conjunction with training.

We Can Work It Out!: Problem Solving Through Mediation, Elementary Edition. 1996. Linda Barnes-Robinson, Sue Jeweler, and Judith Zimmer. *We Can Work It Out!: Problem Solving Through Mediation, Secondary Edition.* 1993. Suzin Glickman and Judith Zimmer. National Teens, Crime, and the Community Program, c/o National Institute for Citizen Education in the Law, 711 G Street SE, Washington, DC 20003. Phone: (202) 546–6644.

Audience: grades 5–12.

Focus: to promote cooperation over competition while pursuing a nonadversarial method of conflict resolution. The lessons teach students to generate nonviolent options when faced with conflict; develop critical thinking, questioning, and active listening skills; analyze and solve problems; find common ground when they disagree; and manage conflict in their daily lives. Lessons culminate in a mock mediation where students role-play the parts of disputants and mediators and are evaluated by members of the community involved in related fields.

Key teaching strategies: critical thinking, problem solving, cooperative learning, role playing, interviews, group dialogue, brainstorming, and other experiential learning strategies.

Type of material: curriculums for grades 5–7 (elementary edition) and 7–12 (secondary edition).

Cost: elementary edition, $40; secondary edition, $40.

Mediation

Classroom Conflict Resolution Training for Grades 3–6. 1995. Community Board Program, Inc., 1540 Market Street, Ste. 490, San Francisco, CA 94102. Phone: (415) 552–1250.

Audience: grades 3–6.

Focus: to introduce conflict management concepts and skills to third through sixth grade classes before a selected group of students is trained as conflict managers.

Key teaching strategies: activities to build communication and problem-solving skills.

Type of material: manual.

Cost: $13.

Conflict Manager Training for Elementary School Students. 1995. Nancy Kaplan. *Mediation Training for Middle School Students.* 1995. Nancy Kaplan. *Mediation Training for High School Students.* 1995. Nancy Kaplan. Conflict Resolution Unlimited, 845 106th Avenue NE, Ste. 109, Bellevue, WA 98004. Phone: (206) 451–4015.

Audience: grades K–6, 6–9, and 9–12.

Focus: to create a comprehensive conflict resolution program for the entire school and parent community.

Key teaching strategies: demonstrations, exercises, and role playing.

Type of material: curriculum manual, video and leader's guide, classroom teacher's manual, and training aids. Videos and student handouts also available in Spanish.

Cost: elementary edition: curriculum manual, $200; classroom teacher's manual, $150; video and leader's guide, $95; package consisting of all manuals, video, and teaching aids, $295. Middle school and high school editions: curriculum manual, $250; classroom teacher's manual, $200; video and leader's guide, $150; package consisting of all manuals, video, and teaching aids, $395.

Conflict Managers Training Manual for Grades 3–6. 1995. Community Board Program, Inc., 1540 Market Street, Ste. 490, San Francisco, CA 94102. Phone: (415) 552–1250.

> Audience: grades 3–6.
>
> Focus: to foster enhanced cooperation and reduce violence through peer mediation, effective communication, and peaceful problem-solving skills and processes.
>
> Key teaching strategies: role playing, group discussion, experiential practice of skills, recordkeeping, and demonstrations.
>
> Type of material: training and implementation manual.
>
> Cost: $17.

Establishing a Viable and Durable Peer Mediation Program: From A to Z. 1995. Louis A. Siegal and Lorraine M. Lopez, The Institute for Violence Prevention, Inc., 155 Landor Drive, Athens, GA 30606. Phone: (706) 548–4932.

> Audience: grades 4–12.
>
> Focus: to establish peer mediation programs; logistics, goals, mediator and adviser selection, training, publicity, and evaluation.
>
> Key teaching strategies: brainstorming, vocabulary games, simulation exercises, role playing, team building, theory, and mediation practicum.
>
> Type of material: program coordinator's manual and training guide, including sample forms, overheads, and list of resources.
>
> Cost: all materials, $199.

Lessons in Conflict Resolution for Grades 4–6. 1994. New Mexico Center for Dispute Resolution, 620 Roma NW, Ste. B, Albuquerque, NM 87102. Phone: (800) 249–6884.

> Audience: grades 4–6.
>
> Focus: to develop an understanding of conflict, styles of conflict, feelings, anger management, communication skills, and problem solving.
>
> Key teaching strategies: small-group and large-group cooperative activities, brainstorming, role playing, personal reflection, and other experiential learning strategies.
>
> Type of material: booklet.
>
> Cost: $20.

Mediation and Conflict Resolution for Gang-Involved Youth. 1992. Sara Keeney, Jean Sidwell, and Melinda Smith, New Mexico Center for Dispute Resolution, 620 Roma NW, Ste. B, Albuquerque, NM 87102. Phone: (800) 249–6884.

Audience: grades 6–12.

Focus: to provide training for those working with gang-involved youth. Contains mediation training activities, lessons in conflict resolution for youth, and recommendations for conducting multiparty youth mediation.

Key teaching strategies: Small-group and large-group activities, role playing, and other experiential learning strategies.

Type of material: standard school materials.

Cost: $35.

Peer Mediation: Conflict Resolution in Schools. 1997. Revised edition. Fred Schrumpf, Donna Crawford, and Richard Bodine, Research Press, Inc., P.O. Box 9177, Champaign, IL 61826. Phone: (217) 352–3273.

Audience: grades 6–12.

Focus: to develop a peer-based mediation program for faculty, student body, and peer mediators through basic and advanced training and through strategic program implementation guidelines.

Key teaching strategies: experiential learning activities, simulations, group discussions, and schedule options for training.

Type of material: program guide with forms, student manual, and video.

Cost: program guide, $25.95; student manual, $10.95; video, program guide, and student manual, $365; video rental, $55.

Starting a Conflict Manager Program. 1992. Community Board Program, Inc., 1540 Market Street, Ste. 490, San Francisco, CA 94102. Phone: (415) 552–1250.

Audience: grades 3–12.

Focus: to provide a complete overview of implementing the conflict manager program in elementary, middle, or high schools.

Key teaching strategies: five-step implementation process to secure support, train teachers, plan implementation, train students, and maintain a successful program.

Type of material: manual.

Cost: $25.

Students Resolving Conflict: Peer Mediation in Schools. 1995. Richard Cohen; Scott, Foresman and Co., 1900 East Lake Avenue, Glenview, IL 60025. Phone: (617) 876–6074.

Audience: grades 6–12.

Focus: to guide educators in implementing peer mediation programs in their schools. Theory and practice of mediation, including overview of conflict resolution and mediation the-

ory, technical assistance for implementing a program, conflict resolution lessons for delivery to all students, program
forms, and mediation transcripts.
Key teaching strategies: role playing, discussion, brainstorming, games, worksheets, and group dialogue.
Type of material: text.
Cost: $14.95.

*Training and Implementation Guide for Student Mediation in Elemen-
tary Schools.* 1990. Sara Keeney and Jean Sidwell. *Training and Implementation Guide for Student Mediation in Secondary Schools.* 1990.
Melinda Smith and Jean Sidwell. New Mexico Center for Dispute
Resolution, 620 Roma NW, Ste. B, Albuquerque, NM 87102. Phone:
(800) 249–6884.

Audience: grades K–5 and 6–12.
Focus: to prepare school staff to implement a schoolwide
mediation program.
Key teaching strategies: small-group and large-group activities,
brainstorming, and other experiential learning strategies.
Type of material: step-by-step staff implementation guide and
mediation training curriculum.
Cost: $35.

Training Middle School Conflict Managers. 1996. *Training High School
Conflict Managers.* 1996. Community Board Program, Inc., 1540
Market Street, Ste. 490, San Francisco, CA 94102. Phone: (415)
552–1250.

Audience: grades 6–9 and 9–12.
Focus: to prepare high school students to be conflict managers
who will help their peers resolve disputes peacefully.
Key teaching strategies: role playing, simulations, group dis-
cussion, experiential practice of skills, and recordkeeping.
Type of material: training and implementation manual.
Cost: $17.

Peaceable Classroom

Conflict Resolution in the Middle School. 1994. William Kreidler, Educators for Social Responsibility, 23 Garden Street, Cambridge, MA
02138. Phone: (617) 492–1764.

Audience: grades 6–8.
Focus: to teach conflict resolution skills.
Key teaching strategies: role playing, writing a journal,
minilectures, brainstorming, microlabs, and small-group
discussion.

Type of material: curriculum and teaching guide, and student
handouts.
Cost: $35.

*Creative Conflict Resolution: More than 200 Activities for Keeping
Peace in the Classroom.* 1984. William J. Kreidler; Scott, Foresman
and Co., 1900 East Lake Avenue, Glenview, IL 60025. Phone: (800)
628–4480.

Audience: grades K–6.
Focus: to teach conflict resolution techniques.
Key teaching strategies: discussion, example, activity, and
worksheet.
Type of material: resource and workbook.
Cost: $12.95.

Creative Controversy: Intellectual Challenge in the Classroom. 1987,
1992, 1995. David W. Johnson and Roger T. Johnson, Interaction
Book Co., 7208 Cornelia Drive, Edina, MN 55435. Phone: (612)
831–9500.

Audience: grades K–12 and adults.
Focus: to increase students' motivation to learn, academic
achievement, creative thinking, and higher level reasoning.
Students research a position, present it persuasively, try to
refute the opposing position, and synthesize the two posi-
tions into their "best reasoned judgment."
Key teaching strategies: experiential and cooperative learning,
simulations, role playing, and perspective taking.
Type of material: book, video, and audiocassette.
Cost: book, $25; video, $25; audiocassette, $10.

Elementary Perspectives: Teaching Concepts of Peace and Conflict. 1990.
William J. Kreidler, Educators for Social Responsibility, 23 Garden
Street, Cambridge, MA 02138. Phone: (800) 370–2515.

Audience: K–6 educators.
Focus: to help students acquire the concrete cooperative and
conflict resolution skills needed to become caring and
socially responsible citizens.
Contains more than eighty activities designed to help teachers
and students define peace, explore justice, and learn the
value of conflict and its resolution.
Key teaching strategies: role playing, songs, writing, discussions, and cooperative activities.
Type of material: curriculum.
Cost: $28.

*The Friendly Classroom for a Small Planet: A Handbook on Creative
Approaches to Living and Problem Solving for Children.* 1988. Priscilla

Prutzman, Lee Stern, M. Lenard Burger, and Gretchen Bodenhamer, Children's Creative Response to Conflict, P.O. Box 271, Nyack, NY 10960. Phone: (914) 353–1796.

> Audience: grades pre-K through 6.
> Focus: to teach conflict resolution skills to those who work with young people.
> Key teaching strategies: experiential activities, including role playing and small-group work.
> Type of material: handbook.
> Cost: $14.95.

Making Choices About Conflict, Security, and Peacemaking. Part I: Personal Perspectives. 1994. Carol Miller-Lieber, Educators for Social Responsibility, 23 Garden Street, Cambridge, MA 02138. Phone: (800) 370–2515.

> Audience: grades 9–12.
> Focus: to explore with high school students the nature of conflict and its relation to public policy; to build a "conflict toolbox" to help students resolve their conflicts without resorting to violence; and to provide practical classroom management tools.
> Key teaching strategies: hands-on activities, role playing, group brainstorming, innovative projects, and problem-solving activities.
> Type of material: curriculum.
> Cost: $25.

Talk It Out: Conflict Resolution for the Elementary Teacher. 1996. Barbara Porro, Association for Supervision and Curriculum Development, 1250 North Pitt Street, Alexandria, VA 22314. Phone: (703) 549–9110.

> Audience: elementary teachers.
> Focus: to incorporate conflict resolution training into a daily program at the moment when students disagree.
> Key teaching strategies: uses fifty-four children's problems to teach them the skills of managing anger, listening, oral communication, and critical thinking.
> Type of material: book.
> Cost: $18.95.

Teaching Students to Be Peacemakers. 1987, 1991, 1995. David W. Johnson and Roger T. Johnson, Interaction Book Co., 7208 Cornelia Drive, Edina, MN 55435. Phone: (612) 831–9500.

> Audience: grades K–12 and adults.
> Focus: to create a cooperative learning community, teach all

students how to negotiate and mediate, rotate the responsibility of mediator so that all students have their turn, and continue to teach students negotiation and mediation skills throughout the school year. Research base is presented.

Key teaching strategies: experiential and cooperative learning, simulations, role playing, and perspective taking.

Type of material: book, student manuals, video, and audiocassettes.

Cost: book, $25; video, $25; audiocassettes, $10.

Teaching Young Children in Violent Times. 1994. Diane Levin, Educators for Social Responsibility, 23 Garden Street, Cambridge, MA 02138. Phone: (800) 370–2515.

Audience: grades pre-K through 3.

Focus: to teach young children to develop the understanding and skills for living peacefully with others.

Key teaching strategies: teacher-led discussions, role playing, class games, and rituals.

Type of material: teacher's guide.

Cost: $16.95.

Peaceable School

Creating the Peaceable School: A Comprehensive Program for Teaching Conflict Resolution. 1994. Richard Bodine, Donna Crawford, and Fred Schrumpf, Research Press, Inc., P.O. Box 9177, Champaign, IL 61826. Phone: (217) 352–3273.

Audience: grades 3–12.

Focus: to create a cooperative school environment through the institution of a rights-and-responsibilities approach to discipline where both adults and students learn to manage and resolve conflicts using the strategies of negotiation, mediation, and group problem solving.

Key teaching strategies: experiential learning activities, learning centers, cooperative learning, simulations, and class meetings.

Type of material: program guide, student manual, and video.

Cost: program guide, $35.95; student manual, $14.95; video, program guide, and student manual, $365; video rental, $55.

Resolving Conflict Creatively: A Teaching Guide for Grades Kindergarten Through Six. 1993. *Resolving Conflict Creatively: A Teaching Guide for Secondary Schools.* 1990. RCCP National Center, 163 Third Avenue, No. 103, New York, NY 10003. Phone: (212) 387–0225.

Audience: grades K–6 and 7–12.

Focus: to reduce violence and promote caring and cooperative schools and communities through showing children that they have many choices for dealing with conflict other than through passivity or aggression, through teaching them skills to make real choices in their own lives, and through increasing their understanding and appreciation of their own culture and other cultures.

Key teaching strategies: Role playing, interviews, group dialogue, brainstorming, and other affective experiential learning strategies.

Type of material: curriculum, videos, resource material.

Cost: curriculum not available for purchase without a three-to-five-year commitment to the program within a school system. Videos are available from $24 to $40.

Selecting Curriculum and Staff Development Providers

It is important for those investigating conflict resolution education curriculum resources or conflict resolution training opportunities to understand that not all that is labeled *conflict resolution* represents an authentic conflict resolution education program. An authentic conflict resolution education program goes beyond providing skill development in the foundation abilities of orientation, perception, emotion, communication, and creative and critical thinking skills that enable one to use the conflict resolution problem-solving strategies to deal constructively with conflict. An important benchmark of an authentic conflict resolution education program is its provision for training in and significant practice using negotiation, mediation, and/or consensus decision making. These strategies require proficient skill development in the foundational abilities to make possible effective utilization of the four principles of conflict resolution: separate people from the problem, focus on interests rather than positions, generate options for mutual gain, and use objective criteria when selecting a plan of action. Programs and curricula that do not embrace and use all four of these principles of conflict resolution to provide strategies for managing and resolving conflicts are not genuine, quality conflict resolution education programs. This is the case even when the program or curriculum deals with aspects of conflict and teaches some or all of the skills embodied in the foundation abilities.

Secondly, it is important for those seeking conflict resolution education curriculum resources or conflict resolution training opportunities to understand that even a quality program may not address the specific needs targeted by an individual school, and it may not be designed to use the identified resources of that school-community.

To assist those seeking conflict resolution education curriculum resources or conflict resolution training opportunities, the consultation and training resources listed in Appendix A and the curriculum resources listed in Appendix B do, in the opinion of the authors, satisfy the criteria for authentic, quality conflict resolution education. The listings in those appendices are, however, likely not to be exhaustive. Other resources may exist. Further, only those people involved in designing the school-based conflict resolution education program can determine if a curriculum or training addresses the needs and resources specific to that school.

The instruments in this appendix are designed to assist school personnel in identifying conflict resolution curriculum and program resources as well as staff development providers who best address the specific needs targeted by the school and that use the identified resources of the school-community.

Curriculum and Program Resources Assessment

The Conflict Resolution Program and Curriculum Assessment Form (Exhibit C.1) is a tool to help school personnel investigate conflict resolution programs. First, it can be determined whether or not a program meets the criteria of a conflict resolution program as set forth in this book; if it does, then (second) it can determine how well the program matches the needs and resources of a specific school. Specifically, the form in Exhibit C.1 (when used with the associated forms shown in Exhibits C.2 through C.6) facilitates assessment of:

- The degree to which the philosophy of conflict resolution is advanced

- The degree to which the foundation abilities for conflict resolution are developed (Exhibit C.2)

- The degree to which the fundamental principles of conflict resolution are incorporated (Exhibit C.3)

- What problem solving strategies are provided (Exhibit C.4)

- The learning processes that deliver the program to students (Exhibit C.5)

- The implementation component (Exhibit C.6)

Exhibit C.1.   Conflict Resolution Program and Curriculum Assessment Form

General Information

Name of program

_____

Author(s) _____

Publisher's name, address, phone   Publication date: _____

_____

_____   Cost: Teacher material $ _____

_____   Student material $ _____

_____   Video material $ _____

                                                Other material $ _____

                                        Specify nature of other: _____

                                        _____

Target audience (check all that apply):

    Students: _____ Preschool   _____ Parents

                                _____ K–2 grades   _____ Teachers

                                _____ 3–5 grades   _____ Administrators

                                _____ 6–8 grades   _____ Other school staff

                                _____ 9–12 grades   _____ Other adults

    Alternative schools: _____ students   _____ staff

    Juvenile justice facilities: _____ youth   _____ adults

Instruction format:

    _____ one-on-one

    _____ small group (<15)

    _____ classroom (15–30)

    _____ schoolwide

Other general descriptive information about curriculum/program:

_____

_____

Strengths and weaknesses:

Use the attached forms to assess the curriculum/program in five critical dimensions.

Exhibit C.2.   Foundation Abilities of Conflict Resolution

The program provides for developing understanding of conflict and peace and for developing orientation, perception, emotion, communication, creative-thinking, and critical-thinking abilities.

Foundation Skill or Concept	Degree to Which Skill or Concept Is Developed by the Program				
	Thoroughly	Well	Somewhat	Not at all	Comments
Understanding conflict	4	3	2	0	
Cooperation	4	3	2	0	
Appreciation of diversity and prejudice reduction	4	3	2	0	
Understanding peace	4	3	2	0	
Empathizing	4	3	2	0	
Dealing with perceptions	4	3	2	0	
Managing emotions	4	3	2	0	
Active listening	4	3	2	0	
Speaking to be understood	4	3	2	0	
Brainstorming	4	3	2	0	
Fairness	4	3	2	0	

Exhibit C.3.   Fundamental Principles of Conflict Resolution

The program incorporates and provides for development of operational understanding of the four fundamental principles of conflict resolution.

Fundamental Principle	Degree to Which Principle Is Incorporated into the Program				
	Extensively	Well	Somewhat	Not at all	Comments
Separate people from the problem	4	3	2	0	
Focus on interests, not positions	4	3	2	0	
Invent options for mutual gain	4	3	2	0	
Use objective criteria	4	3	2	0	

Exhibit C.4.   Problem-Solving Methods of Conflict Resolution

The program provides training in and practice with the problem-solving strategies.

Problems-Solving Method	Major Emphasis		Minor Emphasis		No Emphasis	
Negotiation	yes	no	yes	no	yes	no
Mediation	yes	no	yes	no	yes	no
Consensus decision making	yes	no	yes	no	yes	no

Exhibit C.5.   Learning Opportunities and Styles

Criteria for the learning process relate to the manner in which the curriculum is organized, delivered, and learned.

Learning Process Criteria	Degree to Which Criteria Are Satisfied					
		To some extent				
	Fully	75%	50%	25%	Not at all	Comments
The program uses a variety of learning activities.	4	3	2	1	0	
The program offers opportunities to practice conflict resolution in day-to-day situations.	4	3	2	1	0	
Materials are age-appropriate for the target population.	4	3	2	1	0	
Materials have clear formats and directions.	4	3	2	1	0	
Materials are culturally consistent for the target population.	4	3	2	1	0	
Materials are gender-sensitive.	4	3	2	1	0	
Materials provide ideas for extending activities and learning beyond the materials.	4	3	2	1	0	
Materials offer opportunity or ideas for parental involvement.	4	3	2	1	0	
Materials contain ideas for integrating conflict resolution into standard school subjects.	4	3	2	1	0	

Exhibit C.6.   Implementation

Criteria for implementation relate to the efficacy of the information provided by the program to guide school personnel in using the materials and the program.

Implementation Criteria	Degree to Which Criteria Are Satisfied					
		To some extent				
	Fully	75%	50%	25%	Not at all	Comments
Describes how to use the program	4	3	2	1	0	
Describes appropriate audiences for the program	4	3	2	1	0	
Describes how to address barriers to implementation	4	3	2	1	0	
Offers start-up ideas and suggestions for extending the program	4	3	2	1	0	
Describes how to identify students for participation if only some students will be involved	4	3	2	1	0	
Provides staff with suggestions of resources that offer additional information and strategies	4	3	2	1	0	
Provides schedules and plans for training students	4	3	2	1	0	
Provides practice activities in conflict resolution	4	3	2	1	0	
Offers ideas for promoting program within the school	4	3	2	1	0	
Provides ideas for managing program operation	4	3	2	1	0	
Delineates adult responsibilities in program operation	4	3	2	1	0	
Provides ideas for obtaining sponsorships and financial support	4	3	2	1	0	
Provides tools for assessing program effectiveness	4	3	2	1	0	

Staff Development Provider Assessment

The Conflict Resolution Staff Development Provider Form (Exhibit C.7) and its associated list of assessment criteria (Exhibit C.8) are tools to assist school personnel in investigating a potential provider of conflict resolution training. First, it can be determined if the provider is creditable in the field of conflict resolution; if so, it can then be determined how well the skills and offerings of the provider match the identified training needs of a specific school and of the targeted populations to be trained.

Exhibit C.7.   Conflict Resolution Staff Development Provider Assessment Form

---

General Information

Name of provider _____

Organizational affiliation

_____

Provider Address _____

                  _____

                  _____

         Phone (_____)_____

           Fax (_____)_____

Training based on specific published materials?   Yes   No

              If yes, title of materials: _____

                            Authors: _____

              Publisher and publication date: _____

Materials included in training costs?   Yes   No

      If no, cost: Teacher materials: $ _____

                      Student materials: $ _____   Required?   Yes   No

                      Video materials: $ _____   Required?   Yes   No

                      Other materials: $ _____   Required?   Yes   No

Type of training provided:

_____

_____

Training audience:

_____

_____

Format of training:

_____

_____

Length of training: _____

Scheduling options:

_____

_____

_____

Costs of staff development services:

_____

_____

Other general descriptive information about staff development provider:

Strengths and weaknesses:

Complete the attached form to assess the qualifications and quality of the staff development provider.

Exhibit C.8.   Conflict Resolution Staff Development Provider Assessment Criteria

---

Qualifications and Training in Conflict Resolution:

Training in negotiation theory: Where received? _____   When? _____

Training in mediation: Where received? _____   When? _____

Experience:

Served as a mediator?   Yes   No

If yes, what were the experiences? _____

School-based experience in education?   Yes   No

If yes, what were the experiences? _____

Implemented a school conflict resolution program?   Yes   No

If yes, what types of program? _____

Number of years providing staff development in conflict resolution: _____

Has trained students in conflict resolution?   Yes   No

Has trained teachers in conflict resolution?   Yes   No

Has trained administrators in conflict resolution?   Yes   No

Has trained other school staff in conflict resolution?   Yes   No

Has trained parents in conflict resolution?   Yes   No

Approximate number of people that have been trained by staff developer: _____

Involvement in school reform initiatives?   Yes   No

If yes, what was the involvement? _____

Participated in development of a strategic plan?   Yes   No

Facilitated development of a strategic plan?   Yes   No

Developed published materials?   Yes   No

Provides follow-up technical assistance and support?   Yes   No

If yes, services: _____

Costs? _____

References for performance as staff development provider:

(1) _____

(2) _____

(3) _____

(4) _____

School representative many observe staff development provider conducting a training session prior to the school committing to a contract with the provider: Yes   No

When? _____   Where? _____

Recommended Reading

American Psychological Association. *Violence and Youth: Psychology's Response. Vol. I: Summary Report on the American Psychological Association Commission on Violence and Youth.* Washington, D.C.: American Psychological Association (1993).

Arbetman, L. P., McMahon, E. T., and O'Brien, E. L. *Street Law: A Course in Practical Law.* (5th ed.). St. Paul, Minn.: West Publishing (1994).

Banks, J. *Multicultural Education: Issues and Perspectives.* (2nd ed.). Needham Heights, Mass.: Allyn & Bacon (1993).

Banks, J. *Multiethnic Education: Theory and Practice.* (3rd ed.). Needham Heights, Mass.: Allyn & Bacon (1994).

Blechman, F. *Evaluating School Conflict Resolution Programs.* Fairfax, Va.: Institute for Conflict Analysis and Resolution, George Mason University (1996).

Bodine, R., and Crawford, D. "Our School's Choice: Creating Peace or Struggling with Violence." *Building Leadership Practitioners Bulletin* (Illinois Principals Association), 1995, 2(1–2), 5–6.

Bodine, R., Crawford, D., and Schrumpf, F. *Creating the Peaceable School: A Comprehensive Program for Teaching Conflict Resolution.* Champaign, Ill.: Research Press (1994).

Bradley, S., and Henderson, F. "A Calm Approach to Violence in the Schools." *Popular Government,* Spring 1994, pp. 34–40.

Brekke-Miesner, P. *Keeping the Peace.* Oakland, Calif.: Oakland Unified School District, Office of Health and Safety Programs (1994).

Brendtro, L., and Long, N. "Violence Begets Violence: Breaking Conflict Cycles." *Journal of Emotional and Behavioral Problems,* 1993, 3(1), 2–7.

Brewer, D., Hawkins, J. D., Catalano, R., and Neckerman, H. *Preventing Serious, Violent, and Chronic Juvenile Offending: A Review of Evaluations of Selected Strategies in Childhood, Adolescence, and the Community.* Seattle: Developmental Research and Programs (1994).

Cahill, M. *Beacon School-Based Community Centers and Violence Prevention: A Discussion Paper.* New York: Youth Development Institute (1993).

Cardenas, J. *Multicultural Education: A Generation of Advocacy.* Needham Heights, Mass.: Allyn & Bacon (1995).

Cities in Schools. *Seeds of Hope: A Guide for Program Resources.* Alexandria, Va.: Cities in Schools (1993).

Community Board Program. *Starting a Conflict Managers Program.* San Francisco: Community Board Program (1992).

Crawford, D. *Youth-Focused Conflict Resolution and the Mission of Education.* Update on Law-Related Education, vol. 20 no. 2. Chicago: American Bar Association (1996).

Crawford, D., and Bodine, R. *Developing Emotional Intelligence Through Classroom Management: Creating Responsible Learners in Our Schools and Effective Citizens for Our World.* Champaign, Ill.: Research Press (forthcoming).

Crawford, D., Bodine, R., and Hoglund, R. *The School for Quality Learning: Managing the School and Classroom the Deming Way.* Champaign, Ill.: Research Press (1993).

Curwin, R., and Mendler, A. *Discipline with Dignity.* Alexandria, Va.: Association for Supervision and Curriculum Development (1988).

Davis, A. *Justice Without Judges.* Chicago: National Law-Related Resource Center, American Bar Association (1994).

Davis, A., and Porter, K. *Tales of Schoolyard Mediation.* Chicago: National Law-Related Resource Center, American Bar Association (1985).

Davis, A., and Salem, R. *Resolving Disputes: The Choice Is Ours.* Chicago: National Law-Related Resource Center, American Bar Association (1985).

DeJong, W. "School-Based Violence Prevention: From Peaceable School to the Peaceable Neighborhood." *Forum* (National Institute for Dispute Resolution), Spring 1994, 25, 8–14.

DeJong, W. "Creating a More Peaceful World." *School Safety* (National School Safety Center News Journal), Fall 1994.

Deutsch, M. *The Resolution of Conflict.* New Haven, Conn.: Yale University Press.

Diaz-Rico, L., and Weed, K. *The Crosscultural Language and Academic Development Handbook: A Complete K–12 Reference Guide.* Needham Heights, Mass.: Allyn & Bacon (1995).

"Dispute Resolution, Youth, and Violence." (Special issue.). *Forum* (National Institute for Dispute Resolution), Spring 1994, no. 25.

Dreyfuss, E. *Learning Ethics in School-Based Mediation Programs.* Chicago: National Law-Related Resource Center, American Bar Association (1990).

Fairfax County Public Schools. *Fairfax County Public Schools Task Force on Hispanic Youth and Gang Violence. Preliminary Report.* Fairfax, Va.: Fairfax County Public Schools (1995).

Fisher, R., Ury, W., and Patton, B. *Getting to Yes: Negotiating Agreement Without Giving In.* New York: Penguin (1991).

Frias, G. "Rhetoric and Realism: We Need a National Strategy for Safe Schools." *Harvard Education Newsletter*, 1994, 3(3), 4–5.

Gaustad, J. "School Discipline." *ERIC Digest*, Dec. 1992, no. 78.

Gaustad, J. "Schools Attack the Roots of Violence." *ERIC Digest*, Oct. 1991, no. 63.

General Accounting Office. *School Safety: Promising Initiatives for Addressing School Violence.* Washington, D.C.: U.S. General Accounting Office (1995).

Girard, K., and Koch, S. J. *Conflict Resolution in the Schools: A Manual for Educators.* San Francisco: Jossey-Bass (1996).

Glass, R. "Keeping the Peace: Conflict Resolution Training Helps Counter Violence." *American Teacher* (American Federation of Teachers, AFL-CIO), 1994, 78(5), 6–7, 15.

Grossnickle, D., and Stephens, R. *Developing Personal and Social Responsibility: A Guide to Community Action.* Malibu, Calif.: Pepperdine University Press (1992).

Haberman, M., and Schreiber Dill, V. "Commitment to Violence Among Teenagers in Poverty." *Kappa Delta Pi Record*, 1995, 31(4), 148–156.

Hamburg, D. "Education for Conflict Resolution." In *Report of the President.* New York: Carnegie Corporation of New York (1994).

Hammond, R. *Dealing with Anger: A Violence Prevention Program for African American Youth.* Champaign, Ill.: Research Press (1994).

Hawkins, J. D. *Social Development Strategy: Building Protective Factors in Your Community.* Seattle: Developmental Research and Programs (1992).

Hawkins, J. D., Doucek, H. J., and Lishner, D. M. "Changing Teaching Practices in Mainstream Classrooms to Improve Bonding and Behavior of Low Achievers." *American Research Journal,* 1988, 25(1), 31–50.

Hechinger, F. "Saving Youth from Violence." *Carnegie Quarterly,* 1994, 39(1), 1–5.

Institute for Conflict Analysis and Resolution. *Understanding Intergroup Conflict in Schools: Strategies and Resources.* Fairfax, Va.: Institute for Conflict Analysis and Resolution, George Mason University (1994).

Iowa Peace Institute. *Fostering Peace: A Comparison of Conflict Resolution Approaches for Students Grades K–12.* Grinnell: Iowa Peace Institute (1994).

Jenkins, J., and Smith, M. *School Mediation Evaluation Materials.* Albuquerque: New Mexico Center for Dispute Resolution (1987).

Johnson, D. *Cooperative Learning in the Classroom.* Alexandria, Va.: Association for Supervision and Curriculum Development (1994).

Johnson, D., and Johnson, R. "Cooperative Learning and Conflict Resolution." *The Fourth R,* 1993, 42(1), 4, 8.

Johnson, D., and Johnson, R. *Reducing School Violence Through Conflict Resolution.* Alexandria, Va.: Association for Supervision and Curriculum Development (1995).

Johnson, D., and Johnson, R. *Teaching Students to Be Peacemakers.* (3rd ed.). Edina, Minn.: Interaction Book (1995).

Johnson, D., and Johnson, R. "Teaching Students to Be Peacemakers: Results of Five Years of Research." *Peace and Conflict: Journal of Peace Psychology,* 1995, 1(4), 417–438.

Kirschenbaum, H. *100 Ways to Enhance Values and Morality in Schools and Youth Settings.* Needham Heights, Mass.: Allyn & Bacon (1995).

Kohn, A. "The Risks of Rewards." *ERIC Digest,* Dec. 1994.

Lantieri, L., and Patti, J. *Waging Peace in Our Schools.* Boston: Beacon Press (1996).

Leal, R. *The Next Generation of Campus Mediation Programs.* San Antonio, Tex.: Public Justice Department, St. Mary's University, 1989.

Leal, R. "Conflicting Views of Discipline in San Antonio Schools." *Education and Urban Society,* 1994, 27(1), 35–44.

Levy, J. "Conflict Resolution in Elementary and Secondary Schools." *Mediation Quarterly,* 1989, 7(1), 73–87.

Lockona, T. *Education for Character: How Our Schools Can Teach Respect and Responsibility.* New York: Bantam (1991).

Maxwell, J. "Mediation in the Schools: Self-Regulation, Self-Esteem, and Self-Discipline." *Mediation Quarterly,* 1989, 7(2), 149–155.

Miller, E. "Promising Practices: Peer Mediation Catches on, But Some Adults Don't." *Harvard Education Newsletter,* 1994, 3(3), 8.

Miller, S. *Kids Learn About Justice by Mediating the Disputes of Other Kids.* Chicago: American Bar Association (1993).

Moore, P., and Batiste, D. "Preventing Youth Violence: Prejudice Elimination and Conflict Resolution Programs." *Forum* (National Institute for Dispute Resolution), 1994, 25, 15–19.

National Association for Mediation in Education. *The Fourth R.* (Bimonthly newsletter, published by National Institute for Dispute Resolution, 1726 M Street NW, Ste. 500, Washington, DC 20036.)

National Institute of Justice. *Research in Action: PAVNET Online User's Guide.* Washington, D.C.: National Institute of Justice, Office of Justice Programs, U.S. Department of Justice (1995).

National School Safety Center. *School Safety Work Book. What Works: Promising*

Violence Prevention Programs. Malibu, Calif.: National School Safety Center (1995).

Ohio Commission on Dispute Resolution and Conflict Management. *Conflict Management in Schools: Sowing Seeds for a Safer Society. Final Report of the School Conflict Management Demonstration Project 1990–1993.* Columbus: Ohio Commission on Dispute Resolution and Conflict Management (1994).

Pastorino, R. *The Mediation Process—Why It Works: A Model Developed by Students.* Grinnell: Iowa Peace Institute (1991).

Pettigrew, M. *Confronting Racial, Ethnic, and Gender Conflicts in the Schools.* Boulder: Conflict Resolution Consortium, University of Colorado (1993).

Pruitt, D. *Negotiation Behavior.* Orlando: Academic Press (1981).

Raffini, J. *150 Ways to Increase Intrinsic Motivation in the Classroom.* Needham Heights, Mass.: Allyn & Bacon (1996).

Resolution. (Journal published by Ohio Commission on Dispute Resolution and Conflict Management, 77 South High Street, 24th Floor, Columbus, OH 43266).

Rogers, M. *A Series of Solutions and Strategies: Resolving Conflict Through Peer Mediation.* Clemson, S.C.: National Dropout Prevention (1994).

Roush, D. "Social Skills Training in Juvenile Detention: A Rationale." *Juvenile and Family Court Journal,* 1996, *49*(1), 1–20.

Schmidt, F., and Friedman, A. *Fighting Fair for Families.* Miami: Peace Education Foundation (1994).

Schrumpf, F., Crawford, D., and Bodine, R. *Peer Mediation: Conflict Resolution in Schools.* Champaign, Ill.: Research Press (1997).

Smith, M. *Mediation and the Juvenile Justice Offender.* Chicago, Ill.: National Law-Related Resource Center, American Bar Association (1991).

Steele, P. *Youth Corrections Mediation Program, Final Report of Evaluation Activities.* Albuquerque: New Mexico Center for Dispute Resolution (1991).

Stephens, J. B. "A Better Way to Resolve Disputes." *School Safety,* Winter 1993, pp. 12–14.

Tennessee Education Association and Appalachia Education Laboratory. *Reducing School Violence: Schools Teaching Peace.* Charleston, W.V.: Appalachia Educational Laboratory (1993).

Tolan, P., and Guerra, N. *What Works in Reducing Adolescent Violence: An Empirical Review of the Field.* Boulder: Institute for Behavioral Sciences, University of Colorado (1994).

Townley, A. "Introduction: Conflict Resolution, Diversity, and Social Justice." *Education and Urban Society,* 1994, *27*(1), 5–10.

U.S. Department of Education and National School Boards Association. "Special Hearings on Violence in the Schools." Proceedings of the National School Boards Association's 54th Annual Conference and Exposition, New Orleans, 1994.

Weitz, J. H., President's Committee on the Arts and the Humanities, and National Assembly of Local Arts Agencies. *Coming up Taller: Arts and Humanities Programs for Children and Youth at Risk.* Washington, D.C.: President's Committee on the Arts and the Humanities (1996).

Wilson, J. J., and Howell, J. C. *Comprehensive Strategy for Serious, Violent, and Chronic Juvenile Offenders.* Washington, D.C.: Office of Juvenile Justice and Delinquency Prevention, U.S. Department of Justice (1993).

Wilson-Brewer, R., Cohen, S., O'Donnell, L., and Goodman, I. *Violence Prevention for Young Adolescents: A Survey of the State of the Art.* Washington, D.C.: Carnegie Council on Adolescent Development, Carnegie Corporation of New York (1991).

Wolfgang, C. *Solving Discipline Problems.* (3rd ed.). Needham Heights, Mass.: Allyn & Bacon (1995).

NOTES

Foreword

1. Prothrow-Stith, D. B. *Deadly Consequences.* New York: HarperCollins (1991).
2. Lowry, R., and others. "Adolescents at Risk for Violence." *Education and Psychology Review,* 1995, 7(1), 7–39.
3. Prothrow-Stith, D. B. "The Epidemic of Youth Violence in America: Using Public Health Prevention Strategies to Prevent Violence." *Journal of Health Care for the Poor and Underserved,* 1995, 6(2), 96.
4. Goleman, D. *Emotional Intelligence.* New York: Bantam (1995), p. xiv.

Red Riding Hood Revisited

1. Bodine, R., Crawford, D., and Schrumpf, F. *Creating the Peaceable School: A Comprehensive Program for Teaching Conflict Resolution.* Champaign, Ill.: Research Press (1994), pp. 102–104, 106, 108, 110, 112.

Preface

1. Bodine, Crawford, and Schrumpf (1994), p. 51.
2. "Conflict Resolution Education: A Guide to Implementing Programs in Schools, Youth-Serving Organizations, and Community and Juvenile Justice Settings." Program Report, U.S. Department of Justice and U. S. Department of Education (Oct. 1996), p. v.

Chapter One

1. Goldberg, S. B., and Reske, H. J. "Talking with Attorney General Janet Reno." *American Bar Association Journal,* 1993, 79(46).
2. Crawford, D. *Youth-Focused Conflict Resolution and the Mission of Education.* Update on Law-Related Education, vol. 20 no. 2. Chicago: American Bar Association, (1996), p. 14.
3. Crawford, D. and Bodine, R. *Developing Emotional Intelligence Through Classroom Management: Creating Responsible Learners in Our Schools and Effective Citizens for Our World.* Champaign, Ill.: Research Press (forthcoming).
4. Hechinger, F. "Saving Youth from Violence." *Carnegie Quarterly,* 1994, 39(1), 1.
5. Elliott, D. "Serious Violent Offenders: Onset, Development, Course, and Termination—The American Society of Criminology 1993 Presidential Address." *Criminology,* 1994, 32(1); Federal Bureau of Investigation. *Crime in the United States 1993: Uniform Crime Reports.* Washington, D.C.: U.S. Department of Justice (1994).

6. Hechinger (1994), p. 2.

7. U.S. Department of Justice. *Comprehensive Strategy for Serious, Violent, and Chronic Juvenile Offenders.* Washington, D.C.: Office of Juvenile Justice and Delinquency Prevention, U.S. Department of Justice, 1993, pp. 5–6.

8. Crowley, M. S. (ed.). "Schools, Congress Sound Alarm on Student Safety and Security Issues." *Child Protection Report,* 1993.

9. Bodine, R., and Crawford, D. "Our School's Choice: Creating Peace or Struggling with Violence." *Building Leadership Practitioners Bulletin* (Illinois Principals Association), March 1995, p. 1.

10. Ibid., p. 2.

11. Elias, M. J. "Preventing Youth Violence." *Education Week,* Aug. 2, 1995, p. 54.

12. Bodine and Crawford (1995), p. 5.

13. Haberman, M., and Schreiber Dill, V. "Commitment to Violence Among Teenagers in Poverty." *Kappa Delta Pi Record,* Spring 1995, p. 149.

14. DeJong, W. "School-Based Violence Prevention: From Peaceable School to the Peaceable Neighborhood." *Forum* (National Institute for Dispute Resolution), Spring 1994, p. 8.

15. Crawford and Bodine (forthcoming).

16. Haberman and Schreiber Dill (1995), p. 149.

17. Crawford and Bodine (forthcoming).

18. Haberman and Schreiber Dill (1995), pp. 151–152.

19. Bodine and Crawford (1995), p. 5.

20. American Psychological Association. *Violence and Youth,* Vol. I: Summary Report of the Commission on Violence and Youth. Washington, D.C.: American Psychological Association, 1993.

21. Bodine and Crawford (forthcoming).

22. Ibid.

23. Townley, A. "Introduction: Conflict Resolution, Diversity, and Social Justice." *Education and Urban Society,* 1994, 27, 5.

24. Moore, P., and Batiste, D. "Preventing Youth Violence: Prejudice Elimination and Conflict Resolution Programs." *Forum* (National Institute for Dispute Resolution), Spring 1994, p. 18.

25. Adler, A. "Implementing District-Wide Programs: If I Knew Then What I Know Now." *The Fourth R,* 1995, 57, 5.

26. Bodine and Crawford (forthcoming).

27. Ibid.

28. Amsler, T. "Educating for Citizenship: Reframing Conflict Resolution Work in K–12 Schools." Coulson Festschrift Meeting, Aspen Institute, Wye Conference Center, Queenstown, Md., March 1994.

29. Davis, A. and Porter, K. "Dispute Resolution: The Fourth R." *Journal of Dispute Resolution,* Spring 1985, pp. 121–139.

30. Hamburg, D. "Education for Conflict Resolution." In *Report of the President.* New York: Carnegie Corporation of New York (1994), p. 15.

31. Bodine, Crawford, and Schrumpf (1994), p. 100.

Chapter Two

1. Bodine and Crawford (1995).

2. Ibid.

3. Crawford and Bodine (forthcoming).

4. Brendtro, L. and Long, N. "Violence Begets Violence: Breaking Conflict Cycles." *Journal of Emotional and Behavioral Problems,* 1993, 3(1), 5–7.

5. Bodine, Crawford, and Schrumpf (1994).

6. Ibid.

7. Johnson, D. W., and Johnson, R. T. "Cooperative Learning and Conflict Resolution." *The Fourth R* (National Association for Mediation in Education), Dec. 1992/Jan. 1993, *42*, 1.
8. Crawford, D., Bodine, R., and Hoglund, R. *The School for Quality Learning.* Champaign, Ill.: Research Press (1993).
9. Bodine, Crawford, and Schrumpf (1994), p. 16.
10. Crawford, Bodine, and Hoglund (1993), p. 187.
11. Bodine, Crawford, and Schrumpf (1994), p. 23.
12. Crawford, Bodine, and Hoglund (1993), pp. 99–100.
13. Crawford and Bodine (forthcoming).
14. Ibid.
15. Kohn, A. "The Risks of Rewards." *ERIC Digest* (ERIC Clearinghouse on Elementary and Early Childhood Education), December 1994. EDO PS–94–14
16. Crawford and Bodine (forthcoming).
17. Ibid.
18. DeJong, W. "Creating a More Peaceful World." *School Safety* (National School Safety Center News Journal), Fall 1994.

Chapter Three

1. Crawford and Bodine (forthcoming).
2. Bodine, Crawford, and Schrumpf (1994).
3. Crawford and Bodine (forthcoming).
4. Bodine, Crawford, and Schrumpf (1994).
5. Ibid.
6. Ibid.
7. Crawford and Bodine (forthcoming).
8. Bodine, Crawford, and Schrumpf (1994).
9. Ibid.
10. Schrumpf, F., Crawford, D., and Bodine, R. *Peer Mediation: Conflict Resolution in Schools.* Champaign, Ill.: Research Press (1997).
11. Ibid.
12. Ibid.
13. Ibid.

Chapter Four

1. Filner, J. and Zimmer, J. *Understanding Conflict Resolution: School Programs for Creative Cooperation.* Update on Law-Related Education, vol. 20, no. 2. Chicago: American Bar Association (1996).
2. Crawford and Bodine (forthcoming).
3. Fisher, R., Ury, W., and Patton, B. *Getting to Yes: Negotiating Agreement Without Giving In.* New York: Penguin, 1991, p. 21.
4. Schrumpf, Crawford, and Bodine (1997).
5. Ibid.
6. Fisher, Ury, and Patton (1991), p. 11.
7. Ibid., p. 21.
8. Ibid., p. 22.
9. Schrumpf, Crawford, and Bodine (1997).
10. Fisher, Ury, and Patton (1991), p. 29.
11. Schrumpf, Crawford, and Bodine (1997).
12. Fisher, Ury, and Patton (1991), p. 32.
13. Schrumpf, Crawford, and Bodine (1997).
14. Fisher, Ury, and Patton (1991), p. 11.
15. Ibid., p. 57.
16. Crawford and Bodine (forthcoming).

17. Ibid.
18. Adapted from Bodine, Crawford, and Schrumpf (1994), pp. 179, 219, and 283.
19. Crawford, Bodine, and Hoglund (1993), p. 47.
20. Crawford and Bodine (forthcoming).

Chapter Five

1. The primary school edition is Barnes-Robinson, L., Jeweler, S., and Zimmer, J. *We Can Work It Out! Problem Solving Through Mediation.* Washington, D.C.: National Institute for Citizen Education in the Law (1996). The secondary school edition is Glickman, S., and Zimmer, J. *We Can Work It Out! Problem Solving Through Mediation.* Washington, D.C.: National Institute for Citizen Education in the Law/National Crime Prevention Council (1993).
2. Glickman, S., Johnson, N., Sirianni, G., and Zimmer, J. *The Conflict Zoo.* Washington, D.C.: National Institute for Citizen Education in the Law (1996).
3. Cohen, R. *Students Resolving Conflict: Peer Mediation in Schools.* Glenview, Ill.: Scott, Foresman (1995).
4. Schrumpf, Crawford, and Bodine (1997).
5. The Illinois Institute for Dispute Resolution promotes peer mediation as a viable entry point to establishing conflict resolution education programs in schools. Through continued involvement with those schools that develop and implement peer mediation programs, IIDR promotes extending conflict resolution education to every student and adult within the school rather than the few who are trained as peer mediators within the schools.
6. Kreidler, W. *Elementary Perspectives I: Teaching Concepts of Peace and Conflict.* Cambridge, Mass.: Educators for Social Responsibility (1990).
7. Johnson, D., and Johnson, R. *Reducing School Violence Through Conflict Resolution.* Alexandria, Va.: Association for Supervision and Curriculum Development (1995).
8. Ohio Commission on Dispute Resolution and Conflict Management. *Conflict Management Resource Guide for Elementary Schools.* Columbus: Ohio Commission on Dispute Resolution and Conflict Management, and Ohio Department of Education (1995), pp. 7–8.
9. Lieber Miller, C. *Making Choices About Conflict, Security, and Peacemaking.* Part I: *Personal Perspectives.* Cambridge, Mass.: Educators for Social Responsibility (1995).
10. Johnson, D., and Johnson, R. *Teaching Students to Be Peacemakers.* Edina, Minn.: Interaction Book (1991), pp. 3:52–3:60.
11. Bodine, Crawford, and Schrumpf (1994).
12. Ibid.
13. Ibid.
14. Ibid.

Chapter Six

1. DeCecco, J., and Richards, A., *Growing Pains: Uses of School Conflict.* New York: Aberdeen Press, 1974.
2. Johnson, D., and Johnson, R. "Teaching Students to Be Peacemakers: Results of Five Years of Research." *Peace and Conflict: Journal of Peace Psychology,* 1(4), 417–438.
3. Johnson, D., and Johnson, R. *Teaching Students to Be Peacemakers.* (3rd ed.). Edina, Minn.: Interaction Book, 1995.
4. Ohio Commission on Dispute Resolution and Conflict Management. *Conflict Management in Schools: Sowing Seeds for a Safer Society.* Columbus: Ohio Commission on Dispute Resolution and Conflict Management (1994).

5. Carpenter, J. *Clark County Social Service School Mediation Program Evaluation Reports.* Clark County, Nev.: Clark County Social Service, 1993, 1994.

6. Tolsen, E. R., McDonald, S., and Moriarty, A. *Peer Mediation Among High School Students: A Test of Effectiveness.* Chicago: Center for Urban Research and Development, University of Illinois (1990).

7. Metis Associates. *Resolving Conflict Creatively Program: 1988–89 Summary of Significant Findings.* New York: Metis Associates (1990).

8. Lam, J. *The Impact of Conflict Resolution Programs on Schools: A Review and Synthesis of the Evidence.* (2nd ed.). Amherst, Mass.: National Association for Mediation in Education (1989).

9. Carter, S. *Evaluation Report for the New Mexico Center for Dispute Resolution: Mediation in the Schools Program, 1993–94 School Year.* Albuquerque: New Mexico Center for Dispute Resolution (1994).

10. Deutsch, M., Mitchell, V., Zhang, Q., Khattri, N., Tepavac, L., Weitzman, E. A., and Lynch, R. *The Effects of Training in Cooperative Learning and Conflict Resolution in an Alternative High School.* New York: Columbia University (1992).

11. Nakkula, M., and Nikitopoulos, C. *Preliminary Evaluation Findings for the Fall 1995 Implementation of the Program for Young Negotiators.* Cambridge, Mass.: Graduate School of Education, Harvard University (1996).

12. Hanson, M. K. "A Conflict Resolution/Student Mediation Program: Effects on Student Attitudes and Behaviors." *ERS Spectrum,* 1994, *12*(4), 9–14.

13. Personal communication, M. K. Hanson, Sept. 1995.

14. Personal communication, R. Lewis, results from a telephone survey conducted by the Safe School Center, West Palm Beach, Florida, May 1996.

15. Leal, R., Hollis, P., and Cole, D. *A Collaborative School-University Mediation Program.* Paper presented at the second annual Alternatives to Violence Conference, Sam Houston University, Galveston, Texas, Apr. 1996.

16. Dabson, J. *Internal Report: Youth at Risk.* Washington, D.C.: Section of Dispute Resolution, American Bar Association (1994).

17. Hawkins, D. *Social Development Strategy: Building Protective Factors in Your Community.* Seattle, Wash.: Developmental Research and Programs, 1992.

18. Benard, B. "Fostering Resiliency in Kids." *Educational Leadership,* Nov. 1993, pp. 44–48.

19. Hawkins, D., Doucek, H., and Lishner, D. "Changing Teaching Practices in Mainstream Classrooms to Improve Bonding and Behavior of Low Achievers." *American Research Journal,* 1988, *25*(1), 31–50.

20. Bodine and Crawford (forthcoming).

Chapter Eight

1. Bodine, Crawford, and Schrumpf (1994).

2. Kreidler, W. *Creative Conflict Resolution: More than 200 Activities for Keeping Peace in the Classroom K–6.* Glenview, Ill.: Scott, Foresman (1984).

3. Schrumpf, Crawford, and Bodine (1997).

4. Ibid., p. 75.

5. Ibid., p. 80.

6. Bodine, Crawford, and Schrumpf (1994), pp. 314–316.

Chapter Nine

1. Schrumpf, Crawford, and Bodine (1997).

2. Bodine, Crawford, and Schrumpf (1994).

3. Crawford, Bodine, and Hoglund (1993).

4. Ibid.

A

Abilities: for conflict resolution, 55–58; resources on, 175–180
Academic controversy, in peaceable classroom approach, 77–81
Accommodation, as soft response, 42
Action plans, examples of, 164–170
Addams, J., 79
Adler, A., 208
Administrators, in peaceable school approach, 97
Advisory committee, for implementation, 140, 142
Alaska, peaceable school approach in, 96
American Bar Association, Lawyers Adopt-a-School Program of, 110
American Psychological Association, 10, 208
Amsler, T., 208
Arbitration, for problem solving, 48
Arkansas, peaceable school approach in, 98
Art classes, and conflict, 78
Assertiveness, as alternative, 30–31
Assessment: of conflict resolution education, 106–111; of curriculum and program resources, 192–196; of needs, 135–140; of staff development, 197–201
Australia, peaceable school approach in, 98
Autonomy, and resilience, 113

B

Barnes-Robinson, L., 210
Batiste, D., 208
BATNA (best alternative to a negotiated agreement), and problem solving, 49–50
Behavior management, coercion absent in, 25–31
Behavioral expectations: developmental curriculum for, 117–128; educating about, 158; in peaceable schools, 95; and responsible citizens, 26–27, 28–30
Behaviors: changes of, in education, 4–5; in conflict resolution, 60
Belief statements, for strategic plan, 161–162
Benard, B., 211
Bethune, M. M., 79
Bodine, R., 41, 49, 55, 59, 132n, 140n, 141n, 145n, 147n, 148n, 207, 208, 209, 210, 211, 212
Bonding: and resilience, 113–114; social, 22–24
Boston, process curriculum approach in, 63
Boston Plan for Excellence in the Public Schools, 63
Brainstorming: for conflict resolution, 54, 57; rules for, 161–162
Brendtro, L., 21, 209
Brookline, Massachusetts, peaceable classroom approach in, 87
Bunche, R., 79

C

California: conflicts in, 103; mediation program approach in, 73–76; peaceable school approach in, 96, 98; process curriculum approach in, 63
Canada: peaceable school approach in,

98; process curriculum approach in, 63

Carpenter, J., 211

Carter, S., 211

Catalano, R., 112, 113

Centers for Disease Control and Prevention, 6

Change: and conflict resolution education, 4–5; and staff development, 32–33; systemic, 94–95

Chavez, C., 79

Chicago, research in, 107

Children's Creative Response to Conflict (CCRC), 89–91, 171

Citizenry, responsible: aspects of developing, 17–33; and civil association, 13–14; comprehensive approach for, 17–18; concept of, 38; and conflict resolution education, 12–14, 17–33

Civics classes, and conflict, 80

Clark County Social Service School Mediation Program, 107

Classroom approach, implementation of, 156–158. *See also* Peaceable classroom approach

Climate, peaceable, 98–99, 158

Coercion, absence of, 25–31

Cohen, R., 69, 210

Cole, D., 211

Communication: abilities for, 57; in conflict resolution, 52; developmental curriculum for, 124–125

Community: in mediation program approach, 74–76; in peaceable classroom approach, 91; in peaceable school approach, 100–101; and peer mediation, 151; in process curriculum approach, 63–64

Community Board Program (CBP), 73–76, 171

Conflict: aspects of learning from, 35–44; avoiding, 41–42, 43; background on, 35–36; and choice, 38–39, 44; concept of, 35; hard responses to, 42, 43; and limited resources, 39; nature of, 82, 99; origins of, 36–41; principled responses to, 42, 43–44; responses to, 41–44; soft responses to, 41–42, 43; strategies for, 82–83; and value differences, 39–41

Conflict management: and conflict resolution, 48–49; practices for, 47–50

Conflict resolution: abilities for, 55–58, 175–180; behaviors in, 60; and conflict management, 48–49; as future directed, 49, 60; principles of, 50–55; problem solving for, 58–60

Conflict resolution education: approach-es to, 45–114; assessments of, 106–111; background on, 3–4; case for, 1–44; and change, 4–5; as choice, 30; components of, 47–60; and cooperative learning, 12, 24–25; development providers for, 191–201; developmental curriculum for, 117–128; and empowerment, 8–9; establishing programs for, 115–170; implementing programs for, 129–158; mediation program approach to, 61, 68–76; and mission of education, 3–15; organizations for, 171–173; peaceable classroom approach to, 61, 77–91; peaceable school approach to, 61–62, 92–101; principles of, 9; as proactive, 10–11; process curriculum approach to, 61, 62–68; programs for, 61–101; rationale for, 14–15; readings on, 203–206; research on, 103–114; and responsible citizenry, 12–14, 17–33; and risk factors and resilience, 111–114; and social justice, 11–12; strategic plan for, 159–170; time needed for, 23–24; and violence prevention, 7–11

Consensus decision making: developmental curriculum for, 128; principles of, 160; for problem solving, 59

Control theory, and conflict, 36

Cooperative learning: and conflict resolution education, 12, 24–25; in peaceable classroom approach, 77–81

Coordinators, for implementation, 134–135

Crawford, D., 41, 49, 55, 59, 132*n*, 140*n*, 141*n*, 145*n*, 147*n*, 148*n*, 207, 208, 209, 210, 211, 212

Creating the Peaceable Home, 100

Creative thinking: abilities for, 57; developmental curriculum for, 125–126

Criteria, objective: in conflict resolution, 54–55; in strategic plan, 160

Critical thinking: abilities for, 58; developmental curriculum for, 126–127

Crowley, M. S., 208

Curriculum: development of, 65–66; developmental, 117–128; in peaceable classroom approach, 77; in peaceable school approach, 96–97; resources on, 175–190. *See also* Process curriculum approach

D

Dabson, J., 211

Dade County, research in, 109–110

Davis A., 208

DeCecco, J., 103, 210
Decision making, by consensus, 59, 128, 160
DeJong, W., 32, 208, 209
Deutsch, M., 211
Developmental curriculum: activities in, 119–121; aspects of, 117–128; background on, 117–118; and circle of learning, 118–119; sequence for, 121–128
Discipline: alternative to, 30–31; or punishment, 25–26
Doucek, H., 211

E

Economics classes, and conflict, 80
Education: behavior and system changes in, 4–5; change in, and staff development, 32–33; and citizenship development, 17–33; on conflict, violence, and peace, 9–10; ideal setting for, 3–4; mission of, 3–15; preventive actions in, 8; sense-based system for, 27–30; and violence prevention, 19–20. *See also* Conflict resolution education
Educators for Social Responsibility (ESR), 79, 85–89, 95, 172
Elias, M. J., 208
Elliott, D., 208
Emotions: abilities for, 56; in conflict resolution, 51–52; developmental curriculum for, 124
Empowerment, of youth, 8–9, 22–23
Environment, for cooperative learning, 82
Expectations. *See* Behavioral expectations

F

Faculty: development for, 32–33; and implementation, 137, 150–151, 156
Federal Bureau of Investigation, 208
Fighting Fair for Families, 110
Filner, J., 209
Fisher, R., 49, 50–53, 62, 209, 210
Florida, research in, 109–110
Follow-up: for peacemaking, 87; in process curriculum approach, 65

G

Gain, options for mutual, 53–54
Gedstad, A., 87
Geography classes, and conflict, 80
Georgia, peaceable school approach in, 96, 98
Glasser, W., 36, 37

Glickman, D., 210
Goals statement, in strategic plan, 163–164
Goldberg, S. B., 207
Goleman, D., 207
Group problem solving, in peaceable school approach, 99

H

Haberman, M., 208
Hamburg, D., 208
Hanson, M. K., 211
Harrison, J., 88
Harvard Graduate School of Education, research at, 108–109
Harvard Negotiation Project, 62, 64–65, 172
Hawkins, D., 112, 113, 211
Health classes, and conflict, 78
Hechinger, F., 207, 208
History classes, and conflict, 80
Hoglund, R., 209, 210, 212
Hollis, P., 211

I

Illinois Institute for Dispute Resolution (IIDR), 172, 210; and Creating the Peaceable School, 98–101; and mediation program approach, 71–73
Implementation: aspects of, 129–158; background on, 129–130; and climate of peace, 158; design and plan phase of, 137, 140–146; funding sources for, 144–146; of peer mediation approach, 146–156, 157–158; phases of, 130–158; policies and procedures for, 142–144; and program development, 130; program team for, 133–137; strategy for, 137, 140; time line for, 140–141
Indiana: peaceable classroom approach in, 88–89; peaceable school approach in, 98
Interests, focus on: in conflict resolution, 52–53; in process curriculum approach, 66
International Center for Cooperation and Conflict Resolution, 108, 172
Intervention: early, 22; and prevention, 20–24; service range for, 21–24

J

Jeweler, S., 210
Johnson, D. W., 24, 77, 81, 103–106, 209, 210–211

Johnson, N., 210
Johnson, R. T., 24, 77, 103–106, 209, 210–211

K

Khattri, N., 211
Kohn, A., 31, 209
Kreidler, W., 77, 210, 211

L

Lam, J., 211
Language arts classes, and conflict, 78
Law classes, and conflict, 80
Lawlor, B., 88
Leal, R., 211
Learning: circle of, 118–119; from conflict, 35–44; cooperative, 12, 24–25, 77–81; and transfer, 18–20, 118
Lewis, R., 211
Lieber Miller, C., 210
Lishner, D., 211
Literature classes, and conflict, 79–80, 81
Long, N., 21, 209
Lose-lose approach, 43
Lottery, for peer mediator selection, 149
Louisiana, peaceable school approach in, 96
Lowry, R. 207
Lynch, R., 211

M

Maryland, research in, 110
Massachusetts: peaceable classroom approach in, 87; peaceable school approach in, 96; process curriculum approach in, 63
Math classes, and conflict, 79, 80, 81
McDonald, S., 211
Mediation: developmental curriculum for, 128; in peaceable school approach, 99; for problem solving, 59; in process curriculum approach, 66–67; process for, 68–69, 84; resources on, 183–186; youth-initiated cases for, 76. See Peer mediation
Mediation program approach: concept of, 61; programs in, 68–76
Mediation Showcase, 67
Metis Associates, 211
Michigan, peaceable school approach in, 98
Minnesota, University of, Cooperative Learning Center at, 81–85, 171
Mission statement, for strategic plan, 162

Missouri, peaceable school approach in, 98
Mitchell, V., 211
Montgomery County, research in, 110
Moore, P., 208
Moriarty, A., 211
Music classes, and conflict, 79

N

Nakkula, M., 211
National Crime Prevention Council, 66
National Institute for Citizen Education in the Law, 66
National Institute for Dispute Resolution, 67, 172
Needs: assessment of, for implementation, 135–140; psychological, 37–38, 40–41; and quality world, 38–39
Negotiation: curriculum in, 64–65; developmental curriculum for, 127–128; in peaceable school approach, 99; principled, 63; for problem solving, 59, 83–84
Nevada, research in, 107
New Jersey, peaceable school approach in, 96
New Mexico Center for Dispute Resolution Mediation in Schools, 108, 172
New York: peaceable school approach in, 96; process curriculum approach in, 63
New York City: conflicts in, 103; and peaceable classroom approach, 89; and peaceable school approach, 95; research in, 107, 108
Nikitopoulos, C., 211

O

Ohio Commission on Dispute Resolution and Conflict Management, 78, 173, 210, 211
Ohio School Conflict Management and Demonstration Program, 107
Oregon, peaceable school approach in, 96
Orientation abilities, 55–56, 122–123

P

Palm Beach County Schools, research at, 110
Parents: in mediation program approach, 73–74, 75; in peaceable classroom approach, 91; in peaceable school approach, 97, 100; and peer

mediation, 151–152; in process curriculum approach, 63–64

Patterson, E., 88–89

Patton, B., 49, 50–53, 62, 209, 210

Peace Education Foundation (PEF), Conflict and Peer Mediation programs of, 109–110

Peaceable classroom approach: concept of, 61; programs for, 77–91; research on, 103–106; resources on, 187–189

Peaceable school approach: concept of, 61–62; programs for, 92–101; resources on, 189–190; and systemic change, 94–95; transformation elements in, 93–94

Peacemaking, nature of, 99

Peer mediation: assessment of, 108; implementation of, 146–158; in mediation program approach, 69–70; operation and maintenance of, 154–156; in peaceable school approach, 97; in process curriculum approach, 67; promotion campaign for, 152–153; selection of students for, 146–150. *See also* Mediation

Perception: abilities of, 56; in conflict resolution, 51; developmental curriculum for, 123

Philadelphia, conflicts in, 103

Physical education classes, and conflict, 79

Porter, K., 208

Prevention: and intervention, 20–24; primary, 21–22; of violence, 7–11, 19–20, 63–66

Principled negotiation, process curriculum approach for, 63

Principled responses, to conflict, 42, 43–44

Problem, people separated from, 51–52

Problem solving: for conflict resolution, 58–60; group, 99; negotiation for, 59, 83–84; and resilience, 113

Process curriculum approach: concept of, 61; programs in, 62–68; resources on, 180–183

Program for Young Negotiators (PYN), 62–66, 108–109, 173

Project S.M.A.R.T. (School Mediator Alternative Resolution Team), 107

Prothrow-Stith, D., 207

Punishment: or discipline, 25–26; and rewards, 31–32

Q

Quaker Project on Community Conflict, 89

Quality world, and needs, 38–39

R

Reading classes, and conflict, 78

Reframing, for conflict resolution, 56, 57

Religious Society of Friends, Peace and Social Action Program of, 89

Reno, J., 3

Resilience: and conflict resolution education, 111–114; development of, 114

Reske, H. J., 207

Resolving Conflict Creatively Program (RCCP), 95–98, 107, 173

Resources: for implementation, 144–146; limited, and conflict, 39

Responsibility. *See* Citizenry, responsible

Rewards, and punishment, 31–32

Richards, A., 103, 210

Risk factors, and conflict resolution education, 111–114

Roosevelt, E., 79

S

Sadat, A., 79

Safe School Center, 110

St. Mary's University, Mediation Project of, 110

San Antonio, research in, 110

San Francisco: conflicts in, 103; mediation program approach in, 73–76

San Francisco Unified School District, 74–75, 76

Schools. *See* Education; Peaceable school approach

Schreiber Dill, V., 208

Schrumpf, F., 41, 49, 59, 132n, 140n, 141n, 145n, 147n, 148n, 207, 208, 209, 210, 211, 212

Science classes, and conflict, 79, 80, 81

Shared vision statement, for strategic plan, 163

Sirianni, G., 210

Skills, in peaceable school approach, 98–101

Social bonds: and resilience, 113–114; restoring, 22–24

Social competence, and resilience, 113

Social justice, and conflict resolution education, 11–12

Social studies classes, and conflict, 79, 81

South Bend, Indiana, peaceable classroom approach in, 88–89

Speech classes, and conflict, 78

Staff. *See* Faculty

Strategic plan: action plans for, 164–170; aspects of, 159–170; belief statements for, 161–162; formulating, 159–160; goals statement in, 163–164; mission statement for, 162; shared vision statement for, 163
Street Law, Inc., 66–68, 173

T

Teachers College, research at, 108, 172
Teaching Students to Be Peacemakers (TSP), 81–85, 103–106, 171
Team, for program implementation, 133–137
Teens, Crime, and the Community, 66
Tepavac, L., 211
Texas: peaceable school approach in, 98; research in, 110
Thetford, Vermont, peaceable classroom approach in, 88
Thinking: creative, 57, 125–126; critical, 58, 126–127
Tolsen, E. R., 211
Toronto, process curriculum approach in, 63
Townley, A., 208
Training: for classroom approach, 156; in mediation program approach, 70, 72, 75–76; in peaceable classroom approach, 82–85, 86–87, 90–91; in peaceable school approach, 96, 99–100; for peer mediation, 150, 155; in process curriculum approach, 63–64; for program team, 133–134
Tutu, D., 79

U

U.S. Department of Education, 207
U.S. Department of Justice, 207; Office of Juvenile Justice and Delinquency Prevention of, 66, 208
Ury, W., 49, 50–53, 62, 209, 210

V

Value differences, and conflict, 39–41
Vermont, peaceable classroom approach in, 88
Violence: as pervasive, 5–7; prevention of, 7–11, 19–20, 63–66; psychological, 7
Vision, statement of shared, 163

W

Washington, peaceable school approach in, 98
Washington, University of, research at, 112
Weitzman, E. A., 211
Win-lose approach, 43
Win-win approach, 43–44
Writing classes, and conflict, 79

Y

Youth Peace Corps, 100

Z

Zhang, Q., 211
Zimmer, J., 209, 210